Akhtar Hassan Malik

# TRANSFORMING SCHOOLS IN PAKISTAN
TOWARDS THE LEARNING COMMUNITY

# TRANSFORMING SCHOOLS IN PAKISTAN
## TOWARDS THE LEARNING COMMUNITY

Edited by
### John Retallick and Iffat Farah

# OXFORD
UNIVERSITY PRESS

Great Clarendon Street, Oxford OX2 6DP
Oxford University Press is a department of the University of Oxford.
It furthers the University's objective of excellence in research, scholarship,
and education by publishing worldwide in

Oxford   New York

Auckland  Cape Town  Dar es Salaam  Hong Kong  Karachi
Kuala Lumpur  Madrid  Melbourne  Mexico City  Nairobi
New Delhi  Shanghai  Taipei  Toronto

with offices in

Argentina  Austria  Brazil  Chile  Czech Republic  France  Greece
Guatemala  Hungary  Italy  Japan  Poland  Portugal  Singapore
South Korea  Switzerland  Turkey  Ukraine  Vietnam

Oxford is a registered trade mark of Oxford University Press
in the UK and in certain other countries

© Oxford University Press 2005

The moral rights of the author have been asserted

First published 2005

All rights reserved. No part of this publication may be reproduced, translated,
stored in a retrieval system, or transmitted, in any form or by any means,
without the prior permission in writing of Oxford University Press.
Enquiries concerning reproduction should be sent to
Oxford University Press at the address below.

This book is sold subject to the condition that it shall not, by way
of trade or otherwise, be lent, re-sold, hired out or otherwise circulated
without the publisher's prior consent in any form of binding or cover
other than that in which it is published and without a similar condition
including this condition being imposed on the subsequent purchaser.

ISBN  978-0-19-597900-8

Second Impression 2007

Typeset in Times
Printed in Pakistan by
Kagzi Printers, Karachi.
Published by
Ameena Saiyid, Oxford University Press
No. 38, Sector 15, Korangi Industrial Area, PO Box 8214
Karachi-74900, Pakistan.

# CONTENTS

|  | page |
|---|---|
| *Preface* | vii |
| *Contributors* | ix |
| *Introduction* | xiii |

**Chapter 1**
Transforming Schools into Learning Communities:
Focus on Pakistan — 1
*John Retallick and Al-Karim Datoo*

**Chapter 2**
Becoming a School Science Teacher in Pakistan:
A Female Narrative — 26
*Nelofer Halai*

**Chapter 3**
Science Teacher Development in Pakistan:
A Learning Community Approach — 45
*Harcharan Pardhan and Patricia Rowell*

**Chapter 4**
The Action Research Interest Group:
Building Capacity for Learning Communities — 67
*Shahzad Mithani, Debbie Kramer-Roy,
Bernadette Dean, and Anjum Halai*

**Chapter 5**
Co-Learning Partnership: A Way forward to Develop
Learning Communities in Pakistani Schools — 93
*Razia Fakir Mohammad*

## Chapter 6
Cooperative Learning in Classrooms ... 116
*Bernadette Dean*

## Chapter 7
Teaching and Learning in Multigrade Classes ... 138
*Rana Hussain and John Retallick*

## Chapter 8
Pedagogical Leadership in Pakistan:
Two Headteachers from the Northern Areas ... 162
*Muhammad Memon and Zubeda Bana*

## Chapter 9
Parents as Partners in the Learning Community ... 182
*Qamar Safdar*

## Chapter 10
Building Communities of Practice in Pakistani Schools ... 199
*Fauzia Shamim and Iffat Farah*

## Chapter 11
Networks of Learning: Professional Associations and The
Continuing Education of Teachers ... 215
*Sikunder Ali Baber, Zakia Sarwar, and Qamar Safdar*

*Index* ... 247

# PREFACE

It was in August 1994, that I first visited The Aga Khan University-Institute for Educational Development (AKU-IED) in Karachi, Pakistan. I was one of a small group of professors from the University of Toronto and Oxford University, who were privileged to work as partners with AKU-IED faculty in the establishment of the Institute's M.Ed. degree programme, and in the initial development of a programme of scholarly and policy-relevant education research in Pakistan, East Africa, Bangladesh and Central Asia. What began as a formal partnership evolved into an ongoing professional collaboration over the next decade. During that time, I have witnessed the emergence and continuing growth of AKU-IED as an internationally recognized centre for innovative programmes of professional development for teachers and school administrators. I have also observed and contributed in a small way to the development of AKU-IED's educational research capacity. A decade ago, very little locally-based academic and policy-focused education research was conducted in the countries served by AKU-IED. Now the faculty and research staff are regular participants and presenters of their own research at international conferences and in internationally respected education research journals. They are also being increasingly called upon by government authorities and international agencies to contribute their research expertise towards understanding local education needs and improvement efforts. The emergence of AKU-IED as a high quality education research centre in such a short time is remarkable. This book is the first of what is certain to be ongoing publications based entirely on original research carried out by AKU-IED faculty, research staff and graduates.

While all of the research reported in this book took place in Pakistan, the relevance of the findings extends well beyond the geographical boundaries of the country. The editors and authors of the various chapters have based their work on contemporary theories and research on teacher development and school improvement internationally, with a particular emphasis on the concept and practice of learning communities and collaborative action research. The ideas and findings presented in this book demonstrate the applicability of these concepts to school and teacher development practice and research in the developing world, while offering fresh perspectives and insights into the process and challenges of creating self-sustaining learning communities in schools and school systems in these contexts. The stories are not all tales of success, but need to be told and learned from by policy makers, school and teacher developers and educators worldwide.

Stephen E. Anderson
International Centre for Educational Change
Ontario Institute for Studies in Education of the University of Toronto
April 2004

# CONTRIBUTORS

**Al-Karim Datoo** is an instructor at AKU-IED. His academic background is in Islamic Studies and Humanities (from the Institute of Ismaili Studies, UK), and in educational research methodology (from the University of Oxford, UK). He has teaching and research interests in the areas of social sciences, cultural studies and educational research. He is a co-author of primary level Social Studies textbooks (2001) published by the Sindh Textbook Board.

**Anjum Halai** joined AKU-IED in June 1998 and is currently an assistant professor. Her responsibilities at the Institute include teaching and research. She teaches courses in research and mathematics methods. Her research interests are in teacher education, school improvement and student learning. Her work has been published in national and international journals, newsletters and dailies.

**Bernadette Dean** is an assistant professor and Head, Academic and Student Affairs at AKU-IED. She has teaching and research interests in social studies, education/citizenship, curriculum, teaching and learning, and action research. Her publications include social studies textbooks for primary schools and various articles and chapters.

**Debbie Kramer-Roy** has been a senior instructor at AKU-IED since 1999, where she has been raising awareness about, and developing, a programme on Inclusive Education for Children with Special Needs. Prior to joining AKU-IED she worked as an occupational therapist in a variety of settings in England and Pakistan.

**Fauzia Shamim** is an associate professor at AKU-IED. Her academic background is in TESOL. Her current research interests include teacher development, online teaching and learning, and innovative methodology for teaching and learning of English in Pakistan and other developing countries.

**Harcharan Pardhan** joined AKU-IED in 1994, and is currently an assistant professor. Prior to this, she taught Math/Science since 1970 at different levels (primary to first year university), in a number of countries, including Kenya and Canada. She has also been a teacher educator especially in the area of science. Her area of interest is teacher education, particularly, science teacher development in collaborative/community settings.

**Iffat Farah** is an associate professor at AKU-IED. She has teaching and research interests in the area of school improvement, as well as education and development. She has published several research reports and book chapters.

**John Retallick** has been an associate professor at AKU-IED since 2002. Prior to this, he was in the Faculty of Education at Charles Sturt University, Australia, for 25 years. He has teaching and research interests in teacher learning, learning communities, and educational leadership and management. His publications include an edited volume *Learning Communities in Education* (1999), published by Routledge, and journal articles in the *Journal of In-service Education* and *Teachers and Teaching*.

**Muhammad Memon** joined AKU-IED in December 1993 and is now a Professor and Head of Programmes. He has played a significant role in introducing educational leadership and management as a field of studies in Pakistan. He has conducted a number of research studies in the area of educational leadership and organizational learning and has served as a member of various committees and task forces working on reforming education in the public sector of Pakistan. His work is widely published in national and international journals.

**Nelofer Halai** is an associate professor at AKU-IED. She has more than twenty years of experience in teaching science at both the secondary and post-secondary levels in Government and private institutions. She has been affiliated with AKU for the last fourteen years, initially teaching in the Faculty of Health Sciences and presently, as a Teacher Educator at IED. Her research interests are in areas related to science education, teacher education and qualitative methods of research.

**Patricia Rowell** is a professor of science education in the Department of Elementary Education at the University of Alberta, Canada. Her research interests are oriented to the role of language and discourse in teaching and learning science.

**Qamar Safdar** has been a senior instructor at AKU-IED since 1998. Previously, she was the Principal of Al Murtaza School, Karachi for nine years. In teaching and research, her interests are in educational leadership and management. She is the General Secretary of School Head Teachers Association for the Development of Education (SHADE).

**Rana Hussain** is a senior instructor at AKU-IED. She has a special interest in primary education and has vast experience of working in schools in the capacity of teacher educator and manager of primary schools. Her current research is on multigrade teaching in the northern areas of Pakistan.

**Razia Fakir Mohammad** started her career as a secondary school mathematics teacher in Aga Khan School Kharadar, Karachi. After the M.Ed. Programme at AKU-IED, she worked as a Professional Development Teacher in the AKES schools. Since 1998, she has been a senior instructor at AKU-IED. She has teaching and research interests in mathematics education, teacher learning and learning communities, and student assessment. Her publications include a journal article in *Journal of In-service Education*.

**Shahzad Mithani** has been at AKU-IED since 1995, and is now an assistant professor. He initially joined as a research fellow and later worked as a senior instructor and Project Coordinator - USAID Project III: Capacity Building of NGOs/CBOs in Education. Currently, he is Coordinator M.Ed. Program. His areas of interest in teaching and research include: critical pedagogy, assessment of student learning, leadership and management, and, monitoring and evaluation.

**Sikunder Ali Baber** has been a senior instructor at AKU-IED for the past six years. He chairs the Mathematics Association of Pakistan (MAP). His research interests are: linking mathematics education with critical citizenship, networks for learning and philosophy of education. He has been involved in the development of the primary mathematics text books of Sindh Text Book Board Jamshoro, Sindh.

**Zakia Sarwar** is a freelance professional development consultant, with more than 37 years of experience of teaching English language and literature. She retired as the Head of English Department at PECHS College for Women, Karachi, Pakistan, in 1999. She has a number of national and international awards and publications. She is one of the founding members of the Society of Pakistan English Language Teachers (SPELT), and a leader in the field of ELT and teacher development in Pakistan, since 1984.

**Zubeda Bana** has been Manager Academic for Regional Coordination at the Ismaili Tariqah and Religious Education Board for Pakistan since February 2003. Prior to this, she was at AKU-IED as a senior instructor in educational management. She has extensive experience in teacher education in Sindh, Balochistan, NWFP, Northern Pakistan and East Africa.

# INTRODUCTION

Since the publication of an earlier book involving one of the present editors, *Learning Communities in Education* (Retallick, Cocklin and Coombe, 1999), it has been heartening to find that there has been a growing international interest in the idea of the school as a learning community. The momentum of the idea has grown to the point that one writer says, 'within the past decade, the term 'learning community' has been used with increasing frequency to describe a good school', (Schussler, 2003:498). Of course, good schools come in different shapes and sizes and develop in different ways; some are known as 'effective schools', others as 'successful schools'. At the heart of all good schools is a clear and sustained focus on student learning and the learning community idea continues to emphasize that point. What it adds to other approaches, however, is the focus on 'community'; the idea that a good school is a community of learners. All of the participants; be they students, teachers, administrators and even parents are positioned as learners with a strong sense of belonging and care for others which is the essence of community.

Since most of the interest and momentum towards learning communities has been built on research and practice in western countries, it is now the time to consider the usefulness of the idea in a developing country such as Pakistan. To achieve that purpose, this book aims to present the research and thinking of a group of people who actually live and work in Pakistan. The authors of the various chapters in the book are, with just two exceptions, all current or former faculty of The Aga Khan University-Institute for Educational Development (AKU-IED) in Karachi, Pakistan. One of those exceptions has close working connections with the University, while the other is a Canadian academic who supervised a doctoral study that is the basis of one of the chapters, with the data collection being carried out in Pakistan. Again, with only two exceptions, all contributors to this book are Pakistani nationals, exceptions being the Canadian academic mentioned earlier and one of the editors who hails from Australia, but has now been working at AKU-IED for the past two years. Much of the research reported in the book is based on doctoral studies covering research fieldwork carried out in Pakistan, or based upon the experience of teaching and learning at AKU-IED. We, therefore, have no hesitation in proudly claiming that this book is indigenous to Pakistan and presents a Pakistani perspective on the school as a learning community.

Why have we decided to focus on and take up the challenge of the learning community idea? There are three reasons. Firstly, all those contributing to this book have a deep commitment to improving schools and schooling in Pakistan, in particular, and the developing world in general. Improvements in both quantity and quality of school education are desperately required in Pakistan—one has only to read the daily newspapers to be constantly reminded of this. Serious action and increased fundings at all levels of government in Pakistan are needed to improve the 'quantity' aspect. An increase in the number of schools and teachers is required throughout the country to provide access for all children of school-going age. That aspect is beyond the scope of this book but its importance is not denied.

The concern of this book is with the 'quality' aspect, and the need to find ways to make presently existing schools more successful (Farah et al. 1996). The focus is on capacity building at the personal, interpersonal and organizational levels to improve the internal conditions of teaching, learning and leadership in the schools. In international literature, much is known about school improvement (Beach and Lindahl, 2004), though it is also true to say that significant school reform is notoriously difficult to achieve and sustain due to the multi-dimensional nature of the task and the inherent, dialectical connections between schools and the society to which they belong. Although difficult, that constitutes the work of AKU-IED and the authors represented in this book.

Secondly, we believe that the learning community idea can challenge, reconstruct and transform the 'grammar of schooling', (Tyack and Tobin, 1994). Tyack & Tobin's reasoning is that there appears to be a 'grammar' of traditional organization and teaching practices in schools that dates back more than a hundred years to the industrial revolution—when schools were established using the metaphor of the 'school as a factory'. This has been taken for granted and remarkably consistent throughout the world. Perhaps the defining characteristic of this concept is the organizational form known as bureaucracy, that was brilliantly described by the German sociologist, Max Weber, as an 'iron cage'. Bureaucracy is impersonal and based on hierarchy; it aims to achieve efficiency and control, not to release and develop the potential of individuals through learning. Since the core business of schools is learning, we argue that a different kind of institution is needed to foster values such as care, belonging, trust and collaboration, which encourage learning. These values are more likely to be found in the notion of community rather than in factory or bureaucracy.

The essence of the learning community idea is that all stakeholders or participants in the school are viewed as learners and engaged in reciprocal, rather than hierarchical or 'top-down', relationships. Hord (1997:4) suggests that 'In schools, the learning community is exemplified when people from multiple constituencies at all levels collaboratively and continually work together'. Sometimes, the term 'professional community' is used to focus on teacher collegiality and the need for teachers to be lifelong, continuous learners (Sergiovanni, 1996), though in this book we use the more generic term 'learning community', since our interest is in all participants in the school. Of course, the primary function of schools is student learning and that cannot be overemphasized: 'Although a school can exist as a pleasant community where all students feel valued and cared for, it does not exist as a learning community unless education is emphasized and academic rigour is expected of everyone', and of particular importance, 'the empirical data that exists indicates that students in schools operating as learning communities seem to do better than students in traditional schools' (Schussler, 2003:506-9). The benefit for student learning is, then, our third reason for advocating the learning community approach to schooling.

This book has eleven chapters on a range of theoretical and practical aspects of the school as a learning community. In the opening chapter, John Retallick and Al-Karim Datoo lay the foundation of the book by analysing the depth of the problem with school education in Pakistan, and survey the literature on the concepts of learning organization, community of practice and learning community. It is argued that all of these approaches offer useful ideas for transforming schools into learning communities and that they may be seen as a developmental progression or change process to assist schools who may wish to undertake the journey.

The next four chapters are all related around the theme of teachers as learners. In Chapter two, Nelofer Halai presents findings from her doctoral research, where she used the narrative method to reveal 'Munazza's story'. This is the story of Munazza *becoming* a science teacher in Pakistan; it is a contextualised story of how a person learnt to be a teacher and how biography shapes the life and style of a teacher. Since Munazza is a female, there is a powerful sub-text of what it means for a woman to become a teacher in Pakistan. In this chapter, we have an in-depth portrayal of the individual teacher as a learner which is a key idea in the learning community.

Chapter three moves from the individual teacher as learner, to the social dimension of teacher professional development in a Pakistani context. Harcharan Pardhan and Patricia Rowell provide an overview of Pardhan's doctoral study using action research method to promote and investigate the learning of a group of science teachers. From a critical analysis of science education in Pakistan they pose questions such as: How do teachers learn? What do teachers need to know? They then use action research to explore those questions and conclude with some insightful observations about teachers as action researchers and the possibilities for developing learning communities through this method.

In Chapter four, we continue the action research theme, though this time it is embedded in the life and work of AKU-IED through an informal group known as the Action Research Interest Group. The group comprises of a number of faculty members who came together voluntarily in 2002 to share their experiences with action research in schools. Four members of that faculty have co-written this chapter, each member presenting a brief case study of the work they are undertaking in capacity building and forming learning communities in schools through action research. Shahzad Mithani presents an excerpt from a larger study on the impact of an AKU-IED professional development programme in a school in Karachi. In the second case, Debbie Kramer-Roy explores how children with special needs can be integrated into mainstream classes in Pakistan. Bernadette Dean then broadens the context to Central Asia, East Africa as well as Pakistan in her study of improving teaching and learning through action research. The fourth case, by Anjum Halai, shows how action research was used in an advanced diploma programme at AKU-IED. Taken as a whole, the four studies reveal interesting findings about the efficacy of action research as a strategy for capacity building, teacher learning and school improvement.

Whereas the two previous chapters focused on action research as a strategy for teacher learning, Razia Fakir Mohammad, in Chapter five, adopts a co-learning strategy where a teacher educator works closely with mathematics teachers in assisting the improvement of teaching and learning. Based on her doctoral research, the author both contextualizes (in Pakistan), and analyses the notion of a co-learning partnership in this chapter. Interestingly, the teacher educator is also positioned as a learner in this model and the reciprocity of learning inherent in that is a true expression of the values of a learning community. The idea of the learning community may indeed be extended beyond the school to include partnerships with a university faculty.

Following those chapters on different aspects of teacher learning, the theme of the next set of chapters is about other participants in the learning community—students, school leaders and parents. Bernadette Dean, in Chapter six, introduces the student perspective through her study of cooperative learning in some Pakistani classrooms. Cooperative learning is an important, but not the only, strategy for creating a community of learners in the classroom. In a study concerned with fostering a community of learners in a classroom, Sherin, Mendez and Louis (2004) suggest that there are four principles or conditions for learning: activity, reflection, collaboration and community. 'The idea is that for effective learning to occur, the learner must be an active agent in the learning process and must be able to reflect on this learning. In addition, learners must be able to work together in ways that support each other's learning within a community that nurtures such opportunities' (p. 209). It is not only students who are implicated in cooperative learning but teachers as well and the chapter considers capacity building strategies for teachers who seek a departure from traditional classroom teaching based on a competitive and authoritarian ethos. Dean argues that cooperative learning is a useful strategy for creating a classroom-based learning community and her research reveals some of the problems and possibilities of such an initiative.

Continuing on the classroom theme, Rana Hussain and John Retallick take up the issue of multigrade teaching and learning in Chapter seven. They report on a research study conducted in the Northern Areas of Pakistan where multigrade classes are quite common due to the isolation of many villages and the consequent small schools. The research, carried out by Hussain, was an intervention study into four areas of school improvement in multigrade classes; curriculum reorganization, resource development, community involvement and peer tutoring. The most significant outcomes were in the latter two areas, both concerning student learning: community members coming into the schools to foster student learning, and students learning from each other. At first, both of these ideas were anathema to the teachers who saw their *teacher role* being usurped, but following the intervention the attitudes were very different and positive towards the *learning* that resulted.

Muhammad Memon and Zubeda Bana focus on the role of the head teacher in developing learning communities in Chapter eight. There is no doubt that this is the keystone of the learning community movement for without pedagogical leadership, schools will not be transformed into learning communities 'It seems clear that transforming the school organization into a learning community can be done only with the leaders' sanction and active nurturing of the entire staff's development as a community' (Hord, 1997:3). The role of the head teacher has to change from simply carrying out management tasks to taking up the challenge of leadership. But it is leadership of a particular kind that is required, where there is a central concern for the improvement of teaching and learning. In the chapter, the authors review literature on leadership and management and argue the case for a shift of thinking towards pedagogical leadership. They also present the results of a piece of research they carried out in two schools in the Northern Areas of Pakistan where they found good examples of pedagogical leaders in action.

In Chapter nine, Qamar Safdar, considers the somewhat contentious matter of parents and their relationships with schools and teachers. From the perspective of 'parents as partners' with teachers in the learning community, Safdar examines some of the problematic and troublesome aspects of the home-school connection from historical and contemporary points of view, with a particular focus on the situation in Pakistan. As a school head prior to joining the faculty at AKU-IED, she is able to draw on rich experience of the difficulties involved in forging positive and healthy relationships between parents and teachers. Now, in her faculty role, she has a special interest in improving this aspect of the life of schools and examples are taken from her classes to show how parents can meaningfully participate in schools alongside teachers.

The final two chapters may be viewed as a section that is intended to draw the book to a close. The first of these, Chapter ten, by Fauzia Shamim and Iffat Farah, tells the story of a research project that sought to create communities of practice in three schools in Karachi. The chapter highlights the possibilities and problems inherent in the idea of university faculty working with teachers in schools to develop relationships of trust, care and commitment in a bureaucratic environment. The possibilities are captured in the words of one

## INTRODUCTION

teacher who said: 'it is a good way of building trust amongst the teachers...I feel free now and not previously, to share different stories of my class...I'm no more scared of saying 'I don't know'. These are powerful words that speak to the possibility of transforming schools into learning communities, but problems do not simply go away and changes do not occur overnight. Indeed, such changes will take years of persistent effort and it is important that we gain knowledge from this research.

In the concluding chapter, the theme is professional learning through networks. This theme takes us beyond the individual school to the important capacity building function of learning from other schools and other contexts. As Mitchell and Sackney (2000) point out 'network theory assumes that individuals' thoughts and behaviours are at least partly dependent on the ties they establish with other folk in their social or professional community' (p. 23). In this chapter, Sikunder Ali Baber, Zakia Sarwar and Qamar Safdar provide an analysis of the theory of networking along with its place in teacher learning and school reform. They then illustrate the theory with three case studies of professional networks in which they are personally involved. The significance of networked learning is that it shifts attention from competition and privacy amongst schools to collaboration across schools for the purpose of sharing and learning from each other. Spender (2003) makes this point well when she says: 'One of the major challenges for schools is to abandon hierarchies...and to replace them with new, flexible and open structures which encourage free movement of professional and personal expertise across institutions' (p. 120).

Finally, who do we hope will read this book? The book is for teachers and student teachers, teacher educators and trainers, school leaders and managers, education system administrators and policy makers. In short, anyone who has an interest in improving schools in Pakistan and other developing countries could benefit from reading this book. Our hope is that the book will not only be widely read, but will inspire people to act on the ideas with sincerity and commitment to transform schools into learning communities.

John Retallick
Iffat Farah

# 1

# TRANSFORMING SCHOOLS INTO LEARNING COMMUNITIES: FOCUS ON PAKISTAN

*John Retallick and Al-Karim Datoo*

The question before us in this chapter, indeed in this book, is 'How can the quality of schooling in Pakistan be transformed?' That schooling needs to be transformed, for a majority of Pakistani children, is our focus in the first part of the chapter. We present evidence of drastic problems in the quality of schooling and explore the societal context to uncover some of the root causes of those problems in Pakistan. This sets the scene for the second part of the chapter; an investigation into the existing state of knowledge in the areas of learning organization, community of practice and learning community. We see potential in these ideas to transform the schools of Pakistan. Furthermore, we believe there to be a developmental progression in the ideas, by beginning with the principles of a learning organization, moving to a community of practice and thereon to achieving the ultimate goal of a learning community.

It is pertinent to point out that these ideas are providing the basis for the transformation of schools in many countries, and whilst most exist in western contexts, there is now increasing evidence of the ideas being employed in the developing world as well, and Pakistan in particular (as this book amply demonstrates). We do not suggest that all problems outlined in the first section of the chapter can be solved by the application of learning community theory—it is not that simple and the problems of education in Pakistan are deep-rooted. Our argument is that schools need to improve and we believe that will happen to a significant extent if the ideas outlined here are adopted on a widespread basis.

Education is a key function of all societies. In modern civil societies, education has been formalised through the creation of specific institutions of learning such as schools, colleges and universities through which education has become an official and organised activity. The society, largely through the government, shapes the form and content of education, which in turn shapes the society as generations pass through the institutions. Therefore, there is a dialectical relationship between education and society; one influencing the other. Given this inter-relationship of society and education, it is necessary to consider the socio-economic context that prevails in the country in order to understand the condition of schools and schooling.

## Context and Quality of School Education in Pakistan

Pakistan was created on 14 August 1947. It was almost ten years before the first constitution was agreed upon in 1956, when the nation became the Islamic Republic of Pakistan, with a parliamentary form of government. Since then, parliamentary democracy has been disrupted several times by periods of military rule but was most recently restored following elections held in October 2002. With a current population of more than 140 million ethnically-diverse people, the provision of quality education has always been one of Pakistan's most pressing problems. This is indicated by an adult functional literacy rate of less than 50%, a low school participation rate, with some six million children not attending school, and an unacceptably high drop-out rate. The situation is worse for girls than boys, with a range of socio-cultural and economic factors in Pakistan causing an even lower participation rate for them—recent estimates are 55 per cent for girls and 87 per cent for boys (Farah and Bacchus, 1999).

Pakistan, like other developing countries, faces crucial challenges regarding the quality of life. According to UNDP, Pakistan ranks 135 out of 174 countries on the Human Development Index (UNDP, 2000:149). This index measures dimensions such as life expectancy at birth, adult literacy rate, combined primary and secondary enrolment ratio and per capita income. Perhaps the most crucial factor plaguing development is poverty. In Pakistan, one in every three families is poor (SPDC, 2000: 30), and Pakistan ranks 68 out of 174 on the Human Poverty Index (UNDP, 2000:151).

These figures clearly state the extent of poverty in Pakistan, which causes a significant crisis in both quantity and quality of education. In Pakistan, there are some 43.5 million illiterate adults (15+), primary enrolment is 57%, secondary enrolment is 22% and higher education enrolment is just 1.9% (Hoodbhoy, 1998:2). That current (2003) public expenditure on education is only 2.2% of GDP (recently increased from 1.7%), seems to prove Hoodbhoy's statement that '...education is not perceived as a vital, central need of Pakistani society, it is, therefore, not accorded the protection enjoyed by other [social] institutions' (1998:4).

The school education system inherited from the British Raj was meagre: 'At the time the citizenry of the new country was about 90% illiterate and there were only a handful of educational institutions which were grossly inadequate for the needs of the country' (Hayes, 1987:8). Nowadays, school education is provided by a range of different systems and types of schools of greatly varying quality:

- a government system of primary and secondary schools
- a range of private schools and school systems (some non-profit and others for-profit)
- religious schools (known as *madrasahs*)
- community-based schools.

The major problems with the quality of education are found in the government system that caters for four out of five children who attend school, but has been described as a 'failure' (Hoodbhoy, 1998:5). Furthermore, Hoodbhoy (1998) states that 'Pakistan's education system fails because, in its present form, it is simply not valuable or important enough to the society' (p. 3). The argument is that the rich can afford the fees to send their children to private schools but few care enough for the poor to be concerned about their quality of education.

Besides the lack of government funding available to them, other factors contributing to 'failure' are: political and bureaucratic interference (e.g. staff transfers, lack of merit-based appointments, corruption in contract awarding); lack of accountability and sound management practices; lack of internationally comparative learning outcome standards (i.e. curriculum and assessment); and, lack of high quality teacher and staff training (Bregman and Mohammad, 1998:68). One commentator (Mustafa, 2004), recently summarized:

> From a set of medieval curriculum objectives, to substandard textbooks, a teaching method based on rote learning, a vast network of poorly organised and poorly maintained schools, and a public examination system which is fast losing its credibility, we all know and are agreed that the education sector needs immediate and concerted attention at the highest level of policy making (p. 1).

However, despite this grim picture, all is not lost. This needs to be emphasized because, apparently, against all the odds, some schools in the government sector have shown improvement and are perceived by their local communities as successful schools. For instance, in the 'Roads to Success' research study, Farah et al. (1996) found that the successful schools differed from the control schools 'most consistently in terms of school/classroom climate, teacher ownership/commitment and teacher mastery/competence' (p. 8). They describe a successful school in these terms:

> A task-oriented, orderly, and relaxed school/classroom climate prevails in the successful schools. They contain competent teachers who attend regularly and express ownership of and commitment to the school, are able to implement the curriculum completely and on time, and with concern for student learning. Parents (both fathers and mothers) become aware of these school characteristics through the attitudes and behavior of their children (p. 8).

These features of the internal conditions of schools may be seen as the starting point of a learning community. By building on and extending these features, the schools would embark on a journey of development and improvement which is required in all schools in Pakistan. In the next section of the chapter, we outline the key ideas and strategies supporting the learning community movement and seek to show how schools might embark on that journey.

## The School as a Learning Community

Given the problems of school education outlined in the previous section, we now examine the idea of a learning community as a way of handling some of those problems and transforming the schools. Whilst the idea of 'learning community' has been around for some time (some would argue from the time of John Dewey in the early twentieth century), recently, there seems to be renewed interest in the idea with the publication of a number of books e.g. Retallick et al. (1999) and Mitchell and Sackney (2000), journal articles e.g. special issue of *Education Administration Quarterly*, February 1999, on 'School as Community' and application of the ideas in schools e.g. Thiessen and Anderson (1999). Though it is a shifting, contested and somewhat elusive concept, some points about learning community seem to be agreed:

> The metaphor of the learning community assumes, first, that schools are expected to facilitate the learning of all individuals, and second, that educators are ideally positioned to address fundamental issues and concerns in relation to learning (Mitchell and Sackney, 2000:1).

This quotation draws attention to a number of interesting aspects of learning community theory which is held in general agreement. To begin with, it positions 'learning community' as a metaphor. In our knowledge, this idea was first mentioned by Professor Tom Sergiovanni while addressing a conference in 1993, which was subsequently published as *Organizations or Communities? Changing the metaphor changes the theory* (Sergiovanni, 1994). Sergiovanni has made an important suggestion—he suggests that both 'organization' and 'community' are metaphors i.e. linguistic constructions, rather than realities which are immutable and set in concrete (to use another metaphor). Since these notions are linguistic and social constructions, it is possible for them to change; as we change our way of talking about, and working in a school, we can begin to change it's reality. We can, indeed, change our schools from bureaucratic organizations to caring communities, by changing the discourse and social relationships of their participants.

Traditionally, schools have been viewed as 'organizations' featuring bureaucracy, hierarchy, accountability, procedures, rules and regulations. These are the elements and language of a bureaucratic organization. However, as Harber and Davies (1998), based on research in developing countries, state: 'unfortunately in terms of decision-making, bureaucracy is a rigid, closed and non-participatory form of organization which has severe shortcomings in a contemporary world of rapid change and uncertainty.... In schools its effects are particularly harmful on pupils, who suffer the routinized and authoritarian modes of teaching that it inevitably promotes' (p. 59).

While discussing the concept of community, we use the ideas and language of relationships, meaning, collaboration, inquiry and reflection. These are the ideas that underpin the construct of learning community (Mitchell and Sackney, 2000:6). It has been suggested (Scribner et al. 1999) that bureaucratic organization and community are the opposite ends of a continuum. If so, trying to move schools entirely from the former to the latter in a single step would create considerable, if not intolerable, tensions. A resolution of this tension might be found in terms of balance—schools 'need to locate a balance that provides sufficient communal characteristics while attending to bureaucratic imperatives in ways supportive of continuous and reflective professional learning that has the best interests of students in mind' (Scribner et al. 1999:154). In response to this interesting point, we make two observations. Firstly, we agree that certain features of bureaucracy should be retained in schools even when they are transformed into communities, for example, financial accountability. Secondly, we see transformation as a developmental progression or change process (often referred to as a journey), which will take some time and capacity building; certainly not a one-step process.

The next interesting aspect of learning community theory in the above quotation is that *all* participants in the school are positioned as learners. Of course, the major participants in any school are students, teachers and administrators (with parents often being included as well). In contrast to traditional ideas about school where only students are regarded as learners; in a learning community teachers and administrators are both learners though they play different roles in the community. Teachers may be regarded as 'model learners', in the sense that they demonstrate learning to their students and engage students in discussions about *how* to learn i.e. meta-learning or learning about learning, not only *what* to learn. They project themselves to students as fellow travellers on a learning journey, admit when they don't know something and then show students how they go about finding out. They realise that sometimes students know more than their teachers and in such cases, are prepared to learn from their students. Principals and head teachers may be regarded as 'leading learners' or pedagogical leaders, in the sense that they focus the energy of the school on teaching and learning, working closely with teachers and encouraging them to improve their practice and enhancing student learning. All that implies that they, too, are engaged in a process of lifelong learning. Teachers and principals have to deal with large and complex questions of professional learning and development, which is difficult and problematic in contexts where resources are limited.

The final point made in the quotation concerns the responsibility given to educators to 'address fundamental issues and concerns in relation to learning'. If there is one area of knowledge that sets educators apart from other professionals, or one form of expertise that educators should possess, it is in the area of learning. Some people think that the work of teachers is merely to teach and the rest is left to the students; in a learning community, a teacher's work is to facilitate learning, this being done only when the students have learnt what was intended for them. Teachers accept the responsibility of ensuring that students learn and accept the challenge of continuously updating their understanding of learning. For instance, in recent years significant advances in understanding and facilitating learning have occurred e.g. learning as a constructivist process, the theory of multiple intelligences, cooperative learning, outcome-based education etc. Teachers need to be up-to-date with these developments just as medical doctors or other professionals need to have the latest knowledge about their profession.

Having said that there is some agreement around those points, it should also be pointed out that there is some disagreement about trying to define the notion of learning community. As Wyatt (1997) argues: 'Defining community is somewhat difficult because, to a large extent, what a community is, depends on what its members intend it to be' (p. 80). Each community is, therefore, unique 'and the construction of the community is an ongoing process of active participation and intense communication' (Mitchell and Sackney, 2000:7). What this means is that each school has to embark on its own journey of becoming a learning community and the results will differ from place to place depending on the approaches and emphases of the participants in each school. There is no recipe for building a learning community but it may be possible, as suggested later, to see a number of stages in a change process that may help schools to make the journey.

**A New Vision for Education**

Starratt (1996) also reminds us that the idea of a learning community is a metaphor, which helps us to organize and pursue a new vision for education. He defines a number of characteristics of a learning community, as follows:

- Learning must be situated in a critical community of inquirers who accept that knowledge is always partial and fallible and who support the enrichment of knowledge through sharing of meanings, interpretations, and learnings among all members of the community.
- The learning agenda of the school must be continually related to something intrinsically human—to the exploration of questions important to human individuals and social life.
- The learning agenda of the school must be related to the large cultural projects of our current era as well as to the cultural projects of our history. Thus, school learnings are connected to a significant discourse about the making of history.
- School meanings (i.e. what students learn at school), must be continuously related to students' experience of everyday life (p. 70).

Whilst Starratt acknowledges that every school that undertakes the task of remaking itself as a learning community becomes unique, he argues that learning communities will manifest some common, core processes. He puts forward a 'beginning listing' of those processes:

1. Learning takes place in a caring environment. This refers to all children and teachers feeling that they are cared for and that they care for each other. It also extends to caring for what is being studied in the curriculum, through various cooperative learning processes.
2. Learning involves lots of storytelling. This is important both as a way of communicating and as a way of linking the lesson of the curriculum and the lifeworld of the student.
3. Learning in school is related to everyday home and neighbourhood experiences. This idea connects the lifeworld of the school and the lifeworld of home and neighbourhood.
4. Learning should lead to some product or performance. This ensures that students own their learning and demonstrates that learning is useful both inside and outside the school.
5. There should be periodic and continuous reference to an exploration of meta-narratives. These are the 'larger stories' concerning the

central elements of our culture to which students need to have connection for meaning to occur.
6. The learning community should periodically explore the really big questions. Such questions include: What does it mean to be human? What is the meaning of life, suffering, death? What does it mean to be a community? (pp. 71-81).

Mitchell and Sackney (2000) claim that creating a learning community is about building the capacity of people in schools to relate to each other in communitarian ways, rather than bureaucratic or individualistic ways. They argue that all participants in schools need to be learners and that learning must be positioned at the forefront in debates and decisions about what happens in the everyday life of schools. There is now overwhelming evidence that teacher professional learning is consistently related to increased student learning (e.g. Darling-Hammond, 2000), so their claim is on solid ground.

In the holistic vision of Mitchell and Sackney (2000), there are three inter-related dimensions of capacity building—personal, interpersonal and organizational. Emanating from each of these is a range of strategies that can facilitate capacity building:

- Personal capacity—internal and external searches for knowledge. Learning portfolios (internal—learning through reflection), action research (external—learning from research) and workplace learning (trialling ideas in practice) are methods of knowledge construction used to build personal capacity.
- Interpersonal capacity—building a collaborative learning climate. Affirmation, invitation, caring and trust are essential elements of a learning climate. Breaking down teacher isolation and building up teams of people working together improves interpersonal capacity. The strategies are based on building human relationships and communication. These include mentoring, coaching, developmental supervision and professional conversations to reach shared understandings.
- Organizational capacity—attention to the socio-cultural conditions, structural arrangements and collaborative processes in a school. Schools must be structured to support connection rather than separation, diversity rather than uniformity, empowerment rather than control and inclusion rather than dominance. Strategies could include organizational learning through partnerships, shared

leadership, school reviews, school–wide mentoring and learning circles.

These kinds of professional learning strategies can lead to the reconstruction of professional lives, which is required for building a learning community. Individual and collective learning are embedded in one another and are mutually reinforcing. Learning communities exist where educators think together about professional practice and engage in sustained dialogue about how to improve the learning outcomes of their students.

Mitchell and Sackney (2000) use the term 'learning architecture' to suggest that the elements of a learning community need to be consciously built alongside the 'physical architecture' of the school. The elements are: learning teams, a learning agent, time, feedback, incentives and rewards. They say that 'the development of a learning architecture is one of the critical steps in bringing a learning community to life' (p. 121). This is a big task in the context of present policies and practices of teacher professional development in most school systems around the world which provide few resources, little time and inadequate rewards. This is particularly the case in the developing world, but if we want significant improvement in schools, they must undertake the journey of becoming learning communities. Mitchell and Sackney (2000) conclude:

> For us, a learning community consists in a group of people who take an active, reflective, collaborative, learning–oriented, and growth–promoting approach toward the mysteries, problems, and perplexities of teaching and learning (p. 9).

## The Journey Towards a Learning Community

Having considered the outlook of a learning community in the previous section, we now turn to the question of 'how'. How can schools be transformed and what are the stages in the journey towards a learning community? We suggest that there are three stages in the change process from a bureaucratic organization to a learning community (each stage is likely to take at least a year of professional development and capacity-building before moving to the next stage). The first stage is concerned with adopting and putting into practice some principles of a learning organization. The second stage moves into community by using the idea of a 'community of practice' and the third stage is about building a learning community.

## Stage 1: From Bureaucratic Organization to Learning Organization

Watkins and Marsick (1993), start off by asking the questions, 'Why do we need a learning organization?' and 'What is a learning organization?'. Their answer to the first question is in terms of change:

> The forces compelling organizations to make this shift in perspective include changes in organizations, the changing nature of work, changes in the workforce and changes in how people learn (p. 4).

Their answer to the second question is that 'the learning organization is one that learns continuously and transforms itself. Learning takes place in individuals, teams, the organization, and even the communities with which the organization interacts' (Watkins and Marsick, 1993:8). Whilst learning organizations have different outlooks, they are likely to share some features such as:

- Leaders who model calculated risk taking and experimentation
- Decentralized decision making and employee empowerment
- Skill inventories and audits of learning capacity
- Systems for sharing learning and using it in the business
- Rewards and structures for employee initiative
- Consideration of long-term consequences and impact on the work of others
- Frequent use of cross-functional work teams
- Opportunities to learn from experience on a daily basis
- A culture of feedback and disclosure.

Applying such ideas in schools, with their history of teacher isolation and individualistic work culture (Hargreaves, 1994), may seem rather impractical. However, it should not be too difficult, since 'people can learn by converting ordinary challenges in their work into learning opportunities...learning is a continuous cycle of acting and reflecting that grows out of work' (Watkins and Marsick, 1993: 26-27).

What is required to begin is not so much a wholesale change, but a recognition in the teaching profession that professional learning can and does take place on–the–job i.e., at school. This occurs when problems and difficulties are treated as learning opportunities for teachers. A workplace learning orientation can arise from a change of thinking on the part of a few individuals that may then be sufficient to begin a change process. The first step would be to build teams of teachers working together on projects significant to teaching and learning. Learning to work effectively in a team is the first building-block of the learning organization and the first step towards a learning community.

## Teamwork and Learning

Teamwork and learning processes mostly reflect the work of Donald Schon (1983), who described learning as an interaction of action and reflection. Team learning processes call for integrating thinking and action. Whilst we may be familiar with these processes for individuals, it is rather challenging to think of them as *team* processes where skills of dialogue, discussion and consensus formation are most important.

Whilst it is clear that it is only individuals who actually learn, the team acts as a sharing and reinforcing mechanism that enhances and extends individual learning. When individuals learn they may not share their insights, or even if they do, their insights may not get used by the entire school. However, when a team tries something new, the members reinforce each other's actions and spread the ideas faster and further through their combined contacts in the school. This may be referred to as the synergy of teamwork. 'Teams are crucibles through which opposing ideas can be brought together and confronted—ideas that otherwise would remain within the heads of individuals and not linked together in new combinations' (Watkins and Marsick, 1993:97).

So, in order to take the first step on the journey of transformation, begin by forming the teachers into teams to work together on tasks with one member as the team leader. Many schools would have already done this, though it is important to ensure that teams are working well before taking the next step into double-loop learning.

## Double-loop Learning

Argyris (1992) argues that 'organizational learning is a competence that all organizations should develop', on the grounds that 'the better organizations are at learning, the more likely will they be able to detect and correct errors...and the more likely they will be at being innovative or knowing the limits of their innovation' (p. 1). He defines an error as 'any mismatch between plan or intention and what actually happened when either is implemented' (p. 1). Mismatches may be technical, administrative, or human at the individual, group, inter-group and organizational level.

An important distinction in Argyris's work is between 'single-loop' and 'double-loop' learning. Single-loop learning occurs when an error is detected and corrected without questioning or altering the underlying values of the system i.e. the problem is 'fixed' but may re-occur because the system has not been changed. For example, a teacher may be having problems maintaining discipline in a classroom, but the students are well behaved when the Principal walks into the room. That is to say, we have learnt that the problem is 'fixed' by the presence of the Principal and that is single-loop learning. But the Principal cannot be there all the time so there has to be a more fundamental change to the classroom system i.e. double-loop learning is required. Double-loop learning occurs when errors are corrected by first examining and changing the governing variables of the organization and then the actions. So we need to know why the teacher is having problems maintaining discipline and then take some action, such as changing the seating arrangements of the students or devising a professional development process for the teacher according to the problem. The significance of double-loop learning for our purpose in transforming schools is that it questions the assumptions and values that underpin our practices, bringing about change and improvement, rather than merely reinforcing the status quo.

How then can schools be helped to double-loop learn? Four steps are suggested here. The first step is to help individuals and teams to become aware of their theories-in-use that restrict them to a 'fixing-problems' level of working and single-loop learning. The second step is to help them begin to reflect on the assumptions and values that underpin their practice e.g. this may be started by the introduction of action research or reflective practice in the school. The third step is to see how they might create a double-loop learning system, whereby individuals learn a new theory of action that encompasses an analysis of principles and values before taking action. The fourth step is to introduce new actions, such as new approaches to teaching and learning, and also help others to learn them. Argyris argues that 'research on intervention suggests that it is possible to help individuals learn new theories-in-use and create new learning systems...(through) the creation of a dialectical learning process where the participants can continually compare their theories-in-use, and the learning system in which they are embedded, with alternative models' (p. 37).

There is an important issue here for a capacity-building approach towards transforming schools. Inherent in the idea of capacity-building is learning how to improve one's performance on the job. Such learning is likely to be largely single-loop learning, unless it is possible to confront alternative possibilities for doing one's job. It is, therefore, essential to think of the school as a learning system in a way that reflection on the work being carried out is broadened to include an 'outside perspective' i.e., someone who can bring alternative views and suggestions about how teaching and learning might be done differently. Such alternatives could come from a course, a consultant, a mentor, a critical friend or a professional development teacher, to name a few.

**Senge's Five Disciplines**

One of the most significant approaches to learning organization theory is the work of Peter Senge in his book, 'The Fifth Discipline' (Senge, 1990). In his book, the author puts forward five interconnected disciplines for building learning organizations. Each of the disciplines is briefly outlined in the following paragraphs.

*Systems Thinking*: This is the 'conceptual cornerstone that underlies all of the five disciplines' (p. 69), providing a language and a framework with which to view organizations as complex wholes rather than parts. It enables patterns and cycles to emerge, structures and relationships to be identified in dynamic complexity. Two of the basic ideas of systems thinking are 'feedback'—the idea of a reciprocal flow of influence including both cause and effect, and the principle of 'leverage'. Leverage means observing where actions and changes in structures may result in significant, enduring improvements.

*Personal Mastery*: This is the phrase used to describe the discipline of personal growth and learning. People with high levels of personal mastery are continually expanding their ability in order to achieve their goals in life. From their quest for continual learning comes the spirit of the learning organization. That means building an organization where creating visions is valued and where challenging the status quo is expected.

*Mental Models*: These are the world views we hold, the assumptions we make and the frameworks we believe in. Entrenched mental models often thwart changes and restrict learning. Senge argues that most of our mental models are systematically flawed. 'They miss critical feedback relationships, misjudge time delays, and often focus on variables that are visible or salient, not necessarily high leverage' (p. 203). Systems thinking is, itself, a mental model and the more it is used, the greater the likelihood of organizational learning taking place.

*Shared Vision*: Just as an individual may have a personal vision, an organization may also have a shared vision i.e. a similar picture carried by people throughout the organization of what they are trying to create or achieve. Shared vision is vital for the learning organization because it provides focus and energy for learning. A discipline of building shared vision is emerging along with practical tools for working with it. This discipline extends principles and insights from personal mastery into the world of collective aspiration and shared commitment.

*Team Learning*: Team learning is the process of aligning and developing the capacity of a team to create the results they desire. If teams learn, they become a microcosm for learning throughout the organization. There are three critical dimensions—the need for teams to think insightfully about complex issues, the need for innovative and coordinated action and the interaction of team members with other teams to foster cross–team learning.

As schools begin to grapple with double–loop learning and the five disciplines, it is useful to refer to the work of Marsick (1987), who developed a theory of workplace learning that integrates three domains of learning i.e. technical, practical and emancipatory learning. In Marsick's terms, the technical domain equates with instrumental, task-related learning which is a common focus of most workplace learning in schools. An example of this domain would be a teacher learning to prepare lesson plans. The practical domain is represented by dialogic learning which refers to the creation of consensual norms through dialogue and discussion. Dialogic learning could result from a group of teachers questioning the value of rote learning and discussing how they might introduce constructivist learning. Using this framework, however, enables us to seek out a third domain in emancipatory learning that Marsick refers to as self-reflective learning. Reflective learning refers to the way we learn to understand ourselves and how we are shaped through social interaction involving beliefs, perceptions and values. Reflective learning can be linked with Senge's mental models and Argyris's double-loop learning to provide a comprehensive view of a learning organization.

## Stage 2: From Learning Organization to Community of Practice

Once some of the principles of a learning organization are in place in a school e.g. working effectively in teams or agreeing on a shared vision for the school, it is possible to move to the second stage in the journey towards a learning community. The second stage may be seen as a 'community of practice' and the work of Wenger (1998), has brought this term into common usage. He uses the term in a generic way to refer to all those groupings and institutions of people throughout society who come together for a specific purpose—as in organizations, schools, families etc. In this work, the key ideas of 'community' and 'practice' are brought together to show how interactions amongst people enable the development and accomplishment of the various enterprises of our lives. He argues that 'a practice is, first and foremost, a process by which we can experience the world and our engagement with it is meaningful' (p. 51). It is the negotiation of meaning through participation (doing, talking, thinking, feeling and belonging) and reification (making a thing, object or artefact out of our experience), that enables a practice to begin and develop. Teaching is an example of a practice. A community of practice is both social and individualistic; through social processes each individual develops and shapes their identity i.e. who they are, what they can and cannot do, how they relate with others and so on.

Though we are all engaged in many different practices in our lives, the most important one for teachers is the practice of teaching. When a group of teachers and learners come together to negotiate how to work together, such as in a school and a classroom, it is possible for a community of practice to develop. Wenger has asserted three dimensions or characteristics of a practice that generate the coherence required to constitute a community:

- mutual engagement
- a joint enterprise
- a shared repertoire (p. 73).

The mutual engagement of participants refers to the idea of people negotiating meanings with each other. This is a fundamentally important point in building a learning community; teachers and students must have the opportunity to ask, 'what do you mean?'. In traditional schools, there is very little opportunity for this as teachers sit silently in meetings and students sit silently in class (if they speak at all, it is usually not to ask 'what do you mean by what you just said?'). To belong to a community of practice entails having meaningful conversations with others. This implies the enabling engagement of all members but it does not entail homogeneity—diversity and difference are respected in a community where each person finds a unique place and gains a unique identity. Mutual engagement is created through interpersonal relationships amongst people but does not guarantee the absence of tension or conflict.

The second characteristic of a community of practice is the negotiation of a joint enterprise. A joint enterprise is the result of a collective process of negotiation reflecting the full complexity of mutual engagement; it is defined by the participants pursuing it; and, it creates among participants, relations of mutual accountability that form an integral part of the practice. In a school setting there are many examples of this, with the most obvious being the curriculum. The traditional, bureaucratic school allows no negotiation on the curriculum; the curriculum is 'given' and must be 'implemented'. In such schools, teachers are often heard to say that they must 'cover the syllabus'; it is not learning for understanding that is important, but getting through the textbook by the end of term. As a school moves towards a learning community, the curriculum is viewed as a negotiated, constructed and flexible framework or scaffold on which teaching and learning is built.

The third characteristic is the development of a shared repertoire or set of resources used to constitute the practice including routines, artefacts, words, tools, ways of doing things, stories etc. It includes the discourse by which members describe their experiences and the styles by which they express their identity as members. This is in many ways the heart of the school; it is to be found in the way teachers and students talk about their work in the school, how they relate to each other, how lessons are conducted, what artefacts are displayed in the school foyer or principal's office and so on. It is sometimes referred to as the 'culture of the school' and is obvious when a culture of community exists in a school.

Since a community involves the members belonging to it, the notion of 'belonging' is central and is a basic psychological need. Osterman (2000:324-5) says that 'a community exists when its members experience a sense of belonging or personal relatedness... (this) involves the need to feel securely connected with others in the environment and to experience oneself as worthy of love and respect'. She also points out that 'this experience of belonging is an important factor in understanding student behavior and performance' (p. 325), and her extensive review of the research reveals that there is a positive relationship between sense of community and student motivation and engagement with learning tasks. Wenger (1998:173-187) suggests three distinct modes of belonging in a community:

1. engagement—active involvement in mutual processes of negotiation of meaning
2. imagination—creating images of the world and seeing connections through time and space by extrapolating from our own experience
3. alignment—coordinating our energy and activities in order to fit within broader structures and contribute to broader enterprises.

Each of these modes of belonging has a related form of work concerned with forming and maintaining the community. 'Indeed, it is by combining these three modes that we can form learning communities...' (p. 237).

The work of engagement is basically the work of forming the community and the principal or head teacher of a school plays a key role in this. It requires the ability to take part in meaningful activities and interactions, in the production of sharable artefacts, in community-building conversations, and in the negotiation of new situations. The role of the principal as a 'pedagogical leader' exemplifies this kind of work.

The work of imagination requires the ability to disengage—to observe our engagement as an outsider. It requires the ability to explore, take risks, and create unlikely connections. It demands a degree of playfulness and creativity. It needs the willingness, freedom, energy, and time to expose ourselves to something different and explore new relations. It can also provide a new perspective; the perspective of networking. Networking is now recognised as a powerful tool in teacher professional learning and good examples of that can be found in the various professional associations that have been, and are continuing to be, established at local and international levels.

The work of alignment is coordinating perspectives and actions in order to direct energies to a common purpose. The challenge of alignment is to connect local efforts to broader styles and discourses in ways that allow learners to invest their energy in them. It is about defining visions and aspirations for the school; often seen in the form of a mission statement.

Because engagement, imagination and alignment each have different but complementary strengths and weaknesses, they work best when combined; by combining them effectively, a community of practice can move towards becoming a learning community.

**Stage 3: Designing a Learning Community**

Moving towards the third stage of our journey, we outline two approaches to designing a learning community. Firstly, using the previously mentioned concepts we can discuss the principles for designing a 'learning architecture' that can be seen as the basis of a learning community. An important principle of designing a learning community is that students have varied opportunities and places for engagement. In traditional classrooms everyone learns the same thing at the same time through rote learning, with little attention to the quality of learning. By contrast, in a learning community there could be opportunities for students to participate in different ways related to building their individual identity. For example, students might pursue a deeper understanding of a topic of their choice that might be a part of a negotiated curriculum. Currently, most schools present students with information from textbooks that is abstracted from their lives outside of school. Alternatively, if each school could become involved in a socially meaningful enterprise, learning could be a service of that enterprise and make it authentic. The place of learning can sometimes be outside the school, in the wider community that becomes a resource for organizing the learning, as well as a context in which to manifest the learning. This is known as situated or contextualised learning and is most commonly seen in practice as 'community-based learning'.

For example, Hogan (2002) describes a community-based learning programme in environmental education that had students working as volunteers in an environmental agency. Whilst Hogan reveals some problems encountered in this project, she says that 'community-based and service learning programs offer the full richness of authentic contexts...' for learning (p. 618).

Wenger argues that this has two important implications for schools. Firstly, there needs to be a great deal more interaction between 'old-timers' and newcomers i.e. adults and youth, in the real contexts of everyday life rather than students being sheltered from the reality of actual practice. An important function of educational design is thus to maximize, rather than avoid, interactions among generations e.g. by inviting parents and community members to participate in the academic aspects of the school. Secondly, the role of teachers is diminished when they are unable to act as themselves due to the demands of their teaching responsibilities. For instance, as managers of very large classes, teachers do not have much opportunity to develop a rapport with the students. Rather they have to constantly act as authority figures—that is, as representatives of the institution and upholders of curricular demands, their identity defined by the institutional role.

A second approach refers to the work of learning community consultants, Joan Dalton and David Anderson in Australia. In an earlier publication, one of the present authors (John Retallick), made reference to their work, followed by glimpses into schools where they have had some influence (Retallick, 1999). At that time, in the late 1990s, they had achieved considerable success with schools in the Wagga Wagga Diocese of NSW. Their approach at the time was to conduct a five-day intensive 'Institute on Learning Communities' for principals and teachers, who would then begin transforming their schools. Dalton and Anderson would begin by arguing that:

We must prepare young people to live and thrive in tomorrow's world, one which enables them to:

- grow and develop as complete human beings
- live ethical values
- maximize their talents to achieve their personal best
- become responsible, contributing members of society
- play an active part in shaping a better world for all.
  (Dalton and Anderson, 1998:1)

They would focus on 'the adults our children need to become', in order to provide clear long-term goals for teachers and students in order to align their teaching and learning. These goals are seen as 'the outcomes that ultimately matter', and 'can best be realized through membership of caring learning communities, where the spirit of support and challenge work together in harmony, where relationships glue the community together, and where social-ethical values are the foundation upon which everything else is built' (1988:3).

In 2004, Dalton and Anderson developed their work in an interesting new direction, making it accessible to a wider audience, indeed anyone who has access to the Internet. Of particular importance in the present context is the accessibility of their work in Pakistan and other developing countries, where resource and other constraints often preclude teachers from the latest developments in teacher learning.

In cooperation with Education Queensland and Microsoft Corporation, Dalton and Anderson have launched a website on the internet that has potential to be a valuable resource for teacher education courses and school development initiatives in the area of building learning communities. This is a very extensive website called PLOT: Professional Learning Online Tool. The website may be located at www.plotpd.com and is designed to provide 'hands on', practical support to schools engaging in the process of transforming themselves into learning communities. The website offers a wealth of pedagogy content and processes, workshops, strategies, rubrics and tools for building dynamic professional communities focused on constructivist pedagogy. It combines high quality content with the latest Internet technology. It is a practical resource, offering professional learning tools to help schools:

- Build teacher understanding and expertise in pedagogy
- Develop school wide understandings, shared commitment and consistent approaches to learning and teaching
- Build and strengthen professionalism and a learning community
- Build on current practices toward preferred practices (Dalton and Anderson, 2003).

A brief overview of the website reveals two major sections called 'Pedagogy in action' and 'Professional communities'. Pedagogy in action contains six major areas and teaching practices essential to building and growing an effective learning community:

### Deep understanding

Deep understanding of significant, life-related matters is essential to our students' futures and to improving their learning and achievement. This requires that we clearly understand how learners construct understanding to make meaning from learning.

### Inquiry

As human beings, we are biologically designed to seek to make sense of the world. Inquiry is fundamental to helping us to build our theories about the world, and to becoming lifelong and life-wide learners in a world characterized by change and diversity.

### Communication

Communication is central to learning, and an essential key to life success. It is fundamental to making sense of, and successfully participating in, networked societies in a global world. That world is now awash with new communications media and information technologies, requiring that we are able to use and blend traditional and new literacies simultaneously.

### Collaboration

Collaborative effort is the lynchpin of any authentic community. It is essential for effective participation within the family, society, workplace and will be critical for the future of our world. Working collaboratively not only helps to prepare students for a successful life, but makes a dramatic difference to their learning and achievement.

### Self-responsibility

The development of young people toward becoming self-responsible, self-directed learners and autonomous human beings is a major goal of education. Lifelong and life-wide learning will be essential in a world characterized by change and diversity. The role we play in helping children learn to take increasing control of their thinking, learning and behaviour is critical.

### Human development

Of all the learning and teaching practices we engage in, human development is the cornerstone from which we must work to help our young people become the kinds of adults who will thrive in, and make a positive difference to, the world they will inherit.

The second area of the website, 'Professional Communities', is devoted to processes and strategies for building learning communities and is premised on the notion that 'a whole-school approach to professional development is needed, one that is coherent, on-going, site-based, targeted at improving school-wide practices, aligned with school learning goals, and tailored to suit the people and the place' (Dalton and Anderson, 2003). This section includes a substantial amount of material on:

- Professional learning processes
- Reflection and assessment
- Substantive dialogue
- Adult collaboration
- Implementation.

The website was recently trialled at AKU-IED with an M.Ed. cohort studying a module on Teacher Learning and proved to be a great success with the participants, all experienced teachers. It is possible that in the future, after the M.Ed. students graduate, they will be able to make use of this resource with teachers and schools in Pakistan and a number of countries in Central Asia and East Africa. This is an exciting prospect that could play an important part in transforming schools into learning communities in many countries.

## Conclusion

In this chapter, we have invited schools to embark upon a journey towards becoming learning communities. The metaphor of 'journey' implies a movement, a process of progress towards a vision of another place. When we think of a journey, we necessarily think of a starting point and a destination; where we are now and where we wish to be in the future.

In the first section of the chapter, we described the starting point by highlighting the general state of education in Pakistan and the issues concerning the quality of school education in particular. With this backdrop, we put forward a framework around the idea of the school as a learning community as a basis for transforming schools. This transformation, we suggest, entails a fundamental shift in the outlook and approach towards learning in schools. We argue that such a shift will not occur easily or overnight; it will require schools to work through several stages over an extended period of time.

For this we presented a capacity-building model and a change process; from bureaucratic organization we moved to learning organization, to community of practice and thence to learning community. Through this process, we believe that schools will become spaces where, not only students, but also teachers, heads, administrators and parents will take on various learning-related roles. Furthermore, a serious pursuit will create an ethos where values like trust, collaboration and thirst for knowledge form the cornerstones of the learning community.

When taken seriously, these ideas are robust and powerful. However, to make a difference, good ideas by themselves are never enough; they require the active involvement of people as agents of change to adopt and use them. We suggest that teachers, head teachers, parents and students could all be the agents of change to transform their schools into learning communities. If schools can be transformed, they are likely to have a significant effect on improving the quality of school education for children and ultimately on changing the society and nation they belong to.

The journey we refer to in this chapter holds both challenge and promise—for those who dare to travel. What follows, in subsequent chapters of this book, are the stories of some of the travellers who have begun their journey towards a learning community.

## References

Argyris, C. (1992). *On organizational learning*. Cambridge, Mass.: Blackwell.
Bregman, J. & Mohammad, N. (1998). Primary and secondary education—Structural issues. In P. Hoodbhoy (Ed.). *Education and the state: Fifty years of Pakistan* (pp. 68-91). Karachi: Oxford University Press.
Dalton, J. & Anderson, D. (1998). Today's children: Tomorrow's adults. Unpublished paper, *Hands on Educational Consultancy* (personal communication).
Dalton, J. & Anderson, D. (2003). PLOT website. Retrieved on 24 April 2003 from http://www.plotpd.com/Home.htm.
Darling-Hammond, L. (2000). Teacher quality and student achievement: A review of state policy evidence. *Education Policy Analysis Archives*, 8 (1).
Farah, I. et al. (1996). *Roads to success: Self-sustaining primary school change in rural Pakistan*. Research report. Oslo: IMTEC and Karachi: AKU-IED.

Farah, I. & Bacchus, K. (1999). 'Educating girls in Pakistan'. In E. Leach and A. Little (Eds.) *Education, cultures and economics: Dilemmas for Development* (pp. 225–37). NY: Falmer.

Harber, C. & Davies, L. (1998). *School Management and Effectiveness in Developing Countries: The Post-bureaucratic School*. London: Continuum.

Hargreaves, A. (1994). *Changing Teachers, Changing times*. Toronto: OISE Press.

Hayes, L. D. (1987). *The Crisis of Education in Pakistan*. Lahore: Vanguard Books.

Hogan, K. (2002). 'Pitfalls of community-based learning: How power dynamics limit adolescents' trajectories of growth and participation'. *Teachers College Record*, 104(3), 586–624.

Hoodbhoy, P. (1998). *Education and the state: Fifty Years of Pakistan*. Karachi: Oxford University Press.

UNDP (2000). *Human Development Report*. Karachi: Oxford University Press.

Marsick, V. (1987). *Learning in the Workplace*. London: Croom Helm.

Marsick, V. & Watkins, K. (1993). *Informal and Incidental Learning in the Workplace*. London: Routledge.

Mitchell, C. & Sackney, L. (2000). *Profound Improvement: Building Capacity for a Learning Community*. Lisse: Swets and Zeitlinger.

Mustafa, S. (2004, April 3). 'Analysing Failure of Government Initiatives in Education'. *Dawn: Education Expo Supplement*.

Osterman, K. (2000). 'Students' needs for belonging in the school community'. *Review of Educational Research*, 70(3), 323–67.

Retallick, J., Cocklin, B. & Coombe, K. (Eds.). (1999). *Learning Communities in Education*. London: Routledge.

Retallick, J. (1999). 'Transforming schools into learning communities: Beginning the journey'. In J. Retallick, B. Cocklin & K. Coombe (Eds.). *Learning Communities in Education* (pp. 107–30). London: Routledge.

Scribner, J., Cockrell, K., Cockrell, D. & Valentine, J. (1999). 'Creating professional communities in schools through organizational learning: An evaluation of a school improvement process'. *Educational Administration Quarterly*, 17(1), 130–60.

Sergiovanni, T. (1994). 'Organizations or communities? Changing the metaphor changes the theory'. *Educational Administration Quarterly*, 30(2), 214–26.

Schon, D. (1983). *The Reflective Practitioner*. New York: Basic Books.

Senge, P. (1990). *The Fifth Discipline*. Sydney: Random House.

Starrat, R.J. (1996). *Transforming Educational administration: Meaning, Community and Excellence*. New York: McGraw Hill.

SPDC (2000). *Social Development in Pakistan: Annual Review 2000*. Karachi: Social Policy and Development Centre and Oxford University Press.

Thiessen, D. & Anderson, S. (1999). *Getting into the habit of change in Ohio schools: The cross-case study of 12 transforming learning communities*. Columbus: Ohio Department of Education.

Watkins, K.E. & Marsick, V.J. (1993). *Sculpting the Learning Organization*. San Francisco: Jossey-Bass.

UNDP (2000). *Human Development Report 2000. United Nations Development Programme Report*. New York: Oxford University Press.

Wenger, E. (1998). *Communities of Practice*. Cambridge: Cambridge University Press.

Wyatt, S. (1997). 'Dialogue, reflection and Community'. *The Journal of Experiential Education*, 20(2), 80–85.

# 2

# BECOMING A SCHOOL SCIENCE TEACHER IN PAKISTAN: A FEMALE NARRATIVE

*Nelofer Halai*

In this chapter you will meet Munazza[1], a science teacher who works in a private, English-medium and co-educational school for children from middle-income families in Karachi. As part of a larger life history single case-study,[2] to understand a female science teacher's conceptions of the nature of science, I had prolonged and continuous interaction with her over a period of seventeen months. In my effort to grasp her understanding of her practice, I developed a deep insight into the process she followed in becoming a school teacher. This chapter deals with the process of becoming a teacher at two levels—the first level is how one enters the teaching profession in Pakistan and the second level is about the more profound and deeper issue of *how does one become a teacher*. Woven throughout the narrative is the author's voice; I select the stories and fashion the portrayals for representation.

*Becoming a teacher* is a construct that is different from the more commonly held conception of *being a teacher*. There is very little discussion in our context of this very important process of development. This chapter takes an in-depth look at this development process and connects it to the teacher's biography. The intention is to show that the teacher is a part of the community and as the teacher learns and evolves, so does the community. Hence, I argue that though we may not be fully aware of the concept of the school as a community of learners, we cannot escape it.

Science education researchers have, for a number of years, focused on ways and means to elicit teachers' conceptions of the nature of science. A number of tools are available to identify and characterize this phenomenon (Kimball, 1968; Billeh and Hasan, 1975; Lederman, Wade and Bell, 1998). However, recently, science educators have begun to use more open-ended instruments that use multiple sources of data such as interviews and classroom observations. In this study, I have used a number of methods to collect data including interviews and class observations under the framework of life history. My contention is that teachers' life experiences and biography influence their conceptions of knowledge and science. The data includes thirteen life history interviews[3] and many informal conversations with Munazza, observations of science teaching in classes seven and eight, and interviews with other science teachers and administrative staff of the school. This gave me a deep understanding of Munazza's teaching practice and the process of becoming a teacher.

In this chapter, I have highlighted brief sections of Munazza's life in the form of a story. I have used a number of rhetorical devices to represent the story as obtained from the data. For instance, I have used the word 'I' to represent Munazza's voice. By letting Munazza tell her life story in her own words, I have tried to remove the middleperson, and to bring the reader closer to the teacher. To bring into focus Munazza's teaching practice, I have constructed a composite picture to tell a story about her lessons in the science class. It is a composite story, a mosaic or a collage of her actions, views and theories along with my observations and interpretations of the data both from her life history interviews and class observations.

## Munazza's Story

### Induction into Teaching

I liked the idea of teaching, since I was a young child in play school. I would sit my younger siblings in front of me and teach them. My father bought a full sized blackboard for me to write on, rather than scribble on the walls while teaching. Despite this early fascination with teaching, teaching in school was never my first priority. After my FSc exams there was a long break, so I decided to teach in a school to pass away the long months. Like many other young science students in Pakistan, I wanted to become a doctor. I did get into a medical school but that was in rural Sindh, which meant living away from home for five years. So, I chose not to go into medicine but to pursue a B.Sc.

degree in chemistry and microbiology. My classes in college finished at noon and since I was teaching in an afternoon school, I continued to teach throughout my Bachelors, leaving only near to the final exams.

After my B.Sc., I wanted to work in a pathology or microbiology laboratory at least for some time so that I could make use of my knowledge about vaccines, TB tests, cancer etc., that I had studied in microbiology and biochemistry. However, my father thought that the *mahol* (working environment) in laboratories is not good. He believed that teaching is the best and most respectable profession for women and that is what I should take up. Since I liked to teach and already had previous experience, I accepted an offer from the Karachi Model Secondary School (KMSS),[4] where my younger sister was already teaching mathematics and science. However, I wanted to, and still want to, work at least for some time in a laboratory to learn more about the practical side of science. I regret not being able to do that. However, do not misunderstand me, I do like to teach. I don't work in the school in order to socialize or make friends. I come to school because I enjoy teaching. I enjoy being in the classroom. I feel very strongly that if one chooses to teach, one must do it sincerely.

The Principal of the school, Miss Mehar, has high regard for the academic accomplishments of our family as my younger sister Nosheen was an outstanding student of the school and my other siblings in the school were excellent students as well. She gave me a Board chemistry class to teach the same year that I joined the school. This was a great source of satisfaction for me, but stressful too. Not only was it my first Board class, but my sister Nosheen was also studying in it. She was reputed for asking a lot of questions and I made sure that I prepared my lesson thoroughly, so that I could answer her questions.

The Principal observed the first few classes that I taught, but since that time, four years ago, she has not come into my class. I like the Afternoon's[5] environment and I have deep respect for Miss Mehar. What I like about *Madam*, is that she is very cooperative. I have seen in other schools that teachers are not on easy terms with their principal. However, we feel very free with her. We are not scared of going to her office or talking to her. The school itself has a homely atmosphere; in fact, it feels like a second home. The only point where I think the school could improve is on our salary structure. I think we deserve higher salaries than the ones we presently get.

## Teaching and Learning

I have found that I have learnt more about my subject while teaching than as a student. As a student, I was dependent on the teacher and what she/he thought was important to learn. But as a teacher in a co-ed school, I find that students, particularly boys, come up with all sorts of questions. I have to be very well prepared. I dislike it immensely when I cannot answer students' questions. Hence, I study from my younger brother's and sister's college and university textbooks to be thoroughly prepared for the lesson. I do not think the purpose of teaching is to merely complete the course, the purpose is to teach in a way that students get good marks. This will enable them to get admission in good colleges and get into good professions.

In KMSS, there is no regular system of making lesson plans. In some other schools, such as the Karachi Academy, where I taught before I came to KMSS, there was an expectation that teachers will make formal lesson plans before teaching the lessons. All kinds of teaching materials, from a demonstration activity to worksheets, had to be planned ahead of time. For this purpose, Saturday was set aside for teachers to do their planning and preparation materials for teaching. This was particularly good for me, as I was teaching as well as studying for my B.Sc. degree. I did all my lesson preparation on Saturdays and spent the weekdays studying for my degree.

In contrast, in KMSS the teachers are not expected to make formal lesson plans for submission to the Principal. Hence, now I also do not make a 'fair' copy of my lesson plan, but plan mentally. The night before, I go over the lesson that I have to teach the next day. When thinking about a lesson I am going to teach, I usually do not have a particular approach or teaching strategy in mind. I have no training in teaching in the form of a degree or diploma. When I teach, I keep in mind the way I was taught. But very often I teach in a way that I was *not* taught. Let me explain. When I was studying in school, my science *Miss* did not show or explain anything with the help of activities. She would read from the textbook and give oral explanations, and we were expected to memorize the answers to pre-selected questions. I often did not understand what I was memorizing. At home with my younger sister, I would do some of the activities illustrated in the textbook and observe carefully; then I understood much better. Often, I thought, I wish our teachers would teach us in this way. I wish they would explain more. I wish they would show us things. I can say from personal experience that seeing and doing things helped me to understand. That is why I try to show things to my students.

The Karachi Academy is the school where I got a basic understanding of teaching. The head of the science department was a very competent science teacher and an excellent supervisor. She observed my class and made a diagram to show me the students to whom I directed my questions. She helped me in planning the lesson and explained to me that activities should not be for the benefit of the few children sitting in the front. Another science teacher in the school, Miss Surraiya, was also very helpful. If I had difficulties, I would go to these two people.

I teach in the 'normal' way, that is I do not use any special way to teach. I believe my success as a teacher depends on my ability to transfer my learning to the students. There are a number of teachers in my school who have a great deal of knowledge but cannot convey it to the students so that when after their period, I go to their class, they ask me, 'Miss, we have not understood this 'or' we have not understood that. Could you explain it to us?' It is easier for students to learn something that they have understood, instead of just learning things by heart. I am very happy when my students get good marks. I am happiest when my students' results are announced and I have their mark sheets in my hand to see that they have scored high marks. This year, one student in my Board chemistry class scored 74/75 and the majority of the students scored marks in the 70s. I am very pleased with the good results.

**My Classroom**

In the second period, I teach General Science to Class Eight, Section D. It has a number of students who are older than the average student, as they are repeating the class. They are not as motivated as the rest of the class and I find it very difficult to deal with them, as it seems that they do not want to study, but just pass the Matriculation examination. They say, 'Miss we do not want to study science, we want to study commerce.[6] Why do you bother so much, sometimes you bring this, sometimes you do that, when we do not want to study science in the future'. That is why, out of the 35 only about half of them will 'get' science.

Today, I had to teach a new topic and hence expected that the students, particularly the boys, would be more responsive and less distracted in class. I find that the students in this class always want to loiter around. For some unknown reason, they will get up from their seats and walk about the class. This is something that I have not been able to control. The girls also engage in this kind of behaviour but less than the boys. I thought that since I was a relatively newer and younger teacher, I had difficulty in controlling the class. But this class behaves this way with all teachers except their class teacher, Mrs Jamshed. She has a reputation for being very strict and the whole school is afraid of her.

I do not use the textbooks prescribed by the Sindh Text Book Board, but those published by a private publishing house for schools in Singapore. Senior science teachers of the school selected these because they are well written and affordable. We science teachers have modified the contents of the textbook to suit our needs. We teach some components of the Board Science curriculum to Class Seven and Eight. Basic material, such as the language of chemistry, has been added to the course content so that students become familiar with these important concepts and understand them before reaching Class Nine, which is a Board class.

In the next section, I share some episodes from one of the four lessons I taught on the *Excretory System of Mammals.* In the first lesson, I have focused on the kidneys. I used two different kinds of aids to teach this lesson. One is a chart of the excretory system of mammals and sheep's kidney that I had asked my mother to buy when she went to the market for meat. I had kept it in the freezer to be used by all three science teachers of Class Eight when we teach the excretory system. I always spend my own money to buy such simple aids for teaching science, and I have never asked for any reimbursement from the school.

I first introduced the topic of excretion, listing the organs of excretion on the blackboard. Then I explained each briefly, focusing greater attention on the kidneys with the help of the chart. I described the physical features of the kidney and told them that it is shaped like a bean. I pointed out that the membrane covering the kidney was called the *peritoneum*. I then held the kidney up high to show the class that the inner structure of the kidney is of a different colour than the outside and is called the *cortex*. However, it was difficult for the students to see that because the frozen kidney had changed colour, and there was little difference between the outer part of the kidney and the cortex. Besides, the kidneys were too small for the students to see from so far away. Many of the boys and girls shouted, *Miss dikhain, Miss dikhain,* (Miss Show us, Miss Show us). They were keenly interested.

I was gratified by their curiosity. I took the two sections of the kidney and started circulating in the class, showing the section of the kidney to groups of four students. I tried to show the cortex and the fine vessels inside the kidneys to the class. I also realized that, at this rate, all the students would not be able to see the kidney, so I gave one row of students a section of the kidney to see and pass on. What frustrated me was that I soon had to take that kidney section back from the students because they started to play with it.

There were some students, mostly girls, who refused to handle the now wet and slimy sample of the kidney, as they could not bear to touch it. They asked the boys to show them the specimen from afar. The noise in the class rose to an unacceptably high level and I admonished the students who refused to touch or see it. I truly could not see what there was to be squeamish about! Some students wanted to go and wash their hands, some held up their noses against the smell. I scolded them and told them that I did not find the specimens smelly or dirty. Finally, I threatened to call Mrs Jamshed, their class teacher, to restore order. Tomorrow, I must ensure that all the students write the answers of the selected questions in their registers (notebooks).

### End of a long day

By the time the school ends, it is almost *Maghrib* (sunset) and both my sister and I are keen to get home. It takes us over an hour to reach our home in North Karachi. I say my prayers and eat dinner with my family. After that I watch some TV. Then I open my books either to study for my Masters or to prepare my lessons for the next day.

### Successes and Challenges of Teaching

In the very brief life story of Munazza sketched above, some patterns can be seen. These are discussed in this section, where I try to make sense of both the successes as well as the challenges faced by Munazza in her teaching.

## Induction into Teaching

From Munazza's and my own experience, it is seen that it is easy to enter into teaching in Pakistan. Teaching is often seen as a way to fill in time between exams, between admissions to institutions of higher learning and even between other jobs. Many teachers, like Munazza, teach while they themselves are students in a university or college. Often recruiting for teachers is by word of mouth. It is perhaps due to this reason that one often sees a number of members of a family in the teaching profession. In the words of Miss Mehar, the Principal of the school, teaching runs in families. For instance, in KMSS one teacher had three sisters working in the school and nine members from her family had taught in the school at various times. Munazza and I, both were invited to teach because a sister was already teaching in the school.

However, Munazza and I did not go into teaching willingly. Often teaching is taken up as there are almost no other options available. I did not want to teach but wanted to go into television production which twenty years ago, was a field that was taboo for women. However, even where opportunities are available for doing something other than teaching, the principle of the noble profession is still invoked as seen in Munazza's story. In Karachi, she could have easily found an opportunity to put her learning to use in a pathology/microbiology laboratory, but her father believed that teaching would be best for her. She still yearns to go into a profession where she can 'do science'.

## Patterns in Teaching—Biographical Echoes

My interviews and observations showed a pattern. These patterns are not capricious or arbitrary, but represent Munazza's 'best-solutions' (Wallace and Louden, 2000:22) to the expectations that students, colleagues, administrators and parents have of her, as a teacher with a wealth of teaching knowledge. She calls these patterns her normal way of teaching. When asked to explain what she meant by a normal way, she said that she had not had any teacher training and hence taught from her past experience.

The pattern that can be seen in her teaching is a not so subtle shift from a demonstration-based science teaching to the recitation method. By recitation method, I mean a teaching technique where the teacher explains a topic, dictates answers to selected questions for the students to copy into their notebooks and learn for later regurgitation. This rather abrupt shift is due to, at least in part, her own experience of science learning in school. She experienced and learnt through the recitation method, hence she continues to feel comfortable using it. During the interviews, she alluded to specific teaching strategies that she drew directly from her experiences as a student in the classroom. If this method worked for her, she has a good reason to believe that it will work for her students who are working within a similar system. Grossman (1990) studied the pedagogical content knowledge of three beginning, secondary school English teachers who had had no teacher education. She found that all three teachers relied strongly on their memories of themselves as students and referred to their experiences as both high school and college students for instructional strategies to use in their own classroom. Similarly, at times, Munazza imitates the way her teachers behaved as teachers. However, at times, she has also made a conscious effort *not* to follow in her teachers' footsteps. In both ways, memories of how she was taught influenced the way she now teaches.

It is after an innovative demonstration-based science teaching that she switches to the recitation method of teaching which she was exposed to while studying in school. To make sure that the students 'know' the answer to the pre-selected questions, she dictates the correct answers to the questions. She assigns homework at the end of the period, which is usually in the form of learning the dictated answers and completing their registers. Assessment consists of checking that the students can reproduce the correct answer and this is done either orally, or in the form of written tests. Part of the reason for switching back to the recitation method is that the students and parents are socialized into thinking that the real work of the school resides in the written work in the students' notebooks. Munazza and at least two other science teachers of KMSS told me that when they do activities with the students, the parents and many students themselves believe that no work of value has been done in class. She is caught between two worldviews: the traditional and the more progressive.

Another reason that Munazza switches back to the tried and tested recitation method, is her need to cover the syllabus and remain synchronized with other sections of the same class. In my conversations with the science teachers of the school, all of them laid strong emphasis on covering the syllabus. That meant completing the required topics to

*[handwritten margin note: v.v. good]*

*[handwritten bottom note: yes. emphasis is always on passing the exam. Than learning!]*

teach and ensuring that the students had copied the answers to a given number of previously determined questions into their registers before the start of the term exams. Munazza's determination to bring activities into her classroom was particularly laudable as the three term exams and one final exam with its concomitant preparation and correction time took up a large amount of time.

## Strategizing for Success in the Board Exam

I also observed a few lessons where Munazza was teaching chemistry to class Nine, a Board class. I concluded from these observations that both Munazza and her students knew that this was a 'game' that they had to play to beat the system that expected them to memorize the answers to a list of questions. The most economical way to win this game was to learn the answers to selected questions that had a greater likelihood of inclusion in the Board exams. Since the setting of the paper follows a set blueprint, it is considered fair to guess and prepare the students thoroughly for the expected questions. Teaching to the test is not new and is practiced everywhere, but here it seemed to dominate the lesson planning completely. The reasons for these practices are not hard to find; there is enormous pressure on the schools from parents to ensure that students obtain high scores. High marks will increase the chances of the students to get admission into the few good colleges in Karachi. Competition is intense. Students themselves want to get good marks because their future is at stake. Hence schools, teachers and students do not allow anybody to interfere with this goal.

For Munazza, the disadvantage of not obtaining sufficiently high scores is a lived experience. She felt awful when a difference of a few marks, rendered her ineligible for admission to a medical school in Karachi. Hence, she understands the dilemma of the students and does her best to see that students get high marks. If the Board exams dominate and affect the teaching in the Board classes, it might be easier to accept and even excuse the practice. However, the Board system of exams carries at least two other grades in its wake: grade 7 and grade 8.

In an effort to see that students get the highest marks possible, at KMSS and many other private schools, the syllabus of classes Seven and Eight is enriched with topics that belong to the class Nine and Ten Board science curriculum. I have called this practice 'teaching science to classes Seven and Eight with an eye to class Nine and Ten'. This practice, in my view, gives rise to a number of issues, (a) students are exposed to concepts and ideas for which a sufficiently strong foundation has not been built, (b) students are burdened with additional topics in an already heavy curriculum, and (c) the students who will not 'get' science in grade Nine have to study content which is not a part of the official curriculum. However, this practice is not only entrenched at KMSS, but in other schools, in and outside of Pakistan (Kanu, 1996; Tan, 1991).

## Subject Matter of Science

Munazza has a good understanding of school science, and her colleagues and the Head teacher acknowledge her strength in the area. However, like the three teachers in Grossman's (1990) study, mentioned above, she equates class preparation with subject matter preparation. For example, when preparing her mental plan of teaching, she usually thinks of the content to be taught, based on the textbook. Then she chooses the classroom activity and thinks a great deal about the conceptual issues that might arise pertaining to the planned activity or demonstration. But she does not think about the practical aspects of doing an activity in class. Mundane details such as where she will put the apparatus before she gets to the activity so as not to distract the students, or how will she ensure that all students are able to see what she wants them to see in a demonstration, or where and how will she dispose of litter such as used filter paper, matchsticks, water etc., are not thought out in advance. They are unplanned and dealt through on-the-spot improvizations. While such improvizations are a necessary part of a complex activity such as teaching, over-reliance on impromptu planning suggests that Munazza conceives of thinking about content knowledge as lesson planning and tends to disregard practical implications of her method of teaching. She is not alone in thinking this way.

## Order and Class Management

Munazza has difficulty in managing her class; noise and out-of-seat behaviour being the particular issues that she has found very problematic. The students in class Eight D especially perturbed her. After observing her teach in a number of different grades, I concluded that she was right about her analysis of having much more of a problem with class Eight than in the other classes she taught; but the difference was one of degree rather than the nature of the problem. What was surprising for me was that Munazza took the confusion and chaos in her classroom very calmly. It almost seemed that it had become invisible to her. At other times, she appeared to be very frustrated because a great deal of class time and her energy was spent in settling down the students. She ascribed student misbehaviour to her inability to use the more draconian forms of discipline that the other teachers used. The important thing is that she mostly saw the problems in terms of factors external to herself. She attributed the class management issues she faced to the fact that the majority of her class were boys. She said, 'In an all-girls classroom, order and discipline must be non-issues. But I have always taught boys sections so I have always had to deal with these difficulties'. She also attributed the lack of discipline in her class to the lack of motivation and interest in science due to the low ability of students.

I see another factor at work. When bright, intelligent graduates set out to teach, they assume that their students are like them. Grossman (1989:200), while working with three beginning teachers who had not undergone teacher education coursework, found that 'All three share a conception of teaching that presupposes bright, motivated students who are eager to learn from a knowledgeable teacher, a conception that matches the teachers' undergraduate experience'. Munazza and all her nine siblings are bright, intelligent, and have had very successful school experiences. Hence, she takes her experience to be representative and typical of all students. When Munazza comes across students not nearly as motivated or intelligent and eager to learn as she was, she attributes it to their general intellectual ability rather than a reflection on her ability to reach all the students in the class (if that were even possible).

## Understanding Comes Slowly and in Stages

During the interviews, it became clear that Munazza separated learning into two forms: memorization and understanding. She knew that her methods of teaching encouraged memorization, but she believed that understanding would come, albeit slowly. She knew that during her teaching only a small percentage of the class understood the science concept, while most of them learnt it by heart. However, she believes that as they proceeded with their studies, they would slowly understand more of the science.

Hence, for Munazza, learning science has a short-term goal of learning the answers by rote, passing the exams and getting good marks; the long-term goal is understanding. Understanding will come to those who take up the study of science in the higher classes. Understanding of science concepts also comes through teaching them. She expressed that as, 'Each time I plan to teach a lesson, I learn something new'. Munazza said she enjoys the 'learning' aspect of teaching science and said that she has understood far more science now that she has started to teach it. As a student, her learning depended on the questions that the teacher wanted her to learn, but as a teacher she has to know everything about a topic to be able to teach it well. She always tries to be a few steps ahead of her students and prepares the content thoroughly, using books that belong to her siblings who are studying in college and university.

**Preparing Students for Success is her Moral Responsibility**

Professional rewards and social pressures are connected to conventional school performances. Hence, it becomes the teacher's moral responsibility to see that the students succeed in the conventional way, as defined by society. Munazza accepts the success of her students in the exams as her prime goal and lets the understanding of the students take secondary importance. Munazza's own experience with the recitation method has resulted in success for herself and her siblings. Her methods of teaching have ensured students' success in the examination and reaped appreciation from the administration of the school.

Munazza's major goal of teaching is to transfer the knowledge that she has to her students. She attributes her success as a teacher to the fact that she could transfer her knowledge to the students, while a number of her colleagues, though very knowledgeable, could not do so. This is the area where my own worldview clearly differs from Munazza's. For me, it is very important that students understand what is taught; while for Munazza, it is essential that students pass their exams with flying colours. However, it was not that she encourage rote learning without thinking. She understands the difference between teaching for understanding and rote memorization, and that both occupy a different plane on the teaching learning landscape. She believes that to succeed in the exams, it is necessary to commit to memory large sections of the text, and hence proceeds to teach in that way. She is very proud that, rarely do her students take outside tuitions (coaching) in her class Nine, Board. She recalled that her schoolteachers took full responsibility for preparing them for success in the exams and she must do the same.

Munazza feels that it is her responsibility to see that *all* students in her class have learnt the lesson. She feels strongly about teachers who do not care whether students have the required notes in their registers. Her ardent interest in student learning is obvious from the passion in her voice and the fire in her eyes when she talks about this issue. She has strong views about teachers who do not try to fulfill this responsibility. She sees this responsibility in three ways. One, she has to make sure that all the students have necessary materials to learn, that is, they have the notes in their registers. Second, she ascertains that the students have learnt the required questions by going to each student in the class and requiring them to respond orally to a question she has put before them. I observed four teaching periods when Munazza utilized different ways to see that this goal was achieved. If she thought that time would run out before she got to all the students, she used the method she saw her teachers use in class. She, as a monitor, was often asked to 'hear the lesson' from other students. Twice, I saw her request a monitor in her class to work with her and hear the lesson from one end of the class, while she worked with students at the other end. The third way that she tries to fulfill her responsibility towards student learning is to teach all the three disciplines of science as well as she can. Though her strength obviously lies in chemistry and biology, as she has studied these two subjects at the B.Sc. level, she tries her best to teach exemplary lessons in physics too.

### If you Teach then You Must do it Sincerely[7]

During the interviews, Munazza and I had a number of discussions on what teaching means to her, and her thoughts on how teaching of science could be improved. She quoted what Elbaz (1983) has called the 'rules of action' to guide practice. She believed that as a teacher she must do what she has come to do in the school—teach. She does not believe in wasting time, and more importantly, in wasting the students' time. She views teaching as a noble profession, a calling. She takes a dim view of teachers who have other agendas attached to coming to school.

For Munazza, sincerity (or as she put it 'sincerely *parhana*') is an important attribute of a teacher. One cannot be a teacher and at the same time not be sincere to the profession and the students. For Munazza, sincerity also means to teach to the best of her ability. She said, 'If one does not know something, then it is the teacher's *faraz* (duty) to ask somebody or find out. *Na aane mai koi sharam nahi hai, agar hai tu na poochhne me hai*'.[8] She does not feel that not knowing is something to be ashamed of. That is why she often sought help from other teachers and was willing to learn from me as a researcher.

### *Agar chhorni pari tu chhor doongi*[9] - Issues of Relational Autonomy

Munazza's life story shows that she has made an attempt to live her life in such a way that she balances what she wants to do with what society expects of her. Living in a patriarchal society like Pakistan, she has been able to deploy a finely tuned blend of personal autonomy and interdependence that has worked well for her. Her parents greatly value education. Their views match the views of the large Urdu-speaking *mohajir* population of Karachi. They migrated and came to settle in Karachi empty-handed, to build a new life for themselves. Education is seen as a means of social mobility, to get access to better jobs and a better life. These values enabled Munazza to value the school and learning as very essential for life. She has had a very successful experience in school and wants to replicate the same experience for her students. She values success in the conventional terms of high marks and admission to good professional institutions and tries her best to help her students achieve these goals.

Munazza has had to struggle to get access to places and people in a way that is socially safe and personally acceptable to her. She wanted to go to St. Michael's College, but did not. She wanted to do medicine, and she was one of the few lucky women in Pakistan who had access to this opportunity—but in her eyes she did not have access, as she was offered admission to a medical college in interior Sindh, where she was unwilling to go. She wanted to work in a pathology laboratory but her father said 'no'. The issue of access is connected to personal autonomy. If personal autonomy is defined as self-determination and self-sufficiency and choosing to live according to one's own values and standards (Friedman, 2000), or being self-supporting and self-reliant (Reindal, 1999), then it is clear that Munazza does not have it. I want to argue that not only is the concept of personal autonomy in this sense obsolete and incomplete, but Munazza deploys a form of autonomy and agency that is more suitable to the environment and more effective. I have called it relational autonomy.[10] Friedman defines this idea as development of autonomy through social interaction, keeping the context, such as personal values, in mind. Munazza feels personal relations are more important than access or personal autonomy. She has made many decisions in favour of maintaining good relations with those she loves and respects because she believes that her sense of autonomy is embedded in the society in which she lives. Society in Pakistan is segregated and males and females cannot and do not associate with each other except in very prescribed circumstances. The hesitancy to 'walk through streets filled with *ajeeb* and *khofnaaq* men' is understandable. Much as she might have wanted to deploy her autonomy to fulfill her ambitions, her values are embedded in a society that abets this segregation and allows only grudging access to public space for women. Hence, relational autonomy rather than autonomy works for her.

Munazza is at a very difficult stage of her life, a 'waiting stage' where she cannot make many long-term decisions about her life because the big decision of her marriage is yet to be made. However, instead of being rooted into this passive way of thinking, she has shown clear signs of moving ahead; she has decided to do her Masters in Islamic History. The decision has been made keeping in mind the various constraints of balancing a full-time job and her studies. Islamic History is probably not her first choice, yet it is something in which she is interested. Whether she continues to teach in a school or seeks out an opportunity to teach Islamic History in college remains to be seen.

In fact, I sometimes felt that Munazza's marital status was getting in the way of my study. I could not discern how a really committed school science teacher thought of her practice, until the question of her marriage was out of the way. My participant should have been either married, with a commitment to continue teaching science in a school, or she should have been a person at an age where marriage appeared to be a distant possibility. Suddenly, it dawned on me that I was staring at one of the issues that the teaching profession faces in Pakistan. It reminded me of a cartoon where a policeman spent an hour searching a car for illicit arms when a canon was lashed on to the rooftop. One of the difficulties with female teachers in Pakistan is that they cannot commit to the profession until they are married and know their new circumstances. Not knowing the course of their life, they continue to flow with the tide until circumstances force them to become more serious about the profession. That is why Munazza said, '*Agar chhorni pari to chhor doon gi*'. (If I have to leave [my profession] I will).

Lortie (1975) has also shown his awareness of a gender division in teaching. He has reported that women teachers in their twenties do not get deeply involved in their careers as they are hedging their bets to cover contingencies related to husband and children. These socio-cultural dimensions affect teaching as they have an impact on the professional development of teachers.

The 'waiting period' where the teacher waits either to get married or to go into another profession affects her thinking about the profession and professional development. The yearning to get out of school teaching never goes away completely. Munazza, when given an opportunity, chose to do her MA in Islamic history rather than in teaching.

## Conclusion

Research findings are consistent about teachers using their prior personal and professional experiences to frame their classroom teaching. The maxim 'teachers teach who they are' appears to resonate with teachers all over the world. Hence, it is not surprising that for Munazza, too, teaching is autobiographical. The challenge in Pakistan and in AKU-IED is to harness and utilize this powerful understanding about teachers and to develop a better understanding of how teachers learn and contribute to the community of learners.

## NOTES

1. All teachers/administrators mentioned in this chapter are addressed by their pseudonyms.
2. See, Halai, N. (2002). Munazza's Story: Understanding science teaching and conceptions of the nature of science in Pakistan through a life history study. Unpublished doctoral dissertation of the University of Toronto.
3. All interview data was bilingual, as Munazza used both Urdu and English to express herself. The interviews were translated into English by the author.
4. All schools mentioned in this chapter are addressed by their pseudonyms.
5. Generally, the afternoon section of the Karachi Model School was referred to as the 'Afternoon'.
6. Referring to Arts, Science and Commerce, the three major subject groups available to class Nine and Ten. KMSS offers its students the last two options.
7. The word 'sincerely' was the exact word Munazza used. It is not a translation from Urdu.
8. 'There is no shame in not knowing, but there is shame in not trying to find out'.
9. 'If I have to leave teaching' 'I will leave it'.
10. It is after I had named it thus that I came across Mackenzie and Stoljar's (2000) excellent work on this same concept.

## References

Billeh, V.Y. & Hasan, O.E. (1975). 'Factors Affecting Teachers' Gain in understanding the nature of science'. *Journal of Research in Science Teaching*, 12(3), 209–19.
Elbaz, F. (1983). *Teacher Thinking: A Study of Practical Knowledge*. London: Croom Helm.
Friedman, M. (2000). 'Autonomy, Social Disruption and Women'. In C. Mackenzie and N. Stoljar, (Eds.). *Relational autonomy: Feminist perspectives on autonomy, agency and the social self* (pp. 35–51). New York: Oxford University Press.
Grossman, P.L. (1990). *The Making of a Teacher: Teacher Knowledge and Teacher Education*. NY: Teachers College Press.
Grossman, P.L. (1989). 'Learning to teach without teacher education'. *Teachers College Record*, 91(2), 191–208.
Kanu, Y. (1996). 'Educating Teachers for the Improvement of the Quality of Basic Education in Developing Countries. *International Journal of Educational Development*, 16(2), 173–84.
Kimball, M.E. (1968). 'Understanding the Nature of Science: A Comparison of Scientists and Science teachers'. *Journal of Research in Science Teaching*, 5(2), 110–20.
Lortie, D.C. (1975). *Schoolteacher: A Sociological Study*. Chicago, IL: University of Chicago Press.
Lederman, N.G., Wade, P.D. & Bell, R.L. (1998). 'Assessing the nature of Science: What is the Nature of our Assessments? *Science and Education*, 7(6), 595–615.
Reindal, S.M. (1999). 'Independence, Dependence, interdependence: Some Reflections on the Subject and Personal Autonomy'. *Disability and Society*, 14(3), 353–67.

Tan, S.B. (1991). 'The Development of Secondary School Science Curriculum in Malaysia'. *Science Education*, 75(2), 243–50.

Wallace, J. & Louden, W. (2000). *Teachers' Learning: Stories of Science Education*. Boston, MA: Kluwer Academic Publishers.

# 3

# SCIENCE TEACHER DEVELOPMENT IN PAKISTAN: A LEARNING COMMUNITY APPROACH

*Harcharan Pardhan and Patricia Rowell*

Since the 1980s, traditional top-down and quick-fix approaches to teacher development have been questioned and alternate field-based, bottom-up approaches have been advocated by teacher educators around the world. One approach conceives practitioners in 'learning communities' (Cochran-Smith and Lytle, 1992). This approach is grounded in the premise that 'professional development is a teacher activity requiring commitment, time, and support' (Guilbert, 2002:78). Current literature on teacher professional development places emphasis on 'teachers as collaborative inquirers into classroom teaching and learning' (ibid). Hargreaves (1995) describes professional development through 'cultures of collaboration among teachers'. Such cultures allow teachers to collectively share and employ alternate paths 'to promote comprehension among students' (Shulman, 1987:8). This chapter builds on these ideas and reports, on the establishment of a learning community in a small group of in-service science teachers in Karachi, Pakistan.

## Science Education in Pakistan

Teaching and learning of science in Pakistan is predominantly teacher-centered and traditional. The teaching/learning scenario is well described by one of the M.Ed. course participants at AKU-IED:

Reflecting on my experiences as a learner, I remember that the teaching/ learning of science at all levels of education in Pakistan is 'teacher dominated',...I clearly remember that we spent many hours and days memorizing scientific concepts from the textbook in order to pass the examination. I found science 'boring', 'useless' and unrelated to everyday life. As a beginning science teacher, I taught science to my pupils exactly the way I was taught. Various sources revealed that in Pakistan, science teaching in the primary, middle and secondary level is done generally using a transmission mode of teaching (Journal entry, June 1995, quoted with permission).

Furthermore, teachers are generally unmotivated and either untrained or poorly trained. This bleak picture was documented in research findings of the USAID funded BRIDGES project in 1987-88: 'Teachers are poorly paid and often poorly motivated.... Though teachers usually have 10 years of general academic training, a good number do not have pre-service training, especially in Balochistan, where all teachers are hired directly as untrained teachers' (Rugh, Malik and Farooq, 1991:8). The project also revealed that, because of poor teacher training, there were no observable differences in the learning outcomes of students taught by trained and untrained primary teachers. Indeed, the number of years of formal schooling was found to be a far more significant variable in a student's academic performance (ibid). Warwick and Reimers (1995:143) have also reported 'that the general education of teachers proves to be a far better predictor of a student's mathematics and science achievement than professional certification at teacher training institutes.' Kizilbash (1998) expressed the following concern about public teacher education courses in Pakistan:

> The courses have been described by students as only vaguely relevant to the work they have to do in school, and the use of the lecture method seems to be in universal use in colleges of education (p. 110).

Since the 1970s, the Government of Pakistan's attempts to bring about changes in the teaching of science have not been successful in accordance with worldwide trends. This is reflected in the description by the M.Ed. participant quoted above and Iqbal's (1994) commentary on science curricula and prevalent teaching practice in Pakistan:

> Teachers were not made familiar with the new approach and methodology envisaged in the new curricula...emphasized the content and the product of science instead of the processes of science. As a result, experimental

work was hardly made part of science teaching (p. 37)....Until recent past, didactic method of teaching, lack of audio-visual-aids, lack of laboratories, incompetent and unmotivated teachers, poor quality of text-book, emphasis on factual materials and rote memorization, an ineffective system of examination and evaluation and above all, the lowest financial allocation to education have been the major weaknesses of science education in Pakistan (p. 34).

The top-down efforts of the government have not resulted in the desired changes. Because of the difficulty of effecting improvement in the quality of education on a significant scale, the government has encouraged non-government organization initiatives such as AKU-IED. The Institute is a non-government, not-for-profit organization which, in collaboration with the Pakistan Government, has a vision to be instrumental in education reform and improvement in Pakistan. Since its start in 1993, AKU-IED has offered a variety of field-based in-service teacher development programmes based on contemporary practices in education. The programmes include: a two-year M.Ed. programme; a field-based one-year diploma programme; and an eight-week teacher certification programme. Programmes for school heads and other administrative and policy makers are offered concurrently with the programmes for teachers. The overall goal is whole school improvement. One of the present authors (Pardhan, a faculty member of the Institute since 1994) had the opportunity to undertake central leadership roles (coordinator, facilitator, and mentor), to implement the first two concurrent one-year diploma programmes in Science and Mathematics offered by the Institute during 1997-98. Most of the programme took place in the participants' home schools and emphasized content, but pedagogy was also addressed appropriately. Reflecting upon practice through success stories and learning by sharing were the distinguishing features of the diploma programme. This helped the participating teachers to voice their contextual needs and concerns in an encouraging and inviting environment. Significant improvements were witnessed as a result of the participants' experiences. The teachers' observations (gathered during group sessions and conversations and evaluation) provide evidence of this (Pardhan, 1998):

> There was a change in my teaching after attending this program. I realized that now I can give the students better teaching and better ways of conceptual understanding. I also noted that students were taking a keen interest in the activities.

One of the concepts underpinning the programme was constructivism and we will now turn to an exploration of this concept.

## How do Teachers Learn?

Constructivism is a contemporary theory of learning which emphasizes the importance of the psychological and experiential domains in learning rather than just the rote memorization of the content. Consequently, there is a shift in emphasis from students' rote or factual learning to conceptual understanding (Shulman, 1986) and learning is viewed in part as a conceptual change. Early research on constructivism focused on students' formal school learning, which has recently been extended to teacher education (Skamp, 1998). It has also been realized that many students do not actually change their ideas about how their world works through formal schooling, and some pre-service science teachers at the end of their teacher education do not change their views about learning and teaching (Kagan, 1992). This counters the view that knowledge is 'out there,' and supports the view that learning is embodied in, and through the learner. Thus, teacher learning is seen as a process of conceptual change. An appropriate beginning to effect change is to first identify the existing ideas of teachers, and then engage them in tasks to help them bridge the gap by questioning their own practices. This is the premise of constructivism; it maintains that knowledge is generated through a cyclic/spiral process where the focus is on the individual to take responsibility for learning. Today, research on *how* teachers learn favours a constructivist position. Thus, teachers' conceptual understanding and cognition of the concept is crucial to student learning. The implication for teacher development is to recognize teachers as 'thinking selves' who internalize and utilize knowledge about how students learn in constructing their instructional discourse.

The constructivist approach to teaching and learning has also been very useful in bringing to the surface the complex nature of the process of learning to teach science. It emphasizes the central role of students' understanding of science constructs. This places special demands on teachers. Extensive research on constructivism has brought a realization that not only do students construct ideas, but teachers as well. This means that teachers must also construct ideas about teaching and learning science. Constructivism introduces complexity and multiplicity by adding the context and active participation of the students in addition to the importance of teachers' knowing the subject matter knowledge.

However, the constructivist argument for promoting teachers' and students' personal construction of knowledge needs to be considered carefully and critically. Teachers have the challenging job of negotiating science concepts developed by scientists, with students' existing understandings. When the two are at variance, a teacher enters a problematic zone and may seek safer ground; i.e. a traditional didactic method. This perpetuates the survival and self-concern model. To avoid this, teachers must have pedagogical content knowledge that integrates the content and pedagogy appropriately and carefully.

**What do Teachers need to Know?**

Shulman (1986) developed a theoretical framework for analysing the knowledge that teachers have and use for the purpose of teaching. The categories of the knowledge base in teaching, according to Shulman, include content knowledge, pedagogical content knowledge, curriculum knowledge and knowledge of learning. Schulman's unique contribution has been in identifying the significance of pedagogical content knowledge.

Pedagogical content knowledge entails the transformation of subject matter knowledge to make it comprehensible to others, and in doing so, 'embodies the aspects of content most germane to its teachability' (p. 9). Thus, pedagogical content knowledge can be conceptualized as a blending of pedagogy and content in such a way as to translate or transform content into curriculum. Shulman's construct of pedagogical content knowledge suggests that 'a teacher's role emerges from an understanding of both subject knowledge and the ways children learn' (Carre and Ovens, 1995:5). Since the late 1980s, several studies have been reported on the importance of pedagogical content knowledge of science teachers. For example, Smith and Neale (1989) studied the important role of subject matter knowledge in primary science teaching. They reported that as their ten primary science participating teachers changed their understanding of the subject content and effective teaching methods, they modified their teaching. The authors described the outcomes of their project as follows:

Teachers' knowledge of the content, their translation of that content into appropriate and flexible usage in lessons, their knowledge of children's likely preconceptions to be encountered in lessons and the effective teaching strategies for addressing them, and especially their beliefs about the nature of science teaching, all proved to be critical components in the changes they were able to make in their teaching (Smith and Neale, 1989:17).

The authors emphasized the role of appropriate activities to enhance the teacher's knowledge base. Knowledge may be individually or socially constructed. Knowledge may also be seen to co-emerge through human interaction with others and the environment. Thus, group discussions and interactions may provide sites for interactions and critical reflection on experiences and shared meanings. It makes sense to carry on the search for better learning and teaching models collectively with others. That is, to share our collective and personal learning to construct a contextual perspective. As will be discussed next, this is the premise of action research that encourages change through collaborative action amongst teachers. The aim is to empower teachers to develop their own theoretical perspective of good classroom practice, by reflecting on their personal and collective experiences and to strive for shared meanings and understandings.

## Action Research

Early educational action research emerged from the 'teacher as researcher' movement (Stenhouse, 1975). Despite the wide range of approaches to action research and the differing theoretical underpinnings, all action research shares a systematic process of inquiry into practice. Practitioners, as action researchers, identify problems for inquiry and formulate strategic planning through deliberation. Each action research cycle requires that participants monitor, reflect and evaluate. The cycles are repeated to move to higher levels of thinking in a collaborative and cooperative environment. Collaboration is one of the key tenets of action research:

> Action research extends beyond individual engagement in the process.... Action research therefore precipitates collaborative involvement in the research process, in which the research is extended towards including all those involved, or affected by, the action. Ultimately, the aim of action research is to involve all these participants in communication aimed at

mutual understanding and consensus, in just and democratic decision-making, and common action towards achieving fulfillment for all (Carr and Kemmis, 1986:199).

Carr and Kemmis's conception of collaboration extends beyond individuals merely working cooperatively. It encourages a sense of community among all those involved.

In this project, the researcher as an external person to schools, was to work with the internal school teams comprising teachers, heads of schools and students. Inherent in this was the possibility of putting forward different views. Although the researcher was to work with the teachers most of the time, interactions with the heads and the students could not be ignored. Experiences of AKU-IED colleagues in other action research projects (e.g. Kanu, 1997) helped the researcher to realize that the major challenge for collaboration would be on how to cope tactfully with the issues of power relationships. A basic requirement for establishing a community is to strive for trusting relationships. Consistent with Kanu's teaching approach, the researchers negotiated project goals with the teachers so that these were compatible with the teachers' personal goals. This was to help the teachers re-examine their conceptions of collaboration and develop a positive attitude and stance towards collaborative approaches. Davis and Sumara (1997) also favour collaboration for teacher growth with an emphasis on culture-making:

> ...researcher identity that pre-figures involvement in sites of collaborative action research...activities themselves function to generate individual and collective identities. Action research understood in this way, is not merely a set of procedures that enable the interpretation of culture; action research in an instance of 'culture making' in which the various actors are wholly complicit (p. 301).

For these authors, action research is not an act of exploitation of data by the researcher, but the work of a community of responsible individuals. However, the authors acknowledge that one cannot escape from imposing one's value judgements; rather, one must negotiate those judgements within the personal experiences of others.

This action research project was envisioned as a learning opportunity for all involved (self, teachers and others), with the distinguishing feature of action research as 'not merely research that occurs in educational settings, nor merely that it is focused on educational issues.

Rather, it must be regarded as research that educates, that makes culture' (Davis and Sumara, 1997:309). The project set out to examine closely the changes in science teachers' practice as a result of teachers' stories and reflective dialogues for different settings: planning, preparing, organizing and implementing activities and strategies in the teaching of science. The purpose was to explore teachers' conceptual changes in their pedagogical content knowledge in science in the Pakistan context, and through this process, contribute to an understanding of teacher professional development.

Project research participants were three committed and willing in-service science teachers from a class of the one year Advance Diploma in Subject Specialization from AKU-IED. PT and Saira were primary teachers, and Nina a secondary teacher (all pseudonyms). In the project, qualitative observations of teachers engaged in science activities (planning, preparing, teaching, reflecting...and repeating the cycle) were juxtaposed with conferences and conversations about instances and events. To pursue reflective practice, the researcher scheduled one-to-one conferences, conversations and discussions with each teacher, as well as narratives, discussions and tutorial sessions (as needed) as a group with all three teachers at appropriate times. With the teachers' permission, conversations were audio-recorded and a select number of lessons were video-recorded. During the group sessions, transcripts of the audio-taped sessions were used to explore ways to portray the ways teachers think, make meaning and reflect upon their development. Audio recordings were transcribed and shared on a regular basis with the participants for comments, accuracy and validation. In addition, narratives/stories about teachers' teaching and learning designed to explore meanings that these experiences hold for them, were also used. And, in order for the participating teachers to apply their new understandings in the classroom, the researcher worked alongside the participating teachers to advise, guide, choose, design and prepare tasks and strategies for the science classroom.

## Moving Towards a Learning Community

The action research model was followed by the following themes for different stages: Entry Gaining and Exploration; Collaborative Actions with the Teachers; and Critical Reflections and Relationships. This is consistent with moving towards a learning community. Active planning and preparation prior to and during the fieldwork was highly important. Additionally, consolidated communication efforts with the concerned teachers and heads (as and when appropriate) throughout the project was practiced.

## Entry Gaining and Explorations

Although the researcher knew the schools and the participating teachers, there still remained an element of uncertainty for gaining entry to the classrooms, due to personnel changes. However, visits to the schools and interactions with the heads and teachers by the researcher, in which a written overview of the project (with consent letters) was shared, together with discussion and clarification, proved an encouraging beginning. The heads showed interest and willingness to collaborate:

> These teachers need such experiences.... They have not learnt to take decisions or solve problems...but...they do as they are told.... It is wonderful that you decided to come personally to school...this is the first step to collaboration and shows personal interest and commitment. I like the idea of invitation; it is not commitment or saying, go do this'...(Head of a school, 13/4/2000)...'what will be the incentive for these teachers? Will they be a part of your research? Will they appear in your thesis? (another school head, 13 April 2000).

At an orientation meeting of invited teachers that followed these visits, the teachers showed interest, openness and willingness to join the project:

> Of course, we are asking these questions so we should be aware of all these things before participating in this research....are we able to give time or not'...'time is the main problem...teaching...then other responsibilities... sometimes we don't even know our schedule'...'if you can manage the research during school time and Saturdays...so I am very pleased to do this research...you know life is so difficult after marriage....' (Group Session, 21 April 2000).

The teachers had many relevant questions and concerns. The major concern was time commitment and that too had personal and cultural dimensions to it. What surprised the researcher was the confidence and openness that these teachers demonstrated. Three years ago, at the start of the one-year diploma programme, the same teachers would not utter a word. This change was attributed to the teachers' diploma experiences and the responsible leadership positions they have held since then. This strengthened the researcher's belief that providing an enabling environment and opportunity for teachers to come together and learn makes a difference. Though these teachers had made significant advancements in their teaching career (especially as a result of the one-year advanced diploma programme), they saw the project as an opportunity for further development through interaction, reflection and support:

> ...this year I am given to teach a Cambridge Class instead of Matriculation. It is more content-oriented and very challenging....I have just started... learning...Matric (biology) I can tell you even without having to go and look for syllabus. But Cambridge is new...I have yet to know a whole lot. Working with Charan (researcher)...will be interesting and timely because her critical appraisal will further enhance my development as a science teacher...my science teaching especially for Cambridge classes. I am looking forward to...working and learning together.' (Nina's Journal Entry 8 September 2000).

> Saira: I want to improve my personal growth and know how I can reflect myself. It will affect my teaching...become more effective...how can we observe our students and then how can we reflect on teaching. Nina and PT (pseudonyms of the other two partners) who were listening attentively... 'yes'...'I want to learn English...' (group session, 15 September 2000).

The researcher's earlier relationship with the teachers in a facilitator role, together with the heads' collaboration, made the entry a smooth one. A trusted relationship is apparent from the above anecdotes but at a student-teacher and facilitator level. Now that the teachers had joined the project, they were to be respected as research partners.

These insights made the researcher realize the need for being sensitive to the diversity involved, and hence, to pay attention to individual concerns and aspirations, over and above the project expectations of a collaborative effort. To gain further insights into the teachers' concerns about their practice and to help them articulate these, the first couple of classroom visits for each teacher (27 September 2000 to 14 October 2000) were negotiated during the first project group session. It was mutually agreed that the researcher would play the role of an observer in a non-evaluative but supportive manner so as to stimulate post lesson reflections, share thoughts and ideas, and articulate emerging questions and concerns. The researcher would work together with the teachers to reflect, plan and take more purposeful actions, and simultaneously enable the teachers to gain a sense of ownership. This was consistent with the teachers' expectations and a logical move towards identifying concerns and working together as a community with a common purpose.

**Enacted Classroom Practices**

At the beginning of the project, the researcher expected the teachers to be more inclined to student-centered and reflective practice. This was suggested in their oral responses to questions such as 'How do you think children learn? And how may you know?'. Samples of teachers' responses were, 'by observing,...practicing...they want to understand...so we provide activities...by doing those activities themselves, they learn better than teacher give them lecture' (PT)... 'by solving problems...problems mean scientific activity, but in different situation' (Saira)... 'from situation or question created for the concepts to be learnt' (Nina)... '...we observe our students and how...we reflect on teaching' (Saira, Nina and PT).

Despite these responses, however, the lesson transcript segment below suggests that the enacted classroom practice of one teacher had reverted to a transmission mode:

PT: Tell me what is matter?
S1: There are three states of matter.
PT: I have not asked about states...
S2: Miss, anything that is like stone.
PT: (no response to the student S2's answer) anything that has... (expecting students to respond...students quiet or some talking) what it has...Sara, what it has...(no response from Sara).... Anything which has mass and occupies space...now say together...
PT and SS: (in chorus) anything that has mass and occupies space (repeat a couple of times).
PT: What are three states of matter?
SS: (almost all in chorus) Solid, liquid and gas.

PT: (repeats) Solid, liquid and gas...can you give me example? (field observation lesson transcript).

(Key: S1, S2...represent individual students; SS, all students in chorus; and PT, the participating teacher).

Furthermore, in a conversation after the lesson, the participant indicated, 'I am satisfied' (conversation transcript 27 September 2000). This was a challenging moment for the researcher. To avoid 'telling' an alternative to stimulate PT's self-reflection was needed. Since PT was to teach the same lesson to a parallel class, to video the lesson seemed a sensible suggestion. This was agreeable to PT, '(It) would be interesting. Let us see how one can remember things.' PT and PT's head agreed to sign a written consent to this effect. To the researcher's surprise, towards the end of the discussion, PT even agreed to write about her day's lesson: 'I shall try to write about my today's lesson.' Although PT agreed to have the lessons recorded, there seemed a worry in PT's words that the researcher was able to know only after reading PT's reflection of the lesson:

> It is not easy to keep in mind all the things that children said and it is very difficult to do it immediately. It takes time to recap all the events (PT's lesson reflection, 26 September 2000).

PT's reflection pointed to the researcher, the difficult and time consuming task of a teacher attending to what children say and then trying to recall it. The process of dialoguing, convincing, negotiating, and making appropriate and timely arrangements for videotaping and viewing herself teaching, enabled PT to think differently. The discussion, after having watched the video-taped lesson, was a turning point in PT's thinking. The change was from 'I am satisfied' to self identification and realization of four problematic areas:

- questions...that students were not quite comprehending. For example when I (PT) asked them, 'how much mass has the matter?' and 'how can we measure it?'
- other problem...when I gave them the shopping bag with materials, they (students) started quarrelling with each other and there was a problem in controlling them.
- when I asked them to 'drop the pencils' (seemed a strategy or a rule, one of the few rules in class, which this teacher used to get student

attention) still some girls were not listening and I had to interrupt the conclusion and go there to draw their attention....
* finally, when I asked them to collect the things, they again started quarrelling with each other (conversation transcript after viewing video 27 September 2000).

The conversation then continued as follows:

> PT: Teacher (meaning herself) gets angry easily. Teacher has much anger inside.
> R: Why would that be?
> PT: I don't know.
> R: Let us go back to the video...when did you get angry?
> PT: When students were working in groups...and when I asked them to drop their pencils...this is when I get really angry but I do try to control...also when students were talking very loudly (conversation transcript 27 September 2000).

This afforded the following insight for the researcher:

> PT's words 'teacher has much anger inside her.' I need to pay attention to and be sensitive to this and not press her as I proceed to work with PT for the rest of the project unless in anyways it will happen to affect professionally (Researcher's Journal Entry, 2 October 2000).

Field observations and interactions with Saira and Nina started at a different level. Both had unit plans with detailed lesson plans and were anxious to share them as the segment below suggests:

> Saira: (opening the conversation) My lesson plan has these sections (points at the three columns; Student, Teacher, and Resources)
> R: (pointing at 'Teacher' column) so you start the lesson by...(immediately Saira carries on).
> Saira: By asking questions...actually it varies...depending on topic... sometimes questions...sometimes activity...sometimes worksheet. In every lesson I also mention process...skill...which skill/s I want to develop in the students...for example in this lesson I have to: identify, labelling, drawing, discussion, writing, involving (conversation transcript).

Although Nina and Saira's espoused descriptions of practice had closer correspondence with verbal practice descriptions than PT's, they still had concerns and problems:

> Saira: Time is constraint...I had to achieve all the objectives...I could not...reading process for the students is a problem...discussion in some things becomes long...so could not give enough time for reading. Students wanted to give answers...but some couldn't. Students...some of them are not interested in reading.... So I am thinking, how to create interest in them in reading. Also syllabus is a problem...some discussions become long and we rush to complete the syllabus (Field notes, classroom visit).
>
> 'While teaching biology, when it comes to any math concepts/ideas e.g. graphs, ratios like surface area is to volume/anything to do with calculations' I find it difficult to teach because my own concepts are not clear and I don't understand them...I have no one...to help but I collect books...read and try out exercises...again and again until I feel I am getting a better understanding...it is hard' (Nina: Informal conversation, 4 November 2000).

English as a medium of instruction is a challenge for both teachers and students in Pakistan. Thus, it was not surprising that the teachers identified 'I must also learn English', as one of the benefits of joining the project. PT and Saira also encountered English language reading and speaking problems with their students. This intensified the struggle to maintain the pace and flow of the lesson and as a result, time management suffered. A segment from Saira's lesson transcript on 'food preservation' supports this:

Saira: ...*Lakin* (But) some foods can be saved by for the long time by another process which is called sterilized. What is the spelling of sterilized? (immediately calls upon a student S1).
S1:   S t e
Saira: Okay
S1:   er
Sk:   er
S1:   il
Saira: il
S1:   ized
Saira: ized, sterilized. *Yani* (that is) that means *kay woo ju* tin *kay* box *main hamara* food *atta hai jisay hum* germs say...*Kaar saktay hain* (that food of ours that comes in tin or box and we can...it

from germs)...that (a student is saying something) means you are not listening to me (students still talking; Saira is now a bit angry) what's wrong with you (a student is coughing) okay so second way of food preservation is a sterilize and another way is...*eek aur* (one other) way *joo aap ki* text *main* (which is in your text) mention *kiyaa hai*...(is mentioned) *Jis nay* text *khoor say padha hoo gay uus koo pata hoga kaa ek aur* way *jo yahan* mention *kara hai*, (Only the ones who have read the text carefully will be knowing one more way mentioned there...Saira repeats in English) (calls upon another student S2...but many students start speaking) Miss, chemical...chemical...physical... (another student, loud and fast) chemical, physical, pesticides... chemical.

From these exploratory experiences of the three teachers, the unpredictable, uncontrollable and paradoxical nature of teacher development became increasingly apparent. It also became evident that not only do different teachers grow differently, but even the same teacher develops differently within different times, places and conditions. Teacher development is a continuous process, a life-long learning process, and there are many avenues for continuous improvement; 'expansion, advancement, maturation, elaboration, conversion, evolvement, and progression' (Burke, 1987:xi).

No matter what avenue a teacher follows, it is ultimately the teacher's experience that is the 'teacher'. It is a teacher's lived experience that can make a teacher grow. According to Britzman (1991), lived experience is 'our capacity to bestow experience with meanings, be reflective, and take action. Without an awareness of potential and given meanings, and our capacity to extend experience through interpretation and risk, without this active side, our capacity to participate in the shaping of experience is limited' (p. 34). It is this active process that is central to the Action Research cycle and the Pedagogical Content Knowledge. It is with these new insights and guiding principles that the researcher moved onto the next phase of the project.

## Collaborative Actions with the Teachers

The areas identified in this project for specific development differed for each group member. PT's concern was to engage students in learning and to manage this in a large class of Primary Two students; 'the problem of large classroom strength of students...nobody can solve... so it is better to compromise with it' (PT's journal entry 21 September 2000). Saira was concerned about maintaining student interest in reading and having active student participation in the lesson without rushing it. Nina wanted to enhance her own conceptual understanding of biological concepts and to link concepts from other disciplines like chemistry, physics and mathematics. Each teacher in the project was special and needed to be approached individually. Thus, the nature and extent of the researcher's method of working with each of them varied. At the same time, the researcher had to attempt, as much as possible, to have the teachers make and take decisions affecting their teaching.

This was the stage where the researcher worked alongside the teachers, playing multiple roles in accordance with the nature of the concern and preference. To test PT's hypothesis (above) about the large class size, the researcher negotiated with PT the roles of co-planner, co-teacher and critical friend; with Saira, co-planner, co-teacher, as and when invited, participant observer and critical friend; with Nina, predominantly co-thinker, participant observer and critical friend.

The systematic action research cycles were followed individually, jointly (teacher-researcher) and collectively (group sessions). Significant successes were witnessed:

> We (R and PT) had done our planning and teaching and we have changed and added many new activities.... Some activities which were really challenging, we gave it to the children and you (meant for the group) know...children were really involved in thinking to a level that...there was...optimum (acceptable) level of noise as whatever children were discussing was according to the task given to them. Children didn't quarrel...I was really amazed and impressed...after this activity, I realized that 'activity should have challenge' and we should not underestimate children (PT: group session 1 December 2000).
>
> I felt some inner happiness because students gave good responses and followed the social skills very well.... Teacher talked less and students talked more. In this way in the end I didn't feel tired...I achieved my effort that I make interest in reading materials...students took interest in reading and showed enthusiasm in activities (Journal entry, Saira 8 November 2000).... Clear instructions very beneficial for teacher in this way she talks less and gives more time to students to talk and more time to their understanding (Journal entry, Saira, 6 December 2000).... Activity should be tried out before doing in class (Journal Entry, Saira, 24 January 2001).

Over a time period of five months (September 2000 to January 2001), a trusting and open relationship had developed amongst the group members. A new relationship of community of learners had emerged:

PT: Now we are colleagues and partners.
Nina: We discuss everything...if we had problems we were a bit hesitant there (SST) but...here [project] we discuss every thing openly and share everything.... Now it is totally different and see we came to you and shared all problems that we cannot do this or that naturally we are learning.
PT: And we discuss freely there is no hesitation.
Nina: You are doing your own work...studying and learning and we are also going through the same cycle. We are not going to get a degree but definitely we are learning.
Saira: ...about SST in the start we had hesitation and...now we discuss freely.... Yes, indeed we have come closer and...it feels good (group session transcript, 12 January 2001).

**Teachers as Action Researchers**

Teachers can and do engage in action research through systematic observation and reflection if a conscious and deliberate effort is made to provide them with an opportunity and support to do so. Though the teachers with whom the researcher worked were already overburdened by their teaching load and other personal and professional responsibilities, they participated in the research with willingness, interest and commitment. For example, in spite of unexpected interruptions at short notice that required the teachers to make adjustments, they preferred to carry on with project classroom visits and group sessions. They were the ones to suggest the use of the telephone as a tool to communicate effectively and practically. Such use of the telephone is not a cultural practice in Pakistan, 'teachers only communicate at school...do not do this (communicating by phone).... In fact, talking...mainly social...is done mainly when people meet at gatherings' (Phone Conversation, Workshop Planning, Salima, 4 April 2001). The teachers were prepared to risk it to achieve their goals.

Writing personal stories about teaching as a career or making grids over and above journal writing were thought provoking and time-consuming exercises that are a concrete evidence of teachers' willingness to learn. For viewing videos and listening to audiotapes in the evenings or weekends, the teachers had to make special arrangements, hence extra time for resources; 'today I have Saturday off which I am spending at my sister's house to use her cassette player to listen to my audio recorded lesson' (Journal Entry, Saira, 14 October 2000).... 'After listening to the tape at home, I felt I did not miss anything of the group session of 1 December 2000...I had got all the handouts of the cycles...but when I listened to the tape these handouts became more clear to me' (Journal Entry, Saira, 6 December 2000)...'viewing of the video at home was very helpful for writing my reflection and getting a total picture of what was happening in the classroom...(Journal Entry, Nina, 6 October 2000).... 'Today before group session I was listening to the audio tape...the students used to be silent while listening but make a noise when they are asked a one word answer question...questions need to be framed in such a way that it makes students think and not to give the answer in chorus' (Journal Entry, PT 10 November 2000). PT, though required by family responsibilities to be home immediately after school, made extra time before group sessions to listen to or view her lessons recorded on tapes. Although the research was taking much of their free time (non-contact time), because no extra time was provided for the project, they were willing to spend more time for various reasons as the above interactions and descriptions suggest.

**Possibilities for Teacher Development in Learning Communities**

Much research cites three levels of teacher development; professional, personal and social. Professional development entails ideas and practice. Personal development is about teachers' feelings of being teachers and their perspective of the change process. Social development involves teachers developing new ways of working with their colleagues or other teachers. As can be concluded from the above anecdotes and discussions, all three teachers involved in this project experienced significant development in each one of the three levels to varying degrees. What contributed to this? Not the individualistic culture of teachers that exists in most schools and that leads to teacher isolation, but the collaborative efforts. This was recognized even by the teachers themselves: 'At schools most teachers are busy with their own teaching and preparation'... 'I liked this sharing session'... 'I do miss discussing with other persons, being in the project I can now discuss...it helps understanding a lot'... 'Sharing always helps in lessening the pain.' Implicit in this is the teachers expressing their need for a sense of community.

We argue for a culture of collaboration and collegiality in teaching rather than an individualistic culture. However, we suspect teachers do not always perceive teacher isolation as a constraint on their personal growth. Cochran-Smith and Lytle (1992) point out that some teachers take it as a blessing in disguise because it gives them privacy and autonomy. The culture of collaboration and collegiality of teachers is perceived by many as having the potential for interference with their functional autonomy. For example, PT's co-teacher (a novice teacher assigned to PT by her school head) stopped coming to classes after the first co-taught lesson by the researcher and PT. PT explained that this was due to the 'co-teacher' having other things to do, like copy correction and making reports. PT also added that perhaps if she were in her place she would do the same.

## Conclusion

We have come to believe that teachers should become researchers in their own classrooms and contribute to self-development and school improvement. This is where the concept of action research comes in. Today, action research is used in professional development, school improvement and curriculum development. The common feature is strategically planned activities that are implemented and then subjected to observation, reflection/evaluation, and change. In this process, the research group members are integrally involved in all the activities under consideration. We contend that change can occur through this cyclic process of observation, reflection and action. This is what was greatly responsible for the success of this project.

In the project, the teachers' beginning practice was predominantly a traditional transmission mode of teaching. The teachers' descriptions reveal how their school culture and educational system largely perpetuated a discourse of traditional teaching. Their practice changed when they took part in the in-service teacher development programmes at AKU-IED. These programmes employ constructivist and reflective practice approaches to teacher development. All three teachers acknowledged that the programmes had greatly influenced their taken-for-granted practice. Furthermore, the programmes provided them with approaches and strategies to make their science teaching more participatory, meaningful, and relevant to the lives of their students. The teachers' implementation of new learnings indicated their perception of teaching as an individual activity where the teacher has the autonomy of making decisions about pedagogy and curriculum. Their descriptions also indicated their belief of teaching as a dynamic process that demands active inquiry into their own practice. In spite of some change in their practice, at the beginning of the project, the teachers still saw teaching and teacher development as individual activities rather than social ones.

However, reflecting upon the teachers' descriptions and the researcher's personal experiences in teaching the in-service programmes has made us realize that social, cultural and institutional imperatives that could constrain the implementation of their learnings, were inadequately addressed. As a result, concurrent to struggling with their pedagogical content knowledge, the teachers had to struggle to change the structure and beliefs in the school that resisted to their efforts. However, engaging in the process of action research, the teachers became integral members of a community of fellow learners and researchers. This enabled the participants to 'struggle along with others to construct meaningful local knowledge and where inquiry is regarded as part of the larger effort to transform teaching, learning and schooling' (Cochran-Smith and Lytle, 1999:278) in a supportive and encouraging environment. Another significant development of this action research effort was the formation of a primary and secondary science teachers' learning community at Saira's school. This in turn leads to our networking with other science teachers in Karachi other than in outside Saira's school boundaries, in collaboration with the Science Association for Pakistan. There is every reason to believe that the action research group members will continue their efforts and commitment for their own and fellow teachers' pedagogical content knowledge growth even though the project has formally ended.

We have come to appreciate that action research, in which teachers document and analyze their own direct classroom experiences individually and collectively, allows them to talk about subject matter, students and learning, and teaching. That is, teachers working together to reflect upon their practice and to learn how to enhance their knowledge categories that are necessary for generating Shulman's (1986; 1987) pedagogical content knowledge. Cochran-Smith and Lytle (1999:262) have conceptualized this knowledge as 'knowledge-in-practice' that teachers acquire 'through experience and through considered and deliberative reflection about or inquiry into experience.' This is consistent with the process and expectations of action research.

Action research is an important avenue for teachers to improve their teaching and curriculum. We believe that what teachers learn through the action research process can be shared with others. Learning communities are appropriate sites and contexts for teacher sharing and learning. This can help to sustain teacher learning through teachers teaching other teachers by encouraging and supporting their intellectual and pedagogical growth. However, lack of time, resources and differences between teacher/practitioner research and academic research can act as limitations to the use of action research as a way of sustained teacher learning. We contend that if action research is collaboratively conducted amongst teachers to foster learning communities, committed and willing teachers will strive to sustain on-going learning.

## References

Britzman, D. (1991). *Student Makes Student: A Critical Study of Learning to Teach*. NY: SUNY Press.
Burke, P. J. (1987). *Teacher Development: Induction, Renewal and Redirection*. NY: Falmer.
Carr, W. & Kemmis, S. (1986). *Becoming Critical: Education, Knowledge and Action Research*. London: Falmer.
Carre, C. & Ovens, C. (1995). *Science 7–11: Developing Primary Teaching Skills*. London: Routledge.
Cochran-Smith, M. & Lytle, S. (1992). 'Communities for Teachers' Research: Fringe or Forefront?' *American Journal of Education*, 100(3), 298–324.
Cochran-Smith, M. & Lytle, S. (1999). 'Relationships of Knowledge and Practice: Teacher Learning in Communities'. In A. Iran-Nejad & P. D. Pearson (Eds.). *Review of Research in Education*, 24 (pp. 249–305). Washington, DC: AERA.
Guilbert, S. (2002). *Elementary Science and Teacher Development: Examining a Situation*. Unpublished PhD Dissertation. Alberta: University of Alberta.
Hargreaves, A. (1995). 'Development and Desire: A Postmodern Perspective'. In T.R. Guskey & M. Huberman (Eds.). *Professional Development in Education: New Paradigms and Practices* (pp. 9–34). NY: Teachers College Press.
Iqbal, H. M. (1994). 'Science Education in Pakistan: Retrospect and Prospect'. *Bulletin of Education and Research*, XVI (1–2) (pp. 34–40). Lahore: University of the Punjab.
Kagan, D. M. (1992). Professional Growth among Pre-service and Beginning Teachers. *Review of Educational Research*, 62, 129–69.

Kanu, Y. (1997). 'Understanding Development Education Through Action Research: Cross Cultural Reflection'. In T. Carson and D. Sumara (Eds.). *Action Research as a Living Practice* (pp. 167–83). NY: Peter Lang.

Kizilbash, H. (1998). 'Teaching Teachers to Teach'. In P. Hoodbhoy (Ed.). *Education and the State: Fifty years of Pakistan* (pp. 102–135). Karachi: Oxford University Press.

Pardhan, H. (1998). *Subject Specialist Teacher Program Evaluation Report*. Karachi: AKU-IED.

Rugh, A. B., Malik, A. N. & Farooq, R. A. (1991). Teaching Practices to Increase Student Achievement: Evidence from Pakistan. *BRIDGES Research Report Series*, No. 8. Harvard: Harvard University.

Sumara, D. & Davis, B. (1997). 'Enlarging the Space of the Possible: Complexity, Complicity and Action Research Practices'. In T. Carson and D. Sumara (Eds.). *Action Research as a Living Practice* (pp. 299–310). NY: Peter Lang.

Shulman, L. S. (1986). 'Those Who Understand: Knowledge growth in Teaching'. *Educational Researcher*, 15, 4–14.

Shulman, L. S. (1987). 'Knowledge and Teaching: Foundations of the New Reform'. *Harvard Educational Review*, 57, 1–22.

Skamp, K. (1998). *Teaching primary science constructively*. Florida: Harcourt Bruce.

Smith, D. C. & Neale, D. C. (1989). 'The Construction of Subject Matter Knowledge in Primary Science Teaching'. *Teaching and Teacher Education*, 5 (1), 1–20.

Stenhouse, L. (1975). *An Introduction to Curriculum Research and Development*. London: Heinemann.

Warwick, D. P. & Reimers, F. (1995). *Hope or Despair? Learning in Pakistan's Primary Schools*. West Port, CT: Praeger.

# 4

# THE ACTION RESEARCH INTEREST GROUP: BUILDING CAPACITY FOR LEARNING COMMUNITIES

*Shahzad Mithani, Debbie Kramer-Roy, Bernadette Dean, and Anjum Halai*

Being connected to others and being connected to institutions we value is a way to become connected to ourselves; to know that we belong; to know that we count for something; and to know that we are valued.

Thomas Sergiovanni (2001: 63)

In this chapter, we explore the evolution and some of the work of the Action Research Interest Group at AKU-IED. To provide a foundation for this, it will be useful to understand the idea of an 'interest group'. The Oxford Advanced Learner's Dictionary (Crowther, 1995) defines a group as: 'a number of people gathered or acting together' (p. 526); similarly the word 'interest' has been defined as: 'a state of wanting to learn or know' (p. 622). Therefore, an interest group may be seen as a group of people acting together in a state of wanting to learn or know collectively. The 'wanting to learn or know' in this case refers to action research and its processes; something for which a group of AKU-IED faculty and researchers were keen to learn and seek support.

Kemmis and McTaggart (1998) describe action research as 'a form of collective self-reflective enquiry undertaken by participants in social situations, in order to improve the rationality and justice of their own social or educational practices' (p. 5). The definition lends itself to the idea of participation and sharing as processes involved in an action research project and in learning from an action research process.

Several faculty members were in the planning phase of a project, or at the reconnaissance stage or had just completed the M.Ed. dissertation process with students using action research. The interest in action research and a number informal discussions led to the formation of the Action Research Interest Group (ARIG) in 2002.

The broad purpose of ARIG was to provide a forum for faculty and researchers to enhance their understanding of action research, enhance their capacity in undertaking action research and exchange ideas and allow confidence-building through seeking professional critique. The aims of ARIG are:

1. To enhance understanding and improvement of action research in educational contexts.
2. To collaborate with teachers to systematically research and improve classroom practice in their own schools.
3. To strengthen relationships and build school-based learning communities of teachers and AKU-IED faculty.
4. To study the impact of AKU-IED programmes in schools using action research methodology.
5. To provide a forum for reflection on various action research initiatives of AKU-IED faculty.

Since its inception in 1993, AKU-IED has focused its work on school improvement through in-service teacher education. While preparing teachers and head teachers through the M.Ed., Advanced Diplomas and Certificate programmes, the faculty has recognised the fact that in order to prepare reflective practitioners in the school, we (and our graduates) would have to undertake action research projects to pursue development of various pedagogical and school improvement initiatives.

In addition to this, during the recent past, at least seven national faculty members have rejoined AKU-IED after completing their doctoral studies. They have taken a lead role in academic scholarship along with other colleagues. In comparison, contributions by overseas faculty members from partner universities[1] have declined significantly. Developing ARIG has allowed faculty and researchers to collaborate, support each other and provide critique on each other's work. Thus, it has become an important initiative at AKU-IED and has become a learning community itself, focused on the theory and practice of action research.

## Capacity Building for Learning Communities

One of the aims of ARIG is to build school-based learning communities. Underpinning this aim is building the capacity of faculty members to recognize this notion, to be able to develop this interest group into a learning community at AKU-IED and to work with schools to create a community of learners ethos. Mitchell and Sackney (2000) suggest three dimensions to this capacity building ideal:

- Personal Capacity—building the individual's capacity through knowledge and skills to perform new tasks and roles in a learning community
- Interpersonal Capacity—building the capacity of groups and teams to work effectively in a collaborative climate
- Organizational Capacity—building the capacity of the school as a whole through structural arrangements that support connection rather than separation and empowerment rather than control.

Mitchell and Sackney (2000) write, 'a learning community consists of a group of people who take an active, reflective, collaborative, learning-orientated and growth promoting approach towards the mysteries, problems and perplexities of teaching and learning. The learning of critical importance is that of the students, the teachers and the school administrators' (p. 9).

ARIG has been successful in providing such a forum[2] to its members where they have sought expression and critique of research ideas and in allowing its members to initiate action research.[3] Moreover, ARIG has also facilitated access to international resources and a listserver to facilitate its members to exchange ideas at international forums. For ARIG members at AKU-IED, it has been a knowledge-sharing and knowledge-generating forum.

## The Action Research Projects

The next section of this chapter illustrates four action research projects that ARIG members have undertaken or are currently undertaking. These research projects have all been initiated by individuals rather than emerging directly as a result of ARIG but all of them have been presented and critiqued at this forum. Moreover, the principal researchers have had significant support to improve the quality of their research scholarship. Amongst the four being illustrated, a study by co-researchers Shahzad Mithani and John Retallick, and the study by Debbie Kramer-Roy have already been completed. Studies by Bernadette Dean and Anjum Halai are underway at the time of writing this chapter. Each study is a unique action research experience and together they reveal how varying degrees of capacity building and learning community was, or is being achieved.

**Action Research Project 1**

**The Role of a Mid-level Manager in leading in-service professional development**

*Shahzad Mithani*

This case is an excerpt from a project titled: 'The Impact of Selected Advanced Diploma in School Management (ADISM). Strategies on Mid-level Managers and School Reforms'.[4] Mid-level managers are school administrators usually at one level below principal e.g. vice-principal, department coordinator, section-in-charge. There is evidence of increasing interest in the role of mid-level managers in school improvement with a particular focus on teacher development (Wise, 2001) and the present study was designed to extend that line of research in the context of Pakistan.

The research question was: How, and to what extent do selected ADISM strategies impact on mid-level managers and their school reform efforts? Action research methodology was chosen as the project is concerned with school reform and that implies change in a school. As Calhoun (2002) points out 'action research can generate data to measure the effects of various programs and methods on student and staff learning' (p. 18). In this case, the focus is on the learning of the mid-level managers in ADISM and the impact of that learning on the school reform processes in which they are engaged. Action research is a cyclic process that is concerned with researching interventions whereby both action (i.e. change) and research (i.e. understanding) are simultaneously achieved. It is a negotiated approach to research where researcher and subject are both participants and partners in the process.

The researchers initiated the project by approaching the schools/teachers, conducted regular interviews with the participants to collect data, provided input to stimulate action and improvement in the strategy being investigated, and analysed and interpreted the data on an ongoing basis to develop understandings regarding the research questions. The research participants provided the interview data, initiated action with teachers in their schools within the framework of the project, wrote a reflective journal and met with the researchers for discussions about the project and their developing understandings of the strategies being studied.

## Case Study

Ms X started working in this private school as a senior mistress a few years ago and is currently working as a vice principal of the pre-primary section. The school is a non-profit school with 30 teachers and 400+ students, with each class having 32–33 children and two teachers. The school mission is for students to become confident and able to compete with the world and be critical thinkers.

Ms X completed the ADISM course in June 2002, and as a result, she feels that 'instead of asking teachers to do something by hook or by crook or telling them to do a task in a particular way, I give them the reason for how I would like this thing to be done, so the response to us is more positive than I believe other heads will get'.

## Introducing Reflective Practice

Ms X identified reflective practice as a strategy she learnt during ADISM and that she has introduced in the school. She started work on reflective practice by asking teachers to write their reflections and submit them to her on Fridays:

> but the thing is not very clear to them, what we mean by reflections. What they are writing is just the review, these are things that we did or are doing, just anecdotes. But what we mean by reflections, they are not clear on that issue. So I plan to do a workshop on what I expect them to write on reflective practice.

Moving along the process of reconnaissance, Ms X was asked about her understanding of reflective practice. She said that it is concerned with:

> Whatever I am doing or whatever I have done in fact. That thing happened and what was the reason it happened and what is the next step I could take for that...this is what I believe reflection is.

**Doing Reflective Practice**

The second school visit began with Ms X describing how she learnt about reflective practice during the ADISM course: 'I learnt through our instructors as they were giving us lectures and explaining things. Secondly, whilst doing my assignment on reflective practice I went through many books on reflective practice and that really helped me with what is meant by reflection'.

Ms X mentioned that there were some questions that helped her to reflect: 'What had happened to me? Why had it happened? What action I took and why I took that action? This practice really helped me in different ways. While I am reflecting on something it gives me a chance to think about whatever I have done and the response I received from my colleagues or my head'.

We then read some of the teachers' reflective journals and discussion followed about the nature of the writing. Mostly, it was found to be quite a general overview of the whole week though some pieces concentrated on a particular episode that enabled the writing to be more specific and disclosed feelings about the situation. Two teachers were then invited to join the discussion. One teacher said: 'Writing reflections helps us to see ourselves in a better way, to observe something carefully and then reflect on it...sometimes if we are facing some problems and we need some help from our head and things like that, we can share with our heads. It's a better way that our heads could read this and see what problems we are having'.

We then suggested a strategy that the teachers might like to try. This was the first action step in our action research. The idea was for teachers to focus on a critical incident during the week rather than try to write about everything that happens. There were four questions teachers could use to probe the incident:

- What happened?
- Why did it happen?
- What does it mean?
- What are the implications for my practice? (Hole and McEntee, 1999).

We felt that following this protocol might help teachers to sharpen their writing skills. We also provided an article that explained and gave examples of how teachers might address the four questions.

## Improving Reflective Practice

On the third school visit, we began with a discussion of the article on reflection. Ms X commented: 'Yes, they have really worked on it...though there was confusion over question 3, 'What does it mean?', and they were asking me to explain it but I was not sure about it'. Ms X was concerned about the focus on one incident: 'I was thinking, if I ask them just to write on one or two issues, about their teaching and the problems they are facing in all different subjects. If I am asking them to write about everything in such depth, then it will be too much for them to write and for me also to read'. This was followed by a discussion of the purpose of reflective writing and the focus on meaning: '...by doing this we are going in depth and really getting teachers to think about their practice'.

Ms X was also concerned about another matter: 'Don't you think then my process will be very slow? ...What about the syllabus and curriculum? ...I can't leave some things behind, some children go to another branch and there will be complaints from parents, so how am I going to face that thing?'

While we felt encouraged about the process of reflection in the school, we also had to take account of the difficulties of doing action research and reflective practice in a real school setting where the priorities are different; the priorities are not about teachers reflecting deeply on their practice, the priorities are satisfying the parents and covering the syllabus.

At this stage, the same two teachers who were with us the week before joined the conversation. They produced their journals for us to read and we could see they were doing a fine job of reflective writing about a critical incident though there was still some uncertainty about

Question 3: 'What does it mean...?' After some discussion, Ms X said that she was now more clear about how to handle that question and she suggested: 'One thing we can do is get teachers to sit together and talk about their reflections and all give their suggestions of why it happened and what it means'. We felt that was a very good idea and she said: 'We can do it in a workshop'.

### Final School Visit—The Workshop

The main focus of discussion during the final school visit was the workshop that Ms X had conducted with all thirty teachers in the school. She had given the teachers a handout concerning reflective practice related to our beliefs, our assumptions, our prejudices and actions and their consequences. She also addressed the four questions in the writing protocol by giving an example and asking teachers to write about a critical incident. Later, the feedback from teachers was very positive as the teachers felt it was less time consuming and easier to focus on one issue in depth, instead of describing everything that happened. Ms X felt that this new approach was meeting her needs, as the teachers started thinking more on that particular aspect, which helped them to develop solutions for themselves.

We resolved the troublesome question of 'What does it mean' by considering it from the perspective of the various stakeholders: what does it mean for the teacher, for the students, for the parents and for the school management. This approach seemed to make good sense and enabled teachers to look at the different interests of these groups. Examples from the teachers' journals also indicated that teachers were writing in a more insightful and thoughtful way about incidents in their classrooms. It was also proving to be a very positive experience for Ms X who was greatly encouraged by the success of the workshop and now plans further workshops for the teachers, indicating a change in her practice. She came to realise that by reflection on her own practice she is learning the importance of teachers valuing their practice as a source of learning.

At this stage, we had been through a couple of cycles of action research on reflective practice and felt a need to move on. We agreed that it is important for teachers to continue with writing, as it has been so well accepted and integrated into their work. We concluded the discussion by asking Ms X how she was feeling about the action research process. She responded: 'I am really feeling as if I am learning and this is the evidence. Most teachers have given me good response and I am really learning from this action research'.

## Towards a Learning Community

The case study revealed that the participant did re-conceptualise her roles as leader and manager in the school as a result of ADISM. She moved from an authoritarian, 'telling' orientation, to a role of working with the teachers in a supportive team approach to promote school improvement. She is now more inclined to explain the reasons for the requests she makes, rather than simply issuing orders to the teachers as she did in the past. Such a change from a bureaucratic stance to a leadership approach can be seen as an initial step towards a learning community.

In this case of reflective practice, the process has developed to the point where teachers themselves are now conducting workshops for other teachers to help them improve their reflective writing. Now more than seventy per cent of teachers are writing very clear reflections. Teachers are working and learning together about reflective writing. This is clearly another very significant step in the process of building a community of teacher learners in the school.

## Action Research Project 2

### Exploring how children with special needs can be included in the mainstream school

*Debbie Kramer-Roy*

This research study was planned and implemented to further inform my role at AKU-IED, which is to develop programmes and programme components on 'inclusive education for children with special needs', and to conduct research about them. The working definition of 'special needs' that I have introduced and used at AKU-IED is, 'any characteristic—whether obvious or hidden, whether permanent or temporary—which interferes with the child's learning in school and requires special attention'. This broad definition recognises that a significant minority of children who study in mainstream schools have special needs, which often go unrecognised, e.g. reading problems, mild intellectual impairment ('slow learners') or social and behaviour problems. Instead of receiving support, these children are often labelled and blamed for being 'weak', 'slow' or 'uncooperative'.

My conviction is that the first step towards inclusive education is facilitating the teachers' ability to identify and address the problems of this group of children in a constructive manner. Until this happens, it will not be feasible to suggest that the schools should admit children with obvious special needs, i.e. disabilities. This research, therefore, seeks to explore how these first steps towards 'inclusive education' can be taken. Inclusive education is the situation in which all children, regardless of their ability, study in the same school. For this purpose policies and practices regarding admission, teaching and assessment need to develop a more holistic, child-centred, constructivist and collaborative approach to education. Such an approach would welcome and recognise the potential and actual contribution of all children to building an inclusive community of learners in the school.

**Research Process**

In order to focus the research, I decided upon the following question: 'How can teachers of a mainstream school be supported in gaining knowledge and experience so that they can make their classroom more inclusive for children with special needs? My main purpose of conducting the research was to discover:

- how practicing teachers can start reflecting on their own experience with, and perceptions of, the notion of 'special needs', and,
- how this helps them to be open to learning more about this and trying out new strategies, so that they could start making their classrooms more inclusive.

To accomplish this, I considered it important to work with a team of teachers as they might recognise their own and their colleagues' perceptions and attitudes more easily in the context of group discussions. A change in attitude is the most fundamental requirement for becoming more 'inclusive' in their thinking and this is very difficult to achieve in isolation. Furthermore, forming teams of teachers to work on shared problems is the first stage in building a learning community as shown in Chapter 1 of this book.

At the end of an initial exploratory phase, a stakeholders' workshop was held. It was attended by the head teacher, parents and teachers and the consensus was that 'teacher training' would need to be the first step towards inclusion. This implies that involvement in the research was a positive choice of each teacher. As I was seeking to take an action research approach, I negotiated with the teachers, the knowledge and skills they would like to gain and how we might go about this. It was decided that regular workshops—rather than 'training sessions'—should be held and that the group would agree on an appropriate application activity to be carried out before the next workshop. This was important, as this way the activity was not viewed as homework to be done to please the trainer, but could lead to a more equal and collaborative relationship between the teachers and myself.

Right at the beginning, I shared with the group that I wished to involve them in a research process, rather than a training programme. I emphasized that this process could help them to suggest and implement changes in their own classroom and teaching practice, as well as at management level. One of the teachers volunteered to explain the action research cycle. She did this very well, which helped her colleagues to understand that their involvement in the research could go beyond their own learning at classroom level to influencing the school management.

However, active involvement in the research process did not come naturally, as the teachers were involved in many training sessions organised by their school system, which were very directed and not voluntary. In fact, the school had so many different new initiatives and teaching methods that the teachers suffered from 'innovation overload', which had its knock-on effect on the special needs research as well. Despite a growing realization in the group that children with special needs affect the teaching and learning process for the whole class, and that the application of insights gained and skills learned in the workshop had a positive effect on the class as a whole, it was still very difficult to keep the teachers' sustained interest and commitment to the research. This was especially so on occasions that the school management planned other sessions, the same day.

Other factors hindering the involvement of teachers in the research and their addressing of special needs issues, were the large class size of 40–45 students with only one teacher and the subsequent lack of time to do anything beyond getting through the syllabus. Teachers also expressed their frustration about their meagre pay, which does not encourage them to put in extra effort or time outside school hours.

In terms of openness and willingness to learn from each other, I observed some very positive attitudes. Initially, the teachers expressed that they would like the head and principal to join in the workshops. Even though this never happened, I felt it significant that they expressed their understanding that without the support of the head and principal, it would be difficult to bring changes at the classroom level. The teachers frequently brought up frustrations about lack of flexibility of the school system and frustration with the fact that their ideas were seldom listened to. On other occasions, teachers openly shared a 'failure', like the teacher who admitted to sometimes slapping the children out of frustration. Her colleagues supported her by showing understanding and giving her alternative ideas from their own experience. I did not need to intervene in this valuable shared learning experience, apart from making explicit how it fitted into the theory about behaviour management we had just discussed. This type of interaction started to happen more often, showing that teachers were able to support each other's learning related to their classroom practice.

Another indication of teachers' openness was pointed out by the head teacher, who noticed that the teachers welcomed my classroom observations and understood that the observations were intended to encourage their development and not in any way to criticise or test them. This was confirmed by the questionnaires filled by the teachers at the end of the research process. All indicated that the observations were useful and that it helped them to identify areas for improvement in a positive way.

An example of how the teachers applied what they discussed in the workshops directly in the classroom, was the story about behavioural problems they wrote collaboratively. Each teacher then told the story in the classroom, encouraging the children to discuss the problems and to suggest ways of preventing or addressing them. I observed most of these story telling sessions and although there was a lot of difference between teachers' story telling skills, some very good classroom interactions were seen and all teachers were able to facilitate their classes to make a negotiated list of behavioural 'dos and don'ts'. To ensure that all teachers understood fully how and why stories could be used to discuss sensitive issues with children, we brainstormed all-important things to remember in the next workshop. This gave a very good opportunity for those who had difficulty with the story telling activity, to learn more from their colleagues who were using it more effectively, without putting any one in a negative spotlight. These skills for working together as a positive team were much appreciated by the teachers and made a positive contribution towards building a learning community.

## Outcomes of the Research

At the end of the research period, I concluded that the research was not very successful in terms of achieving more inclusive classrooms in the school. However, as a researcher, I learned a lot about a range of issues:

- the school related factors that hindered teachers learning together
- the motivation of teachers to improve their practice despite these factors
- the effectiveness of action research, even in difficult situations, due to its potential of changing a group of teachers into a learning community
- the factors that hindered the inclusion of children with special needs
- the need for a multi-pronged approach to achieve a more inclusive classroom and school: without the commitment of the school management to improve the basic conditions in the classroom (e.g. class size, student to teacher ratio, more child-centred approaches to teaching and assessment) and to reviewing school policies to enable inclusion of children with special needs (e.g. admission and promotion criteria), there is very little that the teachers can achieve at the classroom level.

It was the opportunity for learning that the research provided to both the participating teachers and myself, that made this research worthwhile. Although my initial focus was not explicitly on the building of a 'critical community of enquirers' (Starrat, 1996 in Retallick et al, 1999), I realised that this process of learning to learn with and from each other is an essential condition for addressing the crucial and ideological issue of 'inclusive education for children with special needs'

## Action Research Project 3

### Researching practice, practicing research:
### Improving teaching and learning in classrooms in developing countries

*Bernadette Dean*

To improve the quality of education in developing countries, AKU-IED developed a model of school improvement through in-service teacher education. In the M.Ed. programme, teachers are educated to become exemplary teachers, teacher educators and researchers. Ten years down the road, a key question is: what is the impact of the teacher education programme on teachers and students. One way of finding out is through classroom-based action research studies in which teachers use a particular teaching strategy taught to them by a graduate of AKU-IED (known as a Professional Development Teacher or PDT) and note the benefits that accrue to students (Anderson, 2001). Such studies would indicate the potential of the strategies taught at AKU-IED for achieving its goals.

As the M.Ed. class of 2002 was completing their studies, I suggested the possibility of engaging in classroom-based action research to a group of students representing different geographical contexts. The aim was to investigate the possibilities and challenges PDTs face in educating teachers in the use of different instructional strategies and in preparing teachers to use action research to study their use of the strategy and note the benefits that accrue to their students.

### The Research Study

I began with this research question: What benefits accrue to students from teachers using student-centered instructional strategies taught to them by the PDTs using action research? There were a number of subsidiary questions; here I will focus only on those which relate to action research directly:

1. What possibilities and challenges do culture and context (school and society) pose to teacher professional development through action research?

2. What changes occur, if at all, in the participants themselves (PDTs and teachers), in those they work with (students) and in the situations in which the actions are carried out?

Action research was chosen for a number of reasons. Firstly, there is evidence that many practitioners (doctors, teachers, psychologists) do very little research (Barlow, Hayes and Nelson, 1984; Martin, 1989 cited in Dick, 1993). Schon (1983; 1987) argues that practitioners would learn more if they subjected their practice to deliberate and conscious reflection, which is a key element of action research. Secondly, action research is usually participatory. There is evidence that increase in better learning accrues from working with others; that a partnership with colleagues is more ethically satisfying and may be more occupationally relevant (Dick, 1993). Thirdly, the PDTs who are leading this research were introduced to the methodology of action research and some have used this methodology for their dissertations, thus gaining first hand knowledge of the possibilities and challenges of undertaking action research.

The action research in this study is being conducted at three levels, all of which proceed simultaneously. The focus of, and outcomes expected, at each level are presented in Table 1.

I began the research by inviting six PDTs to a meeting during which I discussed the idea and sought their feedback. We then decided to co-write the research proposal and to develop a common understanding of action research and the instructional strategies. Over the span of a week, we spent 2-3 hours each day developing a common understanding through presentations, discussion of ideas, addressing concerns and identifying relevant literature that PDTs could take with them. Two members of the group facilitated each session.

Each PDT met with their heads on return to their context, discussed the research proposal and got their consent. PDTs invited teachers to participate in the research. Each taught action research to teachers and an instructional strategy so that teachers could use action research to improve use of the strategy in their classroom. The first instructional strategy PDTs decided to teach was whole class discussion (WCD). The rationale for this was that teachers already use some form of discussion, and therefore, we would be starting from where teachers are. In one case, the PDT introduced inquiry because the curriculum called for the development of the skills of inquiry in students. The PDT supported and challenged the teachers through co-planning, observation and engaging with the teachers in critico-constructive feedback as they used the instructional strategy in their classrooms. In this way, I was able to maintain a sense of community in the group as a whole.

**Table 1**
**Action Research levels**

| Level | Who | Actions | Outcomes |
|---|---|---|---|
| 1. | Faculty | Develop understanding of action research and the instructional strategies. Facilitate research through support and challenge. Document the process. | Challenges and possibilities of action research for of the teacher educator. Nature of impact at all levels. |
| 2. | PDT | Teach action research and instructional strategies. Peer-coach teacher; facilitate critico-creative reflection. Document the process. | Possibilities of using action research for teacher education in their context. Changes in self, others and context. Nature of cooperation, inquiry and discussion. |
| 3. | | Teachers Learn action research and instructional strategies. Use action research to facilitate use of instructional strategies. Document the process. | Possibilities and challenges in using action research and strategies in their classroom. Benefits that accrue to students in terms of knowledge, dispositions, and skills. |

While the PDTs supported and challenged the teachers and each other intra-regionally, I supported and challenged the PDTs through email communication, organizing small group meetings and chatting on the Internet.

**Discussion of findings**

a) **Contextual challenges and possibilities.** Preliminary findings indicate that the culture of schools and understanding of teaching and learning in developing countries is a challenge to the use of action research as a way of improving practice. PDTs and teachers experienced similar challenges, albeit to different degrees and for different reasons. What got the research started was the common interest and commitment of the teachers, but the building of a community of learning through the use of action research is what provided the momentum.

b) **Understanding of teacher education in schools.** In most schools, in-service teacher education consists of one-shot workshops conducted on Saturdays or specially allocated professional development days. Processes like action research or coaching, which are more effective, are not well understood, and not often supported. Thus, when PDTs were given permission to conduct the action research, the permission did not entail providing the conditions necessary for the conduct of the research, that is, the provision of time for training, planning, observation and critico-creative reflection for both PDTs and teachers. An exception was the school in the Northern Areas of Pakistan, where some adjustments were made to provide time for teachers to work together.

c) **Time.** In all contexts, PDTs and teachers kept coming up against the barrier of inadequate time for training and systematic documentation. PDTs felt they did not have enough time to teach action research and the strategy. They lacked 'adequate time to observe teachers' lessons' or 'provide feedback to teachers'. Teachers found planning for discussion very time consuming. Documentation of the research was problematic for both.

d) **Resources.** Both PDTs and teachers identified lack of resources as a constraint. PDTs noted the lack of equipment (cassette recorders, transcribers) that would facilitate the research in all contexts except Tanzania and even more basic stationary (paper, markers, etc) in Tajikistan. The lack of reading material on action research in the local language (Central Asia) and the lack of subject-specific literature on WCD (Central Asia and Pakistan), which would have facilitated the formulation of discussion questions or in addressing concerns was sorely felt.

e) **Other roles and responsibilities.** Both PDTs and teachers felt that the dual roles of teacher and researcher and the accompanying responsibilities with insufficient workload concessions, made it difficult to conduct the research. Most felt overburdened and pressured to successfully complete the tasks of teacher or teacher educator and researcher. Most often the research suffered, as it did not have the immediacy of teaching or other administrative responsibilities. PDTs would have liked more time for initial training. I, however, encouraged them to see the research process as an opportunity to continue educating teachers to deal with issues when they were identified, rather than trying to address all issues during initial training.

f) **Teachers' interest and commitment.** Encountering the difficulties mentioned above would have quickly led to giving up the research had it not been for the teachers' interest and commitment. Teachers were very eager to learn how to engage in action research and the instructional strategies. In all areas, PDTs found a good number of teachers to work with, although some dropped out due to factors mostly not related to the study.

g) **Building communities of learning through action research.** As the PDTs came from six different contexts in five different countries, continuing to build a community of learning was a challenge. The online communications and individual small group meetings between faculty and PDTs and between PDTs intra and inter-regionally, where each had an opportunity to act as critical friend, facilitated the learning. PDTs acknowledged the support and challenge of the faculty and colleagues through constant communication and the sharing of suggested ways to address their questions and concerns. The use of action research with the built-in provision for coaching facilitated the development of a community of learning in the schools and university department where the research was carried out.

The action research methodology of identification of concerns and addressing them was acknowledged as facilitating use of the instructional strategy in the classroom. Through critical reflection teachers came to realize that their work in class was not interactive because they were doing most of the talking themselves or engaging in question and answer sessions. Reflection also helped in the identification of skills lacking in the students. For example, teachers recognized that students joining in discussion did not use agreement or disagreement statements, that students were debating rather than discussing, that some students did not get an opportunity to speak, that discussing issues in a foreign language was problematic. Provision of literature and planning helped them to address the issues systematically.

The PDTs and teachers found the opportunity for learning the strategy together, joint planning, observation of each other's teaching and joint critico-creative reflection facilitated them in learning with and from each other.

h) **Changes in self, others and situation as a result of action research.** Action research is not only about understanding but also about changing self, others and the context in which it takes place. I initially proceeded according to plan but soon realized the need for flexibility and understanding of the differing contextual realities and personalities I was working with. Practicing action research made PDTs realize its true nature. A PDT stated, 'Practicing action research with other responsibilities in real life situation made me recognize the messiness of action research.' They also realize it takes support over time to facilitate change in practice. Teachers were critical of their past practices and reflective of ways to improve their ability to conduct whole class discussion. Most teachers moved, albeit slowly, from controller to facilitator of discussion. With time, discussions became more systematic and coherent. Teachers usually see it as their responsibility to address difficulties faced by students. In the university, however, teachers moved to give students more control by allowing them to gauge their level and quality of participation and to improve it.

Participation of students in discussions improved. More students participated and they were able to express their views clearly and confidently. Students learnt to ask questions, seek clarification and build on or challenge presented ideas using agreement and disagreement statements. Other students enjoyed engaging in inquiry, having learnt the process of inquiry, but did not feel confident in the content acquired through the process until the teacher explicitly taught it to them. Students have learnt to make presentations so as to teach others what they have learnt from the inquiry.

Schools are beginning to see action research as a mean of facilitating professional development. For example, PDTs in East Africa and the

Northern Areas of Pakistan were given a lighter teaching workload to facilitate teacher professional development through research. This needs to be done for teachers as well, if they are to learn from it and improve their practice. In Kyrgyzstan, other teachers of the Department of English are interested in and ask for facilitation in learning to do action research and instructional strategies so as to improve teaching and learning of the English language.

## Conclusion

The research indicates that by its very nature action research facilitates the use of instructional strategies in classrooms in developing countries. However, if teachers are given time and supported by an in-house facilitator such as a PDT, its potential for teacher professional development could increase. Collaborative action research has the potential to create a community of learners in which to bring about change in the context.

## Action Research Project 4

## Action Research Project in the Advanced Diploma in Education: Mathematics

*Anjum Halai*

In this case, I describe the learning community that developed as a consequence of a group of tutors participating in the Action Research Project in the Advanced Diploma in Education: Mathematics, which is a one-year field based programme at AKU-IED. Teachers from sponsoring schools participate in their programme, which is designed to hold seminars during summer and winter breaks and on Saturdays, when most schools are off. During term time tutors visit the participants in the school. The purposes of field visits include provision of classroom support to participants in their efforts to implement their learning in the real classroom, identifying areas where participants require further support and to enable reflection to occur.

I was a member of the group of tutors teaching on the programme and conducting action research into the impact of selected strategies on students' learning of mathematics. On the basis of my participation in this action research project, I assert that certain factors assist in forging a group of professionals into a learning community. These factors include, shared experience of teaching on a common programme, institutional motivations, and availability of support structures.

This section is organised under three broad headings. First, getting started and working together, provides a brief description of the ways in which the group of tutors worked and interacted during the course of the study. Second, under 'what happened?', I share the findings of this research with the process that enabled the group to come together as a learning community. And third, under 'concluding reflections' I share my interpretations and conclusions regarding the factors that led to the formation of a learning community.

**Getting Started and Working Together**

During the past few years there has been an immense interest in generating research-based evidence of impact of AKU-IED programme inputs on schools, classrooms and students' learning. While developing and planning for an advanced diploma programme in the area of mathematics, I conceptualised an action research project with its main focus on studying the impact of selected strategies introduced in the programme. The proposed project consisted of two action research studies: 1) a small-scale action research study conducted by the teacher participants as part of their assignment in the programme, and 2) research undertaken by the faculty who were on the teaching team. The purpose in both cases was to generate local evidence of impact and look for micro impacts that would help justify teaching these methods to teachers more generally.

At the stage of proposal development, for a variety of reasons pertaining to availability of teaching staff, there was a lack of clarity about who would form the team to teach the programme and who could, therefore, be invited to conduct the research project. Once the teaching team was finalised, I invited the members to participate in the research project. The team comprised of four members; two of these (including myself) were full-time teaching staff at AKU-IED and the other two were graduates of AKU-IED, working as Professional Development Teachers (PDTs). The first PDT, Shahid (pseudonym), was a teacher in a government school and the other, Maheen (pseudonym), was a teacher in a local private school.

The project was funded by AKU-IED and provides for the time of the part-time faculty, logistical and other support such as use of internet facilities, secretarial support and transcribers. For the purpose of this chapter, I report the evolution of this group into a learning community i.e. a community where all participants are engaged in a constructive and reflective process of learning. The initial four meetings were scheduled in quick succession, as the primary purpose of these meetings was to develop a shared understanding of the research purpose and process. These meetings were organised so that the part-time and full-time faculty could participate without compromising their other responsibilities. After the initial meetings, regular monthly meetings were organised. The proceedings of all these meetings were tape-recorded. A purpose of these meetings was to share findings from the ongoing fieldwork, identify issues and questions and generally engage in cross analysis that could inform thinking about the study.

## What Happened?

I analysed the transcripts to look at the process of participation of the team members. Findings revealed that during the initial meetings, the two full-time AKU-IED faculty members raised and discussed most of the questions. Also, the stance of the discussion was tilted such that the two more experienced and qualified participants were asked to provide examples and suggestions to address emerging research issues. However, as the project proceeded, all participants participated by sharing ideas, raising issues and asking questions that would enable all members to further their understanding.

## Concluding Reflections

After observing the group of tutors working together, I have concluded that the four tutors began their work as a group but as the project proceeded, the group merged into a learning community. Evidence suggests that certain elements played a key role in enabling the group to forge as a learning community. These include shared experience of teaching on a common programme, political and institutional motivations, and availability of support structures.

*Shared Experience of teaching on a programme.* I believe that all four of us teaching on the same programme provided a shared experience that enabled us to learn together. For example, we could all relate to Maheen sharing the examples from her classroom work with a teacher. A transcript where one of the group members is sharing his/her classroom work is replete with statements such as, 'I had a similar issue...', 'This happened with me also...' or 'This was not the case with me...' and so on. This frequent linking of issues arising in others' classrooms with work in one's own classrooms suggests that the common experience of teaching on the advanced diploma programme was beneficial in enabling the process of learning from each other.

*Support Structures.* Of the four team members, two were full-time employees of AKU-IED and worked in the same building and on the same floor, but the other two worked as PDTs and were geographically at a distance. However, there was regular interaction in monthly meetings (which were supported by the AKU-IED), through telephone or email. While the regular interaction was essential to enable ongoing discussion and learning, it was the availability of support structures such as protected time, transcribers, email and venue for meetings that helped the group to interact smoothly and regularly.

*Institutional Motivations.* All four tutors participated regularly and with enthusiasm in the process of action research. The nature of their participation suggested that they were keen to learn from engagement in the process. But, there was a suggestion in the evidence that they were also interested in the product in the form of presentations and publications. Both process and product of the action research served as a motivation to come together as learners.

To conclude, I believe that the evolution of a community of learners is a process that takes place over time and requires certain elements that forge a group into a learning community. Furthermore, the essence of the action research process is enabling problem solving within the real world situation, which in turn enables the sustainability of this community.

## Analysis and Summary

The four projects described above illustrate the way and the extent to which ARIG is achieving its aim 'to build school-based learning communities'. At the beginning of this chapter, we described how learning communities contribute to capacity building in three dimensions, i.e. personal, interpersonal and organizational capacity. Now we turn to how this was achieved within ARIG as a group, as well as in each of the projects.

In terms of personal capacity building, ARIG provided a forum for its members to discuss their research proposals, processes and findings for feedback and discussion. This process helped members in their planning of and reflection on their research activities, increasing their understanding and research skills. Personal capacity building was also evident in all four studies. For example, in Project 1, Ms X's personal capacity building was greatly supported by the action research; although she had made a start with introducing reflective practice in her school, she was struggling to effectively implement it. The action research helped her to continue this process. Similarly, both researchers and participants in Project 3 developed their skills. Improved capacity of the PDTs to mentor other teachers and to use action research to teach their colleagues new strategies more effectively was evident. The teachers benefited by becoming able to reflect critically on their past and newly learned practices.

Interpersonal capacity building was enhanced through ARIG as it provided faculty and researchers with a regular opportunity to share their research in a non-threatening, yet challenging setting. This has given members more insight into each other's way of working and areas of interest, strengthening supportive relationships beyond ARIG as well. ARIG has made evident that the faculty has a need for shared learning and this contributes to team building. From the four projects, it becomes apparent that personal and interpersonal capacity building often go hand in hand. In Project 2, there was also a lot of interpersonal capacity building, as teachers learned how to support each other's learning through sharing and solving problems together, as well as through sharing individual learning without emphasizing another colleague's failures. For Project 4, the transition from being a group of course facilitators to being a team that perceived all members as equal was a very important part of the research outcome.

Not unexpectedly, capacity building at the organizational level was not as evident as at the other two levels. However, Project 2 describes how the research strengthened teachers' awareness of the need to involve the management in the action research process and make their voice heard. If taken to fruition, this could be an important step in organizational capacity building. Likewise in Project 3, the fact that schools were inclined to reduce teaching time in order for their teachers to develop a deeper learning shows some growth in institutional capacity.

**Conclusion**

The projects show the ways and extent to which ARIG is achieving its aim 'to build learning communities'. Despite the varied focus and approach of each of the action research projects, it is evident in all cases that the research process facilitated the development of learning communities, which built personal, interpersonal and to a limited extent, organisational capacity. Both the reflective nature of action research and the fact that it is necessarily a negotiated approach to research, has led to the development of faculty capacities of a generative nature. This extends to recognizing constructivism as an underlying learning process and shows how it allows development of learning communities as an outcome of these research processes at personal, interpersonal and organizational levels.

## NOTES

1. Since the inception of AKU-IED, Ontario Institute of Studies in Education/ University of Toronto and Oxford University have worked with AKU-IED as partner Universities in the development, planning and delivery of the academic programmes.
2. ARIG activities include: regular meetings among members; proposal development, presentation and critique; feedback on research-in-process; sharing of articles (jig saw reading); and identifying and developing technical resources linkages.
3. Members are currently undertaking action research in the areas of curriculum, mathematics learning, inclusive education, multi-grade teaching, classroom practices and professional development, educational leadership and management and ICT.
4. This research project had two aims: 1) to assess the impact of ADISM and 2) to undertake action research to improve on one of the management practices. For the purpose of this chapter, the discussion will focus more on #2.

## References

Anderson, S. (2001). *Impact Evaluation at IED*. Unpublished paper, Karachi: AKU-IED.

Calhoun, E. F. (2002). 'Action Research for School Improvement. *Educational Leadership*', March.

Crowther, J. (Ed.). (1995). *Oxford Advanced Learner's Dictionary* (5th ed.). Oxford: Oxford University Press.

Dick, B. (1993). *You want to do an action research thesis?* Retrieved online from http://www.scu.edu.au/schools/sawd/arr/arth/arthesis.html

Hole, S. & McEntee, G. H. (1999). 'Reflection is the Heart of Practice'. *Educational Leadership*, 56(8), 34–37.

Kemmis, S. & McTaggart, R. (Eds.). (1998). *The Action Research Planner* (3rd ed.). Geelong: Deakin University Press.

Mitchell, C. & Sackney, L. (2000). *Profound Improvement: Building Capacity for a Learning Community*. Lisse: Swets and Zeitlinger.

Retallick, J., Cocklin, B. & Coombe, K. (Eds.). (1999). *Learning Communities in Education*. London: Routledge.

Schon, D. (1983). *The Reflective Practitioner: How Professionals Think in Action*. Boston: Basic Books.

Schon, D. (1987). *Educating the Reflective Practitioner*. San Francisco: Jossey Bass.

Sergiovanni, T. (2001). *Leadership: What's in it for Schools?* London: Routledge Falmer.

Wise, C. (2001). The Monitoring Role of the Academic Middle Manager in Secondary schools'. *Educational Management and Leadership*, 29(3), 333–41.

# 5

# CO-LEARNING PARTNERSHIP: A WAY FORWARD TO DEVELOP LEARNING COMMUNITIES IN PAKISTANI SCHOOLS

*Razia Fakir Mohammad*

The context of my research is teacher education and its implications for children's learning in secondary school mathematics classrooms in Pakistan. I began this research as a study of how mathematics teachers had implemented their learning into classrooms preceding their participation in the mathematics visiting teacher course at AKU-IED. By analysing Phase 1 of the research, I realized the difficulties faced by the teachers in translating their university learning into classroom activity. The teachers needed support and guidance in the implementation of their learning objectives. Theoretical perspectives (discussed below) leading to the idea of a 'co-learning partnership' suggested to me that establishment of a co-learning partnership itself involves a process of learning for both a teacher and a researcher/teacher educator. The partnership recognises the importance of the teacher educator's learning as well as the teachers' learning. In Phase 2, I extended this research from a study of teachers' implementation strategies to a participatory study of processes involved in supporting teachers' learning and classroom implementation. This model of co-learning partnership could make an important contribution towards building learning communities in schools in Pakistan and other developing countries.

## Context of the Study

Since 1993, AKU-IED has been contributing to in-service teacher development with the aim of improving the quality of school education. The Institute provides courses for teachers and head teachers in which participants are encouraged to look critically at their existing practices and attempt to reconceptualize their roles in schools. One of these courses is a two month, in-service, teacher education programme called the Visiting Teacher Programme. In this chapter, I refer to the Visiting Teacher Programme (VT) in mathematics. The teachers from partner schools who take the course are named Visiting Teachers (VTs). As full time students they learn pedagogy alongside mathematics content and implement their learning experiences in classroom situations.

During the course, mathematics VTs are encouraged to learn in similar ways to those in which they might subsequently work with students in their classrooms. The instructors of the VT programme are professional development teachers, graduates of the M.Ed. programme at AKU-IED, who work (sometimes with guidance from resident or overseas faculty members) within the framework of the philosophy discussed above. During the course, the instructors encourage the VTs to hypothesise, argue, seek patterns while rationalizing rules and facts, and implement new ways of teaching in classrooms in a cooperative environment. The aim behind this approach is to promote VTs' conceptual understanding of mathematics so that they will, in turn, promote their students' conceptual understanding. The VTs learn about co-operative learning strategies and working in collaboration in order to negotiate meanings and exchange ideas to enhance their learning of mathematics. In turn, they promote the value of social interaction in students' construction of mathematical knowledge in their classrooms.

The instructors represent role models for the VTs by modelling behaviours such as active listening, respecting views, encouraging negotiations, developing shared understanding and provoking critical thinking to facilitate the VTs' learning at AKU-IED. It is assumed that visiting teachers returning from in-service education would promote such a teaching approach leading to the promotion of active thinking by students in their classrooms. Considering the culture of Pakistani schools, where teachers have fewer chances to increase self-awareness in their teaching styles and students are expected to reproduce teacher knowledge, the new expectations for teaching aroused my interest. I was interested to explore the impact of the shift in their teaching and learning when teachers returned to their classrooms.

**First Phase of Research**

I adopted an interpretive stance in the phenomenological tradition, to gain access to the VTs' perspectives on their actions as well as to interpret those meanings to gain a new understanding. I observed their teaching and followed it up with open-ended interviews. The findings suggested that, after the influence of an in-service course at a university, they were committed to developing their teaching. However, school life had its own limitations and requirements. There were also limitations in the teachers' understanding of their new role, which put them in a difficult situation. It appeared to me that these teachers were not able to continue their learning at the school according to their new expectations. They were embraced by a powerful culture that had a heavy influence on their thinking and actions. A lack of support and a culture of following routine in schools had discouraged them from continuing change in their practice. At the initial stage of change, teachers needed consistency between their learning and contextual expectations and support; the schools had their own limitations, aims and agenda while the teachers expected the support from AKU-IED, but it was not there. Under the unfavourable conditions of the schools, some of them, though desirous to bring change in their teaching according to AKU-IED ideology, kept their wishes to themselves. The teachers' existing practice also indicated that their learning from the university was going to be a past event, not a process of further development and they felt themselves alone in crossing the road.

These observations made me recognize that change cannot flourish in a vacuum. There were many issues raised by the teachers. Accepting and only discussing them in a thesis means to accept the deficiencies without struggling with them and closing the chapter of developing teaching in the existing context of schools in Pakistan. One teacher questioned the possibility of change in his practice in the school. He asked me: 'Is it all applicable in this situation? If you were allowed to work here, would you be able to maintain the quality of thinking and work you all do at the IED.' I asked myself: For whom does this question stand, was it for me, or for AKU-IED, or for the teacher himself? Should I leave the teachers alone with their problems, and questions? These questions raised another question: How could I adapt myself to make it possible for teachers to work with students in developing conceptual understanding, so that the teachers do not just take the forms of questioning, group work etc., but focus on developing the thinking of students? I, therefore, perceived the first phase of my research as an exploratory stage and made decisions to establish some relationships in which the teachers could acquire confidence to try out their learning in classrooms or to learn from classroom practice.

## The Nature of Co-learning Partnership

In this section, I will examine the basic features of co-learning as a form of collaboration. It may be seen as scaffolding in supporting teachers as they learn from their classroom practice. Wagner (1997) introduces the term 'co-learning agreement' in research relationships between the participants in research. He discussed three modes of co-operation in educational research, namely, those of *data extraction agreement*, *clinical partnership* and *co-learning agreement*. The difference in these three forms of research relationship determines the social arrangement, expectations of the participants, and implications of the research project. In a co-learning partnership, the research is seen as an interactive social approach for the educational reform process. As Wagner states:

> In a co-learning agreement, researchers and practitioners are both participants in processes of education and systems of schooling. Both are engaged in action and reflection. By working together, each might learn something more about the world of the other. Of equal importance, however, each may learn something more about his or her world and its connection to institutions for schooling (p. 16).

From the above statement, it appears to me that the essential feature of the co-learning agreement is that all partners are learners. One way that this could be achieved in teachers' learning situations is by a teacher educator encouraging all the participant teachers to be co-learners along with herself or himself. An educator, in the partnership, does not dictate the directions of the change, nor are the teachers subordinates; all the participants are involved in both the action and reflection, and are responsible for change or development in their respective roles. In this respect, teachers do not work under external control or imposed authority, rather they commit themselves to learn on an equal basis of sharing a mutual agenda and respecting each other's goals of learning.

Jaworski (2000) extends the co-learning idea to the relationship between teachers and teacher educators, as well as between teachers and researchers. She states:

> A co-learning partnership implies an explicit arrangement agreed between participants (p. 6).

According to Jaworski, the consequences of such a negotiation would be a growth of knowledge for both the participants (e.g. teacher and researcher, or teacher and teacher educator) with recognition and resolution of everyday dilemmas of teaching, and teachers' learning. Examining the interaction between the researcher and teachers under the co-learning agreement, she recognised the value of discussion among the participants as a mechanism to deepen the understanding of the teaching practice as well as the researcher's learning about teaching. As she states:

> Interaction between teacher and researcher encouraged the articulation and growth of knowledge on the part of the teacher, and the teacher's communication allowed the researcher to contribute to a wider knowledge base in teaching (p. 7).

Jaworski adds:

> Teachers' engagement in inquiry and reflection at a pedagogical level is central to the development of a co-learning partnership. It is a question for teacher-educators how such activity by teachers originates. In what ways are teachers 'socialised' into the norms of inquiry and reflection? (2000, p. 14)

In such a co-learning partnership teachers become aware of their problems and issues through their own reflection on their practice, and it might involve them in some forms of inquiry into teaching. In addition, in the context of Pakistan where teachers can lose a sense of ownership and become dependent on a partner, for example, a teacher educator, a co-learning partnership may increase the teachers' accountability and freedom to improve their own practice.

It is important to recognise that the quality of relationships is central to achieving a collaborative culture of learning; also, that a commitment to learning together fosters shared understanding through mutual dialogue leading the participants to achieve ownership and confidence in knowledge creation. Trust and compassion among partners reduce their fear of taking risks alone and of negative judgements from external observers. When teachers are committed to the value of change, they give meaning to change. Fullan (1999) discusses the culture of collaborative learning in the following way:

> effective collaborative cultures are not based on like-minded consensus. They value diversity because that is how they get different perspectives and access to ideas to address complex problems. Under such conditions, inequity is far less likely to go unnoticed or to be tolerated. At the same time conflict is brought out into the open. There is a great deal of team building, diverse group working together and intense communication and information sharing (p. 36–37).

According to Fullan, teachers' practice is promoted when collegiality is supported in schools. Collegiality aids shared understanding, shared responsibility in taking risks, shared goals through meetings/projects, or other means that are congruent with teachers' needs in attempting change in the classroom. To support the notion of collegiality, Rogoff (2001) in her study of collaborative partnerships between parents and teachers states that learning through collaboration requires respect for participants' ideas, views and opinions. The differences between participants' views may be viewed as resources to enhance opportunities for learning. However, conflicts and difference in opinions should be dealt with by conversation and problem-solving in trusting non-judgmental environments.

I assumed here that realizing the value of opinions, and listening in order to resolve issues in conversation, provides teachers with constant opportunities for learning and growth in collaborative discussions with a teacher educator. Teachers are neither immobilised nor passive but are self-conscious owners of their learning and have the capacity to reflect. Thus, the purpose of a collaborative culture of learning is two-fold, empowering the teachers to raise their voices and concerns as well as contributing to a teacher educator's own understanding.

The above discussion strengthened my belief that teachers should have autonomy and dignity as learners in the context of working towards their goals for teaching in the classroom. A commitment to learning could be an activator in the sense that it engages teachers in taking actions on the basis of their self-critical reflection, resulting in creating change at a rate which is justified by self-reflection and feasible for practical needs.

In a collaborative partnership, a process of transformation takes place. Teachers feel more committed, responsible and capable of producing meaningful and practical knowledge about teaching and improving themselves through reflection and dialogue with partners. This partnership, between teachers and a researcher/educator, encourages an environment conducive to learning—engaging participants in dialogue, where different points of view are shared and listened to, and in reflection, through which thinking is promoted and consequences are achieved in terms of a shared understanding. Thus, equality is achieved in meaning making through participation in negotiation and reflection. This is parallel to the perspective of students' learning in a mathematics classroom. Students collaborate with a teacher, as discussed in Povey and Burton (1999), where both teachers and learners consult and respect each other's experiences and knowledge as well as question them in order to enhance learning:

> As such, meaning is understood as negotiated. External sources are consulted and respected, but they are also evaluated critically by the knowledge makers, those making meaning of mathematics in the classroom, with whom *author/ity* rests. Such a way of knowing opens up the possibility of understanding knowledge as constructed and meaning as contingent and contextual, and personal in the sense that it reflects the positionings of the knower. The teacher and the learner meet as epistemological equals (p. 234).

Thus, a culture of collaboration focuses explicitly on empowerment of teachers and nurtures their thinking and practice. I see that commitment to learning for both teachers and a teacher educator promotes mutual dialogue resulting from self-reflection and/or a trusting relationship. This commitment then reduces issues of external control and authority over teachers' learning and promotes accountability in self-improvement. However, a recurring question for me is, what are the possibilities and implications of creating such a co-learning partnership in a Pakistani school?

From the above discussion, I realise that a co-learning agreement could not be conceptualised without participants as co-learners. However, this begs the question of what I mean by co-learners in the practicality of teachers developing teaching. My understanding is that the establishment of a co-learning partnership in practice itself involves a process of learning for both myself and the teachers as co-learners.

Therefore, I decided to encourage the teachers to reconceptualise themselves as learners in order to enhance our learning from each other, and more difficult for them, to perceive me as a learner too.

My decision highlights issues of perceptions of my authority, or power accorded to the position of a teacher educator in taking initiatives of creating a co-learning partnership. However, it was the issue of the teachers' difficulties in the practicality of their classroom development which stemmed from their existing problems in their schools. My findings from the first phase identified that teachers faced many problems in developing their teaching (e.g. workload, shortage of time, lack of management support, etc.). I believe that ignoring teachers' needs and failing to provide appropriate support negates the notion of true equality.

I assumed the responsibility to create a trust relationship between two partners (teachers and teacher educator), within which to share their concerns and capabilities in the promotion of development of these respective roles. Following the idea of a collaborative partnership, I shall examine the consequences of a co-learning partnership between a teacher and a teacher educator in the reality of a school setting. In addition, the final part of the chapter contributes to an understanding of co-learning partnerships for the improvement of teacher education, which is the ultimate goal of all Pakistani schools.

## Research Methods

The nature of the collaborative partnership between teachers and the teacher educator emerging in the second phase of my research was reflective and participatory, focusing 'With' rather than 'On' the teachers (Carr and Kemmis, 1986; McNiff, 1991). It was premised on the idea of shared ownership. I assumed that reflection and justification of self-actions would enable participants to understand the reality and difficulties of practice and their own contribution to achieve improvement in practice in a collaborative partnership. In addition, as a researcher, I would be studying these layers of participants' learning in their particular context. One of the features of the second phase of my research could be characterised, as Kemmis and Wilkinson (1988) write:

a form of research which places control over processes of educational reform in the hands of those involved in the actions (p. 189).

Thus, in the second phase of the research, I played two roles: the role of a teacher educator, to activate teachers' learning into practice, and an overarching role of a researcher to analyse processes of teacher development and associated issues. As a teacher educator, I would support the teachers in trying out new ideas and help them gain insights into the issues of their teaching. As a researcher, I investigated the processes of the teachers developing teaching with collaboration of the teacher educator.

I adopted interpretive research methods. I collected data by recording conversations in pre and post observation meetings, maintaining field notes during the teachers' participation in teaching or their learning with the teacher educator, along with the teachers' written comments (when provided) and my own reflective entries. I maintained two kinds of reflective journals, one written as a teacher educator and the other as my reflection on the process of research. The two journals were different. As a teacher educator I maintained a separate journal for each teacher. My medium was Urdu, so it was convenient for a teacher to read. I described the process of collaborative work and also raised some questions which could motivate the teachers to think or respond further. I avoided writing negative judgements but raised the issues in the form of self-questioning. In the journal for myself as a teacher educator/researcher, I attempted to analyse my actions and their limitations, through on-going reflection about my involvement. These reflective entries discussed the nature of my own participation and relevant issues in the collaborative work; for example, how did I decide my actions during collaborative working with the teacher, what were the outcomes or tensions of partnership for me as a teacher educator/researcher. My reflective entries became a form of analysis of the processes and issues of the teachers' learning, as well as creating data of my own learning in these respective roles.

Three teachers, Naeem, Neha and Sahib participated in the second phase of my research. All three teachers aimed to increase the students' participation in their learning and develop students' conceptual understanding of mathematics (adapted from their learning at AKU-IED). This became evident when they responded to my invitation to participate in the second phase of my research. The teachers' aims were:

- Sahib's aim was to talk about the classroom issues and plan lessons according to new methods.
- Neha's aim was to plan and teach lessons according to the ways that she had learned at AKU-IED.
- Naeem's aim was to discuss how to teach mathematics with reasoning.

I worked with them for about ten weeks (from mid-December 1999 to early August, 2001). I met each of the teachers once a week on a regular basis, sometimes, twice a week, if a teacher needed my support. All data was collected and analysed in the teachers' native language, Urdu.

**Analysis and Findings**

My initial analysis in the second phase started by reading the data from a school visit with the teacher. Considering the relevant data, I would write a detailed analytical memo of the meeting between the teacher and myself. An analytical memo was a description about our work together on the particular day in relation to pre and post observation and observation meetings. For example, description might be about how we initiated our work, what the teacher said or did, my reaction to it and what it's limitations or successes.

A range of examples provided evidence of the teacher's learning during my reading of these analytical memos, which were highlighted in tabulated form. I approached these tables to extract certain highlighted examples of the teacher's learning. I also labelled these examples according to a specific aspect of the teacher's learning or engagement in learning, e.g. the teacher's effort in translating of new ideas, understanding of his or her new role. Several examples represented the same aspect of the teacher's learning which I clustered under the same label to form a category describing this learning. In the next section, I present some examples from my wider set of findings that are representative of the teachers' learning of some aspects, resulting from my analysis of data from observations and discussions.

## Teachers' Effort of Translating New Ideas into Practice

Sahib planned to teach lesson 7, 'circles'. He appeared to have two ways of teaching the topic when I invited him to share his planning with me. He had an idea of teaching 'circles' through a practical activity that he had learned at AKU-IED. However, he decided to teach by his routine method of defining and drawing 'circles'. As he said to me:

> If I tell them orally it does not take any time, but if they learn practically the impact will be longer, they will remember the concept forever. However, if I teach practically, then I will not have time for written work and practising drawing 'circles'.

Sahib was aware of the value of teaching through a practical activity, however, for a variety of reasons (e.g., shortage of time and forthcoming examinations), he wanted to teach in the routine way. His concern was that passing examinations did not require conceptual understanding. As he said:

> I have to complete the syllabus before the final examination. A teacher does not need to bother about their [students'] learning; it depends on students how much they want to 'absorb'. We check their memory and skills of drawing in examination; conceptual clarification is not a basic requirement of the examination. If we 'check' [assess] their concepts, none of them will pass the examination.

The teacher's statement clearly indicates a transmission view of teaching, despite his overt emphasis on practical activity. Perhaps the practical realities were obstacles in enriching his lesson planning according to his new aims. The question that faced me was how could I help him to find ways to integrate his new aims of teaching with the realities of practice. I encouraged him to imagine himself in a teaching situation at the school with fewer problems. How would he then teach the lesson with a practical activity? The purpose of my question was to help Sahib articulate the ways of using practical activities in a mathematics classroom. He said:

> I have not tried out any practical activity in teaching the topic previously, whereas, I have been always thinking about teaching it differently.

It appeared that he had not considered integrating his new learning into his teaching practice but merely talked about it. I asked him to give an example of a practical activity in teaching the topic. Sahib talked about an activity on 'circles' that he learned in the VT programme, when the group of VTs were asked to stand at an equal distance from a point, holding a rope. He said that this activity could be a practical demonstration of 'circles' and the students could explore a definition of 'circles' themselves. However, he said:

> I need a full period for taking the students outside the classroom and asking them to arrange themselves. Getting a rope is difficult too. I do not think that then any time will be left for written work.

The issue of Sahib's difficulties in translating that activity (learned at AKU-IED) into the classroom context is evident in the above statement in relation to getting materials, time and space to incorporate the activity in his teaching practice. His statement also signifies his struggle with new ideas, while his thinking was rooted in a transmission view of teaching and learning in the culture of school. However, my presence motivated him to try out the new method in teaching practice, as he said:

> As you are also here, I should try this method in the classroom and you tell me how I can improve myself in that activity.

Thinking about using the activity in the classroom, he said that he could ask one student (for example Kamran) to stand up and stretch his arm, while the others would be asked to stand at the distance of Kamran's arm; in this way they would form a circle themselves. He said:

> I could do this activity inside the classroom in the available space by calling some students. It could be a small circle, and if there will be some space between them I will tell them to imagine no gap.

Sahib acknowledged our partnership which helped him to broaden his mind in order to access new ideas and activities and to discuss the possibilities for applying them.

> We always have previous experiences of learning and knowledge; they are all hidden in our minds. Thinking deliberately means bringing them out. It is difficult to think in isolation. When one talks with someone he discloses

many ideas to himself. However, that someone should have the same vision of teaching.

My analysis is that there were two important factors involved in Sahib's learning in the school context. One was the teacher's teaching in a real classroom situation, the other, the presence of a teacher educator in the school. My presence, as a teacher educator, encouraged him to view himself from the perspective of AKU-IED and reminded him of his learning from the VT course. However, his presence in the school did not let him escape from the limitations of the school context. He was conscious of the school expectations, the limitations of time and resources, and the students' needs and problems, as well as his own focus of teaching. He considered both the school's limitations and his new goals of teaching, and adopted alternative ways to improve the quality of teaching and students' interaction. Thus, new possibilities of teaching occurred to the teacher.

**Improvement of Content Knowledge**

This example is taken from lesson 10, 'decimals'. Naeem's purpose was to teach the methods of converting decimals into common fractions and vice versa, with reasoning. For this purpose, he had planned activities. However, during the lesson, the issue of his limited knowledge of decimals became evident to me. Below I present the relevant part of the lesson:

*Naeem wrote on the board*: **.1 = 1** [I found it hard to understand what he meant here, but it became clear that it aided his idiosyncratic understanding of converting between fractions and decimals].

1 T   You should remember that the decimal point always has a value equal to one.
*He wrote a series of numbers on the board*: **.1, .11, .111, .1111,**
2 T   Observe the values of these numbers in common fractions.
*First he considered '.1'*
3 T   Write the number as a numerator. Remove the point from the number and write one as the denominator. Now count the numbers after decimal and put zeros accordingly in the denominator.

He wrote, $.1 = \frac{1}{10}$. *(His verbal and written explanations were going on simultaneously).*

He solved another question. He wrote, $.11 = \frac{11}{100}$.

4T   We can write this *(pointed to .11,)* in this way.

He wrote $\frac{11}{100} = \frac{1}{10} + \frac{11}{100}$

[I think he wanted to write that 1/10 +1/100=.11, which is another way to represent 11/100, but what he wrote was incorrect].
Then he called one of the students and asked him to write *.111 in common fractions. He guided the student to solve the question in a similar way to the previous examples.*

Naeem had his own idiosyncratic way of thinking about the equivalence of decimal and fraction representations. He had given a mathematically meaningless explanation to the students; it seemed to me that he reasoned as follows:

- Given a decimal such as 0.111, write, $\frac{}{1}$

- Count the figures after the point—in the case of 0.111; there are three figures, so write three zeros after the 1 in the denominator, i.e. $\frac{}{1000}$

- In the numerator, write the figures that follow the decimal point, i.e. $\frac{111}{1000}$.

As I observed his teaching, I asked myself: what would be the consequences of the teacher's limited knowledge for the students' learning? There was another question: should I discuss this issue in the feedback session or should I deal with the issue then in the lesson? I decided to help Naeem during the lesson because I realised a need to demonstrate the method with appropriate mathematical explanations so that he could find the gaps in his understanding and fill them. Also

I felt myself morally obliged to prevent the students from developing a wrong concept about decimals.

I intervened during Naeem's lesson, and asked him if I could take part in the teaching, which he accepted. I intentionally reviewed his first activity before I went on to the second part of his lesson in order to give an appropriate meaning to decimals, since I wanted to reduce any negative impression created by rejecting his methods, and protect him from humiliation. Also, I wanted to maintain continuity in the lesson and wanted to show the teacher ways to link the first activity to the other.

In the feedback session, we discussed the topic further (for example, what is meant by 0.432). Naeem analysed his planning process and his misinterpretation of decimal points. Analysing the impact of his limited knowledge in the lesson, he said that he had not taught the meaning of decimal points before, nor had he himself learned in this way. He said: 'I did not realise I should teach the concept of base 10. Values of numerals depend on 10'.

We discussed various issues, for example, my interruption in his teaching and his learning of mathematics. Naeem said that my taking over the teaching was the right decision. He suggested such support might prevent the students from being given wrong concepts while the teacher could benefit from acquiring mathematical learning. However, he pointed out that learning on his own was difficult within the limitations of the school. Naeem also commented on his efforts of working hard, spending time in thinking and planning the lesson and improving mathematical knowledge in trying out new ideas. Upon my probing into his process of planning, he said:

> I read the exercise, solved some questions and checked answers. I spent a lot of time in thinking about new ways to teach the method by doing calculations myself. I observed that 'one' always removes the decimal point. The number of numerals after the decimal point are replaced by the number of zeros after the 1. I constructed my own number series and applied my explanation. The answers were right. ...For the first activity, I took some ideas from our previous lesson. I added some of my examples.

Naeem had perceived the procedure by which certain decimals could be converted into fractions (correctly) as an approach to generalisation of the rule of converting decimals into fractions. He thought by himself of a table containing a series of decimal numbers. He converted them into common fractions. From the pattern of answers he confirmed that the decimal point was always 'one' and the numbers after the decimal point decided the number of zeros, with the one in the denominator place. With this understanding, he had planned the lesson very thoroughly. His method produced correct answers but the explanation behind those answers made no sense mathematically. This was a case of his reconciling to a new method of teaching with his limited knowledge of the concept. Although his aim was to enable students to seek a pattern from the series of decimal numbers in order to build up the meaning of decimals and the decimal point, he could not succeed because of his own limited knowledge.

He asked me how much he could depend on his own thinking to act according to his beliefs, when his own thinking alone is not enough for his conceptual understanding.

> It is true that I worked very hard, spent hours thinking and planning the lesson but I did not know what my weakness was. I did not want to teach them the wrong concept; I wanted to teach them decimals with reasoning. If I do not know mathematics myself, how can I continue teaching [in a new mode]? For thinking I need [to know] enough mathematics.

An issue seemed to be that, as long as he sticks to the textbook examples, he is offering what has been judged by someone else as correct. With new methods, his own limited understanding is exposed, and he has no way of judging what is appropriate. However, my view is that working together encouraged the teacher to take risks like trying out new ideas but provided safeguards against developing misconceptions.

I raise the issue of my intervention in terms of disclosing Naeem's limited mathematical understanding. The questions remain: Who should take the responsibility to identify a teacher's misconceptions and prevent the students from taking those away with them? If it is a teacher educator's responsibility, then to what extent? If it is the teacher's responsibility, then how far does the teacher educator need to wait for the teacher's self-realization within constraints and ignorance? In my opinion a teacher does not become self sufficient after becoming aware of his or her problems. Awareness of the problems without any resolution may cause pressure on a teacher besides other tensions of the school in Pakistan. A teacher needs some kind of support to improve his or her mathematical understanding in order to gain confidence for further improvement. A commitment to collaboration provides opportunities for partners to share perspectives, exchange roles, identify issues and take responsive actions leading to learning from and with each other.

## Change in Teachers' Behaviour

This example is taken from Neha's planning of her second lesson with me. Neha wanted to teach 'Pythagoras theorem' differently. I asked her to share some of her thoughts about how she would teach the lesson. She said she did not know anything beyond the textbook method. I asked her if we could discuss the theorem first, in order to explore different methods of teaching. She told me that because she had good knowledge of mathematics, she only wanted to know new methods. I encouraged her to discuss the meaning first, because without knowing what the theorem was and how it emerged, it was difficult to explore new methods. She told me that she had never discussed the topic in that manner, and that she could not afford the time. Perhaps due to time limitations, she was in a hurry to focus on new methods of teaching. It might be that she had a problem in dealing with content and methods separately, which would prevent her from planning a rich mathematical activity. I tried to motivate her to explore some ideas of her own, she said:

> I have told you before that I do not have new ideas and activities; neither do I have time to search for books and plan my lessons. I do not have time to think for myself—how can I think of new activities? I think while you are here you could give me new ideas and help in planning. Then I could continue this way. Time is very short for me. I did all my correction at home last night; I knew you were coming today.

Perhaps Neha wanted to save time from the long thinking process and to take advantage of my presence to get as many new ideas as possible. Perhaps there was a tension between her expectations and my expectations. I understood her problems, but I wanted to reduce her possible perception of me as being an expert. My purpose was to engage her in a process of exploring new ways with me instead of my providing ready-made ideas. I suggested to her that new ideas could be developed from different resources, e.g. discussion together, reading books etc. I encouraged her to discuss what the textbook suggested.

We looked at the textbook where there was a written and a symbolic explanation of the theorem. Neha said that she knew the theorem already. I encouraged her to visualize the statement and present her images on paper. There were two purposes behind my strategy; I wanted to engage Neha fully in the discussion, and discourage her from seeking pre-formed ideas, and I believed that her images would lead the discussion further.

Below, I present the part of our conversation that indicates Neha's involvement in the practical proof of the theorem. Here I should mention that our conversation and her written work were happening simultaneously.

1 T  It says 'square of hypotenuse is equal...' It means we need to draw a triangle first. What do you think?
2 R  Ok what else?
3 T  This is a right angled triangle. Hypotenuse, this is perpendicular and base (she labelled the figure). One square on each side.
4 R  Yes
5 T  This is the picture.
*Neha was talking to me and drawing simultaneously.*
6 R  What does this picture tell you?
7 T  I think this is a rough diagram; if I do it properly, then I could say.
8 R  Could we do this again with specific measurements?
*Neha then drew a right-angled triangle with measurements. I asked her to measure the sides and find the square of these sides and seek a relationship*
9 T  We can show the theorem in a pictorial way.
10 R  This could be one way to teach the theorem.
11 T  This will be confusing for students to do so much work, measuring sides, drawing squares and calculating area of each square.
12 R  We could present the idea through different resources.
13 T  Give me an example.
14 R  You could use graph paper or squared paper.
15 T  Yes we have squared paper in the school.

Neha took the responsibility of furthering our discussion and planning a complete lesson. In the feedback session she talked about her further work in lesson planning of the topic.

I drew one triangle and made photocopies so I could provide one triangle to each group. It was difficult to think for different measurements of right angled-triangles and draw them. This planning took such a long time; I spent my two periods [non-teaching] in arranging materials, and sorting out things.

The example discussed shows that there were issues of Neha's busy schedule and the inertia of routine, which had limited her willingness to participate actively. However, our commitment to the partnership enabled us to support each other. I motivated her to take a step ahead from her own perception. She agreed to discuss concepts and methods, and I provided her with the foundation for discussion. I did not reject her opinion; neither had she refused my offer. We listened to each other, valued opinions, and engaged in professional dialogue. The teacher's morale was increased. She recognized the value of self-involvement, increased her intellectual capacity and was motivated to learn and apply new ways of teaching. Nevertheless, it was slow in coming. As her level of knowledge increased, she began to participate, and hence to learn.

**Discussion**

From my wider set of analysis of examples, the teachers' growth was evident. Each of the teachers learned according to his or her own understanding of change, circumstances at the school, previous experiences and emerging needs with the encouragement and support of the teacher educator. The common aspect of their growth was their efforts in making the transition from routine practice to reflective practice with understanding. The guiding principles of the teachers' improvement were not turning their deficiencies into perfection or their blind acceptance of imposed ideas. On the contrary, it was a process of the teachers' questioning routine practice, analysing new ways of teaching and deciding appropriate actions in relation to change within their classroom realities and school circumstances. The teachers' new goal of teaching required them to make efforts and to use their intellectual capabilities in planning, teaching and evaluating the lessons. The shift in the teachers' goal of teaching was not an easy task for them, but they were not alone in coping with the problems and issues of their teaching. As Cooney and Shealy (1996) suggested, the notion of teachers' reform is not the product of inertia, nor blind acceptance of change, but an integration of the existing realities and new ways of teaching as shown in the above examples, unfolding the reform through practical examples.

Under the limitations and imposed authority of the schools, the transition from routine practice was not an easy task for the teachers. The improvement itself was a complex process. Teachers were not in a position to facilitate the process of their learning on their own; neither did they receive positive reinforcement from the schools. The learning partnership provided the teachers with practical support to aid an increase in confidence, extend their routine teaching, respond to the teacher educator's input, and to prevent them from negative evaluation and developing students' misconceptions in their way of taking risks.

It is also evident that the teachers' presence at the schools did not allow them to escape their job expectations while the teacher educator's presence motivated them to be reminded of AKU-IED's theoretical perspectives. The commitment to be a learner encouraged the teacher educator to make efforts to reduce unseen imposition on her part through reflecting (in and on) the teachers' needs in the school setting. The responsibility of the teachers to be learners at their schools increased their confidence in choosing their agenda, setting limits and acting accordingly. As a result of the mutual norms, values and decision, the teachers were able to question their limited experience of teaching at the school, explore practical avenues of developing teaching and identify issues of practice leading to a reduction of any threat to self-esteem.

The moral and practical support built up the teachers' intellectual capabilities and alleviated their frustrations in developing their teaching. Our partnership acted as a bridge between the teachers' learning at AKU-IED and their practice at the school. My study reveals that the teachers did not have any positive input from their schools nor had they understood AKU-IED philosophy in a realistic sense in the limited time of the course. Thinking about change without being able to actually act had created moral tensions for them. It is also evident from the above discussion that leaving teachers alone in school with expectations of change is problematic in teacher development (as cautioned by Pimm, 1993 and Breen, 1999). I found that developing teaching is not independent of the context and that learning is a two-way experience.

The findings of my study suggest that learning opportunities at the university alone may not be sufficient to enable teachers to take responsibility for developing teaching further, but rather limit their thinking and effort to picking up some ideas and dealing with them as an external requirement from teacher education courses. At a university, we (the teacher educators) might want to develop teachers according to our own agenda and perspectives, but this might cause the teachers to ignore the potential of their teaching and contextual considerations. Whereas at a school, the roles of teachers and teacher educators may be those of mutual support, mutual responsibility, mutual understanding, setting of mutual agenda and mutual courage for taking risks.

The study of Sally and Monk (2000) raises issues about improvement of teaching without considering reform in the structure of the school; causing subsequent pressure on teachers' difficult lives in developing countries. Fullan and Hargreaves (1992) suggested focusing on teachers' working environment and on teaching itself for teacher development. My study also highlights important considerations in teachers developing their teaching practice to reform students' learning in a restrictive, authoritarian structure in the schools in Pakistan. In my view, teacher educators need to think about the linkage between our notion of teacher development as 'teachers develop their profession' (as suggested by Day, 1999) at the school and 'teacher is developed' at the university (discussed in Jackson, 1971) in the context of experienced teachers' professionalism. My research suggests that continuing professional growth of the teachers at their schools is vital for:

- Maintaining and developing teachers own commitment and expertise
- Investigating the complexities of context and change itself with appropriate support
- Identifying ways in which teachers learn or not learn
- Preventing the damaging effect on students' understanding in the way of teachers' taking risks.

## Conclusion

Through working together with teachers I, as a teacher educator, saw the possibility of change and professional satisfaction for both the teacher and the teacher educator, if the teachers are supported according to their needs. In addition, the teachers' learning and confidence shows how one can achieve development in a Pakistani school within the school limitations. However, there are problems of the teachers' limited understanding of mathematics as well as what is needed in the development process. The existing school environment is not favourable for teachers to take initiatives and neither do the teachers themselves cope well with problems of mathematical knowledge and mathematics teaching. A comment from one of the teachers indicates this:

> If I move back to my previous style [of teaching] then there will have been some reasons and pressure; it will not only be my fault; we need to work as a group if we want improvement.

This statement raises many questions from a teacher to a teacher educator; from a school to a university or from practice of routine to a theory of change; it is the job of a teacher educator to look critically at ways of teacher change. Furthermore, it raises questions about the direction a university should take in order to ensure teacher development in the Pakistani school context. I conclude that teachers need a support system with the collaboration of school and university after their education from an in-service course. Without provision of practical and moral support in their schools, the teachers cannot sustain their growth. The result would be similar to that of seeds growing on stony ground. However, an issue of time and funding arises: Can such a level of provision be viable for an institution such as AKU-IED?

## NOTES

1. The teacher was implying that she was sacrificing her 'correction time' for co-planning.
2. In a right-angled triangle, the area of the square on the hypotenuse is equal to the sum of the areas of the squares on the other two sides: $c2=a2 +b2$.

## References

Breen, C. (1999). 'Circling the Square: Issues and Dilemmas Concerning Teacher Transformation'. In B. Jaworski, T. Wood & S. Dawson (Eds.). *Mathematics Teacher Education: Critical International Perspectives*. London: Falmer.

Carr, W. & Kemmis, S. (1986). *Becoming Critical: Education, Knowledge and Action research*. London: Falmer.
Cooney, T. J. & Shealy, B. (1996). 'On understanding of the Structure of Teachers' Beliefs and their Relationship to change'. In E. Fennema & B. Nelson (Eds.). *Mathematics Teacher in Transition*. New Jersey: Lawrence Erlbaum and Associates.
Day, C. (1999). *Developing Teachers: The Challenges of Lifelong Learning*. Norwich: Falmer.
Fullan, M. (1999). *Change Forces: The sequel*. London: Falmer.
Fullan, M. & Hargreaves, A. (1992). *Understanding teacher development*. NY: Cassell.
Jackson, W. P. (1971). 'Old Dogs and New Tricks: Observations on the Continuing Education of Teachers'. In L. J. Rubin (Ed.). *Improving In-service Education: Proposal and Procedures for Change*. Boston: Allyn and Bacon.
Jaworski, B. (2000). 'The Student-Teacher-Educator-Researcher in the Mathematics Classroom: Co-learning Partnership in Mathematics Teaching and Teacher Development'. In C. Bergsten, G. Dahland & B. Grevholm (Eds.). *Research and Action in the Mathematics Classroom*. Proceedings of MADIF 2, The Second Swedish Mathematics Education Research Seminar. Linkoping, Sweden: Linkopings Universitet.
Kemmis, S. & Wilkinson, M. (1998). 'Participatory Action Research and the Study of Practice'. In B. Atweh, S. Kemmis & P. Weeks (Eds.). *Action Research in Practice*. London: Routledge.
McNiff, J. (1991). *Teaching as Learning: An Action Research Approach*. London: Routledge.
Pimm, D. (1993). 'From Should to Could: Reflections on Possibilities of Mathematics Teacher Education'. *For the Learning of Mathematics*, 13(2), 22–27.
Povey, H. & Burton, L. (1999). 'Learners as Authors in the Mathematics Classroom'. In L. Burton (Ed.). *Learning Mathematics: From Hierarchies to Networks*. London: Falmer.
Rogoff, B. (2001). *Learning Together: Children and Adults in a School Community*. Oxford: Oxford University Press.
Sally, J. & Monk, M. (2000). *Teacher Development in South Africa: A Critique of the Appropriateness of Transfer of Northern/Western Practice*. Compare, 3 (2).
Wagner, J. (1997). 'The Unavoidable Intervention of Educational Research: A Framework for Reconsidering Researcher-Practitioner Co-operation'. *Educational Researcher*, 26(7), 13–22.

# 6

# COOPERATIVE LEARNING IN CLASSROOMS

*Bernadette Dean*

In most Pakistani schools, learning is characterized by intense and unhealthy competitiveness amongst students. Indeed, classroom learning has become synonymous with competition for grades, teacher recognition and praise. In the typical classroom, each student works alone and in competition with other students. He or she is told, 'Keep your eyes on your own work'; 'don't share'; 'don't talk'; 'don't help'. Students see each other as opponents rather than supportive colleagues. Such an environment is not conducive to learning for students. Students who are not the academic front-runners come to see themselves as losers and drop out of school early. Others seek alternative avenues to bolster their self-esteem or to be noticed e.g., through sports or artistic activities and clowning or getting into trouble. Students who get good grades worry about whether they can continue to outshine everyone else. They fear failure because it may bring a loss of expected love or approval. The average student also suffers because the competitive setting does not allow an opportunity to stand out.

Much of this competitive attitude towards learning originates from the pressure put on students by parents and society, to achieve the highest grades. It is also encouraged and reinforced by the teaching methods emphasized. Most teachers use the method of 'direct instruction', by which the teacher transmits knowledge that the students passively receive, memorize and regurgitate for tests and examinations. If students participate, it is mainly to respond to the questions asked by the teacher. These questions generally check recall or, at best, comprehension. Teachers make interpersonal comparisons and evaluations using as a model, the student who does best academically. In fact, this is the norm by which students are evaluated.

Sometimes, teachers who are aware of the negative effects of competition and want to actively involve students in their learning get them to work in small groups. But such attempts are usually unsuccessful for a number of reasons. The most important reason is that teachers are not trained to manage group work effectively. The groups simply comprise individuals who sit side-by-side at the same table and do their individual assignments. When given group tasks, each group member is accountable for himself or herself and not to the other members. Often high achievers take over the leadership of the group and make decisions that benefit themselves at the expense of the low achievers. Sometimes group members seek a 'free ride', by leaving one member to complete the group's task. Groups fail because of conflicts and power struggles among members, and teachers, unable to handle these issues, revert back to individualist and competitive classrooms.

## Cooperative Learning

Classrooms are generally seen as places where learning occurs though, as suggested above, much of the learning occurs individually and in competition with others. In contrast, the work of Johnson and Johnson (1989; 1991) on cooperative learning suggests a way of developing student learning communities through using cooperative learning and creating a cooperative learning environment.

Johnson, Johnson and Holubec (1993) define cooperative learning as the instructional use of small groups in which students work together to maximize their own and each other's learning. They suggest that in order for students to learn together, five basic elements are necessary; positive interdependence, individual accountability, face-to-face promotive interaction, social skills and group-processing.

- **Positive Interdependence** is promoted when students work together to achieve their goal, realizing that individuals cannot succeed, only the group can succeed. Johnson and Johnson suggest that goal interdependence supplemented with reward interdependence (Mesch, Lew, Johnson and Johnson, 1986), and/or resource interdependence (Johnson, Johnson, Stanne and Garibaldi, 1989) produces higher achievement and productivity.

- **Individual accountability** is realized when every group member contributes to the accomplishment of group goals, and ensures all members of the group are successful in their learning and can individually demonstrate what was learnt in the cooperative group.
- **Face-to-face promotive interaction** is promoting each other's success by becoming involved in important cognitive activities (explaining how to solve problems, discussing concepts being learned) and interpersonal activities (encouraging, praising each other's effort). Face-to-face promotive interaction fostered by positive interdependence influences efforts to achieve, caring and committed relationships, psychological adjustment and social competence (Johnson and Johnson, 1989).
- Placing socially unskilled students in a group and telling them to cooperate does not guarantee that they will effectively do so. Students must be taught the **social skills** (encouraging others, listening, giving help, checking for understanding) that enable groups to function effectively. In order to coordinate efforts to achieve mutual goals, students must get to know and trust each other, communicate accurately, accept and support each other, and resolve conflicts constructively (Johnson and Johnson, 1991; Johnson, Johnson and Holubec, 1993).
- Students do not learn from experiences on which they do not reflect. **Group processing** gives students the opportunity to reflect on their collaborative efforts, and target improvements. Yager, Johnson and Johnson (1985) have pointed out that students in cooperation-with-group-processing achieved higher on daily and post-instruction achievement and retention. Similar findings have been arrived at by Johnson, Johnson, Stanne and Garibaldi (1990).

The study I undertook was an attempt to investigate the possibilities and challenges of developing a teacher learning community to learn about and use cooperative learning methods in schools in Pakistan. It also seeks to identify the elements that help develop a student learning community and the benefits that accrue to students from learning together.

## Developing a Teacher Learning Community to Learn Cooperative Learning

Much has been written about various cooperative learning methods and their effects on students' learning so that schools can use this instructional strategy with confidence. However, little attention is given teachers learning to use this strategy in their classrooms. The danger, as Slavin puts it, is that the method will be oversold and teachers undertrained (Slavin, 1990).

The training of teachers often consists of one-shot workshops (Fullan, 1991) held outside school. These workshops generate much excitement and interest in the innovation but some teachers, when trained, often find it difficult to use their learnings in classrooms. A more useful way of educating teachers may be through developing a learning community:

> A learning community is defined as a group of people who take an active, reflective, collaborative, learning-oriented and growth promoting approach toward the mysteries, problems and perplexities of teaching and learning. The learning that is of critical importance is that of the students, the teachers and the school administrators (Mitchell & Sackney, 2000:9)

Mitchell and Sackney, (2000) suggest that learning communities are best developed by building personal capacity, interpersonal capacity and organizational capacity. The literature on teacher development and change suggests the following factors should be considered in developing the three levels of capacity for use of a new instructional strategy.

## Developing Personal Capacity: Training and Coaching

Showers et al. (1987), and Sacca (1990) refer to several studies which show that training procedures that follow a theory-demonstration-practice-feedback sequence, have typically enabled teachers to attain high levels of skill proficiency. However, even when the training model provides multiple practice opportunities in a training setting, it is highly unlikely that transfer of the instructed skills will occur. Joyce and Showers (1982) suggest that in addition to participating in training, teachers must also have the opportunity to use the innovation in real-life settings and be supported for doing so. They believe that when the coaching component is added and implemented effectively, the new innovation becomes a part of the teacher's active repertoire.

The process of coaching involves the provision of companionship, analysis of application to confront assumptions, beliefs and practices that individuals hold dear, giving of critico-creative feedback, re-creation to suit students and contextual realities and personal facilitation. Showers et al. (1987), estimated that at least 25 teaching episodes involving the new strategy with coaching are necessary to develop personal capacity to use the new instructional strategy and sustain efforts during the early stages of use.

Teachers have, however, been found to express discomfort and concerns with coaching. They are concerned about the lack of time for observations and discussions about teaching due to difficulties with release time, substitute arrangements, and scheduling for coaching. An allied concern of teachers is the issue of evaluation and judgment when the coaching programme is implemented (Watson and Kilcher, 1990).

## Developing Interpersonal Capacity: Building a Collaborative Learning Community

School cultures are generally characterized by isolation. Lortie (1975) describes the school as a cellular organization where teachers work physically apart from their colleagues and struggle with their problems and anxieties, privately. Rosenholtz (1989) corroborates Lortie's observations. She described 'learning impoverished' schools as having a culture of isolation that hinders teacher interaction, and therefore, learning from each other and 'learning enriched schools' as having a collegial culture which facilitates teachers learning with and from each other.

Mitchell and Sackney (2000) suggest that building a collaborative learning community requires attention to the affective and cognitive conditions that support or limit teacher learning. Inviting teachers to participate in a community of learning and affirming their participation are the affective conditions which help to build trusting relationships and facilitate self and collective reflection and professional conversations. As teachers work in collaborative learning teams the individuals within them are empowered to take the risk required to improve their teaching and learning.

Johnson and Johnson (1994) believe that the heart of an effective teacher development programme in cooperative learning is creating collaborating learning teams and giving them the responsibility to ensure that each member learns how to use cooperative learning effectively. They suggest that collaborative learning teams should be small cooperative groups of teachers who help each other to plan lessons, to adapt cooperative learning to their own setting, and solve any problems that may arise during use. These activities must be carried out in a safe and caring environment, the goal of which is to improve each other's competence in using cooperative learning. Edwards and Stout (1990) have noted that collaborative learning teams proved to be a key factor in the continued success of their cooperative learning project.

## Building Organizational Capacity

In a learning community, along with teachers, administrators must also learn. Effective administrators set expectations for continuous improvement by continuing to learn themselves. They participate in in-service training with their teachers, model desired behaviour and give priority to teachers' instructional concerns (Smith and Andrews, 1989). They also provide administrative support in the form of release time for training, observation and feedback, formal recognition for using cooperative learning methods and additional training opportunities for successful implementation.

Ellis (1990) describes how principals and central office administrators learned the necessary attributes of cooperative learning in order to observe teachers and provide informative feedback. She further reports that teachers acquired and used cooperative learning strategies on a regular basis when their principals had attended training sessions and actively promoted their use.

## Research Method

The teacher learning community comprised of four teachers; two from the primary section and two from the secondary section. Learning together involved three stages of activities, i.e. pre-intervention,

intervention and a post-intervention stage. The student learning community comprised 4 classes of students.

**Pre-intervention activities**

To facilitate the study, a meeting with the entire teaching community was held to introduce the idea of cooperative learning. Four teachers were selected to form the learning community, others were encouraged to join in training sessions and observe classroom teaching. To learn how teachers taught, how they involved their students in the class and what areas they sought to improve, a short interview was held. The teachers suggested beginning with demonstrations using topics from their syllabus. The administration facilitated the demonstrations by adjusting the school timetable so that all four teachers were free to observe the demonstration lessons and reflect on them.

**Interventions**

Interventions focused on developing a teacher learning community and a student learning community. The learning community was introduced to cooperative learning through demonstrations conducted in the teachers own classrooms. Each demonstration was preceded by a conference to share the plan of the lesson. The teachers observed the demonstration which was followed by a joint reflection to facilitate understanding, raise questions and concerns and make suggestions to improve the lessons observed. Following the demonstration, teachers were introduced to the theory of cooperative learning. Teachers then co-planned and co-taught lessons with me, which were followed by self and team reflective sessions. By the fourth week, lessons were co-planned but teachers were encouraged to teach these themselves. Each lesson was preceded by a post-lesson conference, during which the teachers reflected on their strengths and challenges and received critical and constructive feedback aimed at the improvement of their practice.

To facilitate peer coaching, teachers reflected on the skills required which were then developed. By the sixth week, most lessons were planned and taught by the teachers themselves with their colleagues acting as peer coaches and myself as an observer. Saturdays were set aside to: 1) learn the theory of cooperative learning; 2) address the concerns of the learning community; 3) share the week's successes and find solutions to problems; and 4) plan lessons for the coming week.

Developing a learning community among students in each classroom began with reflections on their daily life experiences to recognize the importance of working cooperatively. Formation of cooperative groups was followed by providing time for students to get to know each other, decide on a group name and design group logos. The five basic elements were structured and students were given challenging tasks which required teamwork to accomplish them. Self and group processing encouraged reflection on performance and identification of ways to improve.

## Post-intervention

After the interventions, interviews were conducted with all the four participating teachers to find out whether teachers thought adding cooperative learning to their instructional repertoire was valuable, the factors which helped or hindered the use of this strategy, the perceived effects of cooperative learning on the students, and the future of cooperative learning and the team.

Nineteen students, selected by picking every tenth student on the attendance register from all participating classes, were also interviewed. The focus of the interview was to discuss their feelings about working together, the effect on their understanding of the subject, on their interactions inside and outside the classroom, and on their behaviour.

## Problems and Possibilities in Teacher Learning and Using Cooperative Learning

The implementation of any educational innovation produces concerns amongst teachers. This study revealed that the implementation of cooperative learning was no exception. At the beginning of the research, the teachers highlighted several concerns that might inhibit the successful implementation of cooperative learning. However, most problems were turned into possibilities by the teachers during the joint problem solving sessions. The concerns could be subsumed under three categories:

1. Structures—time required for implementation of cooperative learning, administrative interest and support, collaboration with other teachers.
2. Practices/behaviours/skills—the use of cooperative learning to teach all topics, student participation, student assessment and evaluation, noise.
3. Beliefs/philosophies—the role of the teacher, holistic development, cooperation in the classroom.

## 1. Teachers' Concerns vis-à-vis Structures

When teachers begin using cooperative learning, they realize the need for structural changes within the school that will facilitate the implementation of this strategy.

### Time for Implementation

During the research, the concern most frequently expressed by the teachers was time management. When teachers began to use cooperative learning in the classroom, they expressed concerns about the amount of time taken to form groups, teach the social skills, do academic work and process academic and social learnings. They had two concerns: was it possible in a period, and worried that 'Too much time is spent with non-academic work. How will I complete my syllabus.' To address the first concern, I explained that the students were unfamiliar with working cooperatively. They needed to learn, for example, the social skills. But once taught it could be revised in a few minutes. I demonstrated how the social skill could be revised in a shorter time period. The teachers found it impossible to do all that in 30–35 minutes, but when they combined two periods, it worked well with good outcomes. About the second problem, I realized that in most Pakistani schools, completing the prescribed syllabus is of prime importance since exams are based on the syllabus. Most teachers rush to complete the syllabus, at the expense of students' understanding.

When I raised the question of syllabus completion at the expense of conceptual understanding, one of the teachers said:

> We need to complete the grade 4 syllabus because the syllabus in grade 5 is built on what the teacher taught in grade 4. If the students do not cover the topics in grade 4 they cannot cope in grade 5.

I acknowledged the point she was making but questioned the need for completion of the syllabus in the Social Studies and language class. Our discussion centered around the kind of achievements we want for our students and whether students could achieve them by reading, writing and copying from the blackboard. The teachers agreed that their current practice did not facilitate development of the knowledge and skills discussed, but they were at a loss for ways to change their current practice.

One teacher then said:

> The method (cooperative learning) is so important that we should use it even at the cost of chopping a lesson or two. We must pay something to get something.

Another teacher suggested:

> We may have to take away (from the syllabus) at first, but then when we see how it works we may be able to add more.

I recognized that the teachers were beginning to see the possibility that cooperative learning helped them achieve what they wanted for their students. Good scores on exams were required but also learning to work together, to think critically, solve problems, and make decisions so as not only to improve themselves, but also to change society.

## Administrative Interest and Support

Teachers acknowledged the support they received from the administration in the form of timetable adjustments and the provision of materials, but they would have liked to see the administration more actively supporting their use of cooperative learning in several ways. Teachers found they had insufficient time to learn and practice cooperative learning. They would have appreciated their teaching load being reduced. Laila remarked:

I did not have enough time. Sometimes I needed time to do my own work (prepare mark sheet, corrections). I did not get one free moment. I had to plan lessons, teach and reflect. If I have to do this every day for every class, it will be too much.

Laila seemed to be making a comment that is crucial to successful implementation of innovations—the need for administrative support in the form of reduced workload so as to give teachers time to co-plan, observe lessons and provide feedback.

Teachers were also concerned because they did not get clear directions from the administration regarding the use of cooperative learning. They were not told whether cooperative learning was going to be restricted to the research or whether teachers would be encouraged to use it after the study as well. Teachers felt that this clarification from the heads would have been helpful.

## Collaboration with Other Teachers

From day one of the study, the teachers wanted 'each and every teacher to learn to use cooperative learning' and encouraged other colleagues to join the Saturday sessions. Teachers may have been afraid to adopt a change because cooperative learning was very different from their usual way of teaching, and a radical change required other teachers' support and willingness to practice it. If this statement had been made at the end of the study it would have indicated that teachers thought the new practice was valuable but since this statement was made at the beginning of the study, I could not help feeling that the norm in the school required all teachers to use the same strategies. This was confirmed when teachers told me that when they went for a workshop, they were expected to share what they learnt with other teachers, teachers also met together in subject groups to plan for teaching.

I encouraged and promoted these concerns because collaboration fosters implementation of new strategies, professional growth and school improvement. I encouraged collaboration among the participating teachers so that, for the first time, teachers were observing each others' lessons. It was also the first time teachers from the primary section went into a secondary class to observe a lesson, the secondary teachers, however, did not reciprocate.

Collaboration concerns peaked as teachers realized the benefits of cooperative learning for students and their positive response. They even wanted to introduce other teachers to this instructional strategy. Towards the end of the study, they invited other teachers into their classrooms. One of the teachers invited the head and the school's educational advisor to observe her class, hoping to convince them of the importance of the strategy. She shared her plan to continue cooperative learning in her own classroom and to teach one or two teachers the strategy. The other teachers also mentioned their desire to work with their colleagues stating, 'provided we get support from the head as well as time to work with the teacher'.

During the post intervention interview all the teachers felt that learning together had built up collaborative relationships among them and using a similar process would facilitate collaboration with other teachers. Teachers felt that a collaborative relationship would develop because, 'Teachers will share with other teachers', 'We can go to each other for help, we can share ideas with each other and discuss problems with each other'; 'When talking together about work, teachers will become close and can solve personal as well as work problems'.

Teachers seemed to like working together and wanted to see the relationships developed and extended to their colleagues. Given that the study was conducted for only seven weeks, there were indications that coaching facilitated and developed new norms for collaboration among the teachers who participated in the study.

## 2. Teachers' Concerns vis-à-vis New Practices/Skills

According to Fullan (1992), one of the most important findings of research is that structures are the tip of the implementation iceberg. Structures can be changed by policy, but changes in practice and beliefs are more difficult as they cannot be mandated.

### Cooperative Learning to Teach All Topics

A concern which emerged in the study was the feasibility of cooperative learning in the teaching of all topics. After demonstrating the use of cooperative learning in a reading comprehension and composition writing lesson, teachers asked:

'Can I use cooperative learning to teach poems?'

'What other topics can I use cooperative learning to teach?'

'Can I use cooperative learning to teach Islamiat?'

Anderson, Bennett, and Rolheiser (1995) point out that when taking cooperative learning into the classroom for the first time, one of the things teachers find most difficult is to take the concepts and processes of cooperative learning and apply them to curriculum content. This is because initial training in cooperative learning often emphasizes the general principles, concepts and skills associated with it, neglecting its practical implementation by teachers. I feel that this is a serious omission because while some teachers are able to translate theoretically learned concepts and skills into successful classroom lessons, others require practical demonstrations of the strategy and still others support it in practice in their own classrooms. Where demonstration and/or practice are absent, teachers may become frustrated and may come to think that the strategy is impractical and not use it.

## Student Participation

During the initial use of cooperative learning, a concern expressed by teachers was: 'What can I do if a student is not participating in the group'. Teachers were also concerned about students who did 'more than their share of the task'. Related concerns expressed by the teachers were that 'bright students do all the work, give all the answers, while average and below average students are left out'. Others felt that 'the brilliant students don't want to share their ideas, and want to get a high position.' One teacher felt, 'Weak students are too dependent on other group members'. They were concerned that students might not participate willingly and equally.

Once again the suggestions provided possibilities. The teachers suggested that the best way to deal with this problem was to ensure that positive interdependence and individual accountability was built into the lesson. Teachers suggested using the structure of Think-Write-Pair-Share as the writing would ensure individual accountability. They also suggested that each member of the group be given a role or a particular responsibility and every member of the group ensures that the other fulfills his/her role. A teacher felt that using and promoting cooperation required a change in assessment and reporting practices. She said

> Brilliant students would only participate, if we change our way of assessing. If two of us are competing for the first place, why will I share my knowledge; if I do I will not get that position. Therefore, we need a new way of assessing, new report cards and no ranks.

Once again, I noted the effort teachers were making to use cooperative learning successfully, as they managed to turn their concern of student participation into a possibility. I was glad that from depending on me for the 'right' answers, the teachers were finding solutions to their problems.

## Student Assessment and Evaluation

Teachers expressed their concern about assessment and evaluation by asking: 'How can I assess all the students?'; 'How can we keep a record of our observations?'; 'If I have to monitor and assess students for six to seven periods a day, it will be very tiring'.

To address teachers' concerns about assessment, during lesson demonstration, I began using a variety of ways to assess students such as check lists, anecdotal records and collecting students' work. I encouraged the teachers to use different approaches when they were teaching. When sharing methods of assessment, teachers felt that a hindering factor would be their inability to get multiple copies of observation sheets. Later, when the teachers were peer coaching each other, one of them observed another teacher drawing the observation sheet on the blackboard and asking the observer in the group to copy it and use it for their observations. During our joint problem solving session, she mentioned that Naila had found a good alternative to photocopying. I was glad to see that teachers kept the problems mentioned in mind and were searching for solutions. That teachers were finding solutions during the observation of each other's practice showed how much teachers can learn from observing each other.

This led a teacher to suggest that besides the teacher, 'students should also be involved in the assessment process'. I asked her how this was to be done and she replied: 'By having students assess their own and each other's performance'. In response to this suggestion another teacher expressed a concern about students being involved in the assessment process. She said, 'I wonder how good such an assessment will be'. As I listened I was pleasantly surprised by the quality of the exchange. It was critical and seemed reasonable.

**Noise**

Before implementing cooperative learning, teachers said that they did not like to use groups because of too much noise. After the first demonstration lesson teachers began to express concerns about noise. They said,

> Students made a lot of noise when forming their groups.
> There was a lot of noise when the groups were working.
> I don't know if I can manage so many groups and keep the noise level down.

Teachers were apprehensive about the noise generated when students were working together because noise is considered to be a sign that a teacher has classroom management problems and often results in the principal coming to the class to see what is happening (as happened one day during the study). For this reason, no teacher wants 'noise' in his/her class.

Within a few days of using cooperative learning, the students in two grades were working very quietly and all one could hear was the hum of students busy at work. In two classes, work was progressing slowly because of the noise. Teaching and practice of 'using quiet voices' brought a change in one class. However, in the other class the problems with noise continued. We realized it was due to the nature of the task, asking students to answer simple, comprehension questions or filling in missing items. For effective group work with minimum noise, therefore, one needs to practice, observe, and process the social skill of using quiet voices as well as ensure the task is intellectually challenging for the students.

**3. Teachers' Concerns vis-à-vis Their Beliefs**

Cooperative learning requires that teachers learn new skills and behaviours and use them in their practice. However, conflicts were observed during practice which indicated that while teachers learnt and practiced new skills and behaviours, they still held on to their old beliefs and philosophies. This implies that for successful implementation of cooperative learning, a change in teachers' beliefs is crucial.

## The Role of the Teacher

In the traditional model of teaching, the teacher stands in front of the class and lectures the students who are expected to passively absorb the information and regurgitate it on command. In cooperative learning the teacher is a guide. His/her role is to facilitate students learning with and from each other. Students are seen as critical consumers as well as producers of information and ideas which they share with each other when working in their relative groups.

All the teachers in the study expressed concern about the role of the teacher. One teacher said, 'The role of the teacher was secondary. All the time she just kept a vigil'. Another teacher asked, 'Can the students do all the work themselves?' Yet another noted:

> When I write the answers on the blackboard, the whole class writes the same answers at the same time. If they write their own answers they will make mistakes and I will have to check each copy carefully. When they copy what I've written, it is correct, so checking is much easier.

These concerns were felt for a number of reasons. Firstly, some teachers found it difficult to identify their contributions to the education of the student. Many teachers join the profession with the belief that they have something to offer their students, that they can make a difference in the lives of their students. These teachers too mentioned one of their reasons for joining the teaching profession as 'sharing my knowledge'. However, teachers need to see that this sharing, and contribution doesn't have to be made solely through pouring in knowledge but can be made more effectively by facilitating student learning.

Secondly, the subject that a teacher taught also affected the role played by the teacher. In grade V, where we were working in Urdu, which is the mother tongue of most of the students, the teacher found it easier to play the role of guide. In other grades, where the subject being taught was English, teachers felt that they had to transmit knowledge, and therefore, play the role of 'sage on the stage'.

Thirdly, learning is interpreted as knowing facts—not making meaning. Students are not allowed to think for themselves, create and share knowledge. Teachers have little or no available time. They go from class to class, teaching 120 or more students a day, with little time for planning lessons, correcting students' work or reflecting on their practice.

Finally, some teachers did not believe that students were capable of taking control of their own learning.

**Holistic Development**

Most teachers believe that their work is limited to providing instruction in academic subjects and ensuring that students do well in exams. These attitudes caused resistance to cooperative learning, especially because of the 'Learning Together' model implemented in this study. This model emphasizes that social skills can be directly taught in classrooms because these skills are important and valuable in their own right and are a prerequisite for realizing academic gains (Johnson and Johnson, 1991). Helping students develop these skills and attitudes takes time and often conflicts with other teaching responsibilities such as covering content. Teachers just put students into groups to work on a task, then complained that students were not working together and were making a lot of noise. I explained that all the five elements of cooperative learning are important if students are to learn to work together and gain academically.

I found that a teacher who had 'a good achievement record' was more resistant to change. During the study, she brought up the concern of time spent on non-academic work on a number of occasions. She acknowledged students were 'helping each other', 'understanding has been promoted' and 'from the essay and letter writing you can see they are thinking.' However, she was not willing to change her beliefs until 'I will see their examination result.'

Setting a cooperative environment and allowing students to work cooperatively requires a change in teachers' beliefs about how children learn, their role in the classrooms and the goals of education. Teachers must come to believe in the rationale and ideas that underlie cooperative learning if they are to successfully implement it. The benefits to students helped teachers to see its value and potential for successful living in a dynamic and constantly changing society, and for creating a more just and interdependent society.

## Possibilities

So far in the analysis, I have explained the problems converted into possibilities by the teachers during the joint problem solving sessions. However, teachers also mentioned a number of possibilities/facilitating factors such as their motivation, the training method used, learning together and student outcomes.

## Teachers' Motivation

One of the facilitating factors was the teachers' motivation which, in addition to beliefs and skills, is mentioned as a major element on which change stands or falls (Fullan, 1992). The teachers in this study were keen to learn the new strategy and wanted to develop professionally. It was this keen interest which motivated them to learn the new skills involved in cooperative learning, even though this called for a radical reconceptualization of what teaching and learning meant to them.

## The Training Method

The training method used to teach the strategy i.e. the theory-demonstration-practice-feedback and coaching paradigm were seen as an important facilitating factor. A teacher said:

> The demonstrations in our own classrooms made it easy for us to understand the strategy and made us realize that cooperative learning can work.

However, demonstrations are not enough. If teachers are to use cooperative learning effectively in their classrooms, they need coaching to refine their practice. A teacher said:

> The method used was very good. If we had only Saturday workshops and hadn't done any planning, observations and post conferencing, I don't think we would have learnt to use cooperative learning so well.

## Learning Together

Learning together was identified as a key to successful use. Laila said that the opportunity to plan together, to observe each other's practice and discuss ways to improve their performance encouraged her to continue. 'If I learnt with you it would not have been as fruitful as learning together in a group'. Another teacher appreciated learning together because it provided 'the opportunity to reflect together, raise questions, and engage in discussions which enhanced understanding of cooperative learning'.

Teachers wanted to continue working together as a team, as they felt this to provide the social support and forum for teachers to share their successes and problems and find solutions in order to improve the quality of cooperative learning.

## Student Outcomes

One of the most important factors that encouraged teachers to use the strategy was the students' response to their use of cooperative learning and the outcomes that accrued. Teachers and students were extremely positive in their comments about the outcomes from using cooperative learning in their classrooms for such a short period. These outcomes were not achieved immediately. Many problems such as students being reluctant to work together, one student dominating the group and unsuitable tasks were encountered and dealt with. The outcomes that accrued from using cooperative learning can be subsumed under three categories.

## Students' Understanding

Both teachers and students mentioned that cooperative learning had positive effects on students' understanding of the topic/subject. They attributed these positive effects to several things:

a) Receiving help from other group members when they did not clearly understand the concept being taught.
b) Sharing of ideas.

c) Learning and practising social skills was seen by the students as a factor that helped increase their understanding. However, no teacher mentioned social skills as requiring understanding.

## Effects on Students' Interpersonal Relationships and Psychological Health

Both students and teachers felt that students' interpersonal relations had improved. While the teachers mentioned only improvement in interpersonal relations within the classroom, the students gave examples from the classroom, the playground and their homes as evidence that their interpersonal relationships had improved.

The change mentioned most frequently by the students was that they had become friends with more classmates. The friendship was manifested by students sharing not only ideas but also materials. All the teachers and most of the students mentioned the role of social skills in the improvement of the students' interpersonal relationships. They felt that students were listening to each other, encouraging each other, taking turns. Students felt that working cooperatively had also increased their self-esteem. Many of them initially felt shy or lacked confidence which prevented them from talking to others or seeking help when needed.

## Social transformation

The teachers and students believed that if they used cooperative learning in their classrooms there would be some spill-over benefits to society.

> Students will share and help each other in society. They'll learn it in school and then they'll do it in their homes and outside school. This will benefit society.

Another teacher said:

> They'll become more helpful. They'll bury their differences and bear with each other. Many of our current problems in Pakistan are caused because we have become selfish, we can't cooperate. If students learn to cooperate they will care about each other, they will understand each other. The younger

generation are the citizens of tomorrow. If they learn to cooperate, they will become better citizens.

These are realistic statements because students not only mentioned a change in their classroom behaviour but also cited examples of how their behaviour at home and in the playground had changed. For example, one student said, 'At home I encourage my brothers and sisters to share, not fight.' Another said:

> First I used to tell other students when they came to play with us to go away but now I let them play. As we have learnt to work together in class, we play together too.

These positive comments were rewarding as they demonstrated the potential of cooperative learning for developing a student learning community and for helping students develop both academically and socially.

## Conclusion

The study revealed that the use of cooperative learning in classrooms has the potential to develop a student learning community. The classroom as a learning community is a place where the teacher creates and environment in which students learn with and from each other promoting their academic and social development. The study also revealed that when teachers team up to learn an instructional strategy and find ways to address their concerns, a learning community develops among teachers. The possibilities that cooperative learning offer are many. It is my belief that if schools value cooperation and use cooperative learning in their classrooms, teachers and students would become empowered to create schools that are truly cooperative and work together for a better, more equitable society.

## References

Anderson, S.E., Rolheiser, C., & Bennett, B. (1995). 'Confronting the challenge of implementing cooperative learning'. *Journal of Staff Development*, 16(1), 32–8.

Edwards, C., & Stout, J. (1990). 'Cooperative Learning: The First Year'. *Educational Leadership*, 47(4), 38–41.

Ellis, D. (1990). 'Introducing Cooperative Learning'. *Educational Leadership*, 47(4), 34–37.

Fullan, M.G. (1992). *Changing Schools: Insights* (pp. 11–20). Paper prepared for The Office of Policy and Planning: U.S. Department of Education.

Fullan, M.G. (1991). *The New Meaning of Educational Change*. NY: Teachers College Press.

Johnson, D.W., Johnson, R.T., Stanne, M.B., & Garibaldi, A. (1989). 'Impact of Goal and Resource interdependence on Problem-solving Success'. *Journal of Social Psychology*, 129(5), 621–29.

Johnson, D.W., Johnson, R.T. (1989). *Cooperation and Competition: Theory and Research*. Edina, MN: Interaction Book Company.

Johnson, D.W., Johnson, R.T., Stanne, M.B. & Garibaldi, A. (1990). 'The impact of Leader and Member Group Processing on Achievement in Cooperative Groups'. *Journal of Social Psychology*, 130, 507–16.

Johnson, D.W., & Johnson, R.T. (1991). *Learning Together and Alone: Cooperative, Competitive and Individualistic Learning* (3rd ed.). Needham Heights, MA: Simon and Schuster.

Johnson, D.W., Johnson, R.T. & Holubec, E.J. (1991). *Cooperation in the Classroom*. Edina, MN.: Interaction Book Company.

Johnson, D.W., Johnson, R.T., & Holubec E.J. (1993). *Circles of Learning: Cooperation in the Classroom* (4th ed.). Edina, MN: Interaction Book Company

Joyce, B., & Showers, B. (1982). 'The Coaching of teaching'. *Educational Leadership*, 40, 4–8,10.

Lortie, D. (1975). *School Teacher: A Sociological Study*. Chicago: University of Chicago Press.

Johnson, D.W., & Johnson, R.T. (1994). *Implementing Cooperative Learning: Training Sessions, Transfer to the Classroom, and Maintaining Long-term Use*. Draft paper.

Mesch, D., Lew, M., Johnson, D.W. & Johnson. R.T. (1986). 'Isolated Teenagers, Cooperative Learning and the Training of Social Skills'. *Journal of Psychology*, 120(4), 323–34.

Mitchell, C. & Sackney, L. (2000). *Profound Improvement: Building Capacity for a Learning Community*. Lisse: Swetz and Zeitlinger.

Rosenholtz, S.J. (1989). *Teachers' Workplace: The Social Organization of Schools*. NY: Longman.

Sacca, K.C. (1990). Staff Development for Cooperative Learning. *Staff Development*, 153–64.

Showers, B., Joyce, B., & Bennett, B. (1987). 'Synthesis of Research on Staff Development: A framework for Future Study and a state-of-art Analysis'. *Educational Leadership* 45(3), 77–78.

Slavin, R.E. (1990). *Cooperative Learning: Theory, Research and Practice*. Englewood Cliffs, NJ: Prentice-Hall.

Smith, W.F., & Andrews, R.L. (1989). *Instructional Leadership: How Principals make a Difference*. Alexandria, VA: ASCD.

Watson, N., & Kilcher, A. (1990). *Peer Coaching: A Review of the Literature and a Glimpse of Ontario Practice*. Toronto: Ontario Secondary School Teachers' Federation.

Yager, S., Johnson, D.W., & Johnson, R.T. (1985). 'Oral Discussion, Group-to-Individual Transfer, and Achievement in Cooperative Learning Groups. *Journal of Educational Psychology*, 77(1), 60–66.

# 7

# TEACHING AND LEARNING IN MULTIGRADE CLASSES

*Rana Hussain and John Retallick*

Multigrade schools and classrooms are a feature of most education systems around the world. Wherever they are, these schools present particular challenges for teaching and learning, though in a developing country like Pakistan, the challenges may be more intense because of the general shortage of resources and lack of specialized training of teachers for working in multigrade situations. However, such schools by their very nature have strong connections with the idea of the school as a learning community since they are often the focal point of an isolated community in a rural area with close interaction between home and school. They are almost always small schools, often with just one teacher, and usually have a family-like atmosphere of cooperation and mutual support.

One of the present authors, Rana Hussain, was Principal Investigator for a significant piece of research conducted in multigrade schools in the Northern Areas of Pakistan, and that is the basis of this chapter. The chapter will present an account of how teachers were engaged in confirming some principles of adult learning and were creating models of effective teaching and learning practices in the multigrade schools. The second author, John Retallick, provided some conceptual input into planning the project though he did not participate in the data gathering. His interest in the research stems from an experience of many years of teaching in and observing multigrade schools in Australia where they are often known as 'small schools' or 'one teacher schools'. Whilst such schools are always multigrade, there also exist multigrade or 'multiage' classes in larger schools where teachers believe that they provide a more conducive learning environment for students.

## What is Multigrade Teaching?

An international research project based at the Institute of Education, University of London, has been underway for some years to explore the nature and meaning of multigrade teaching in various countries. Their working definition is:

> In multigrade teaching, teachers are responsible, within a timetabled period, for instruction across two or more curriculum grades. In 'one-teacher' schools, the teacher is responsible for teaching across five or six grades of the curriculum. In two or three-teacher schools the teacher is responsible for teaching across two or more curriculum grades. In monograde teaching, by contrast, teachers are responsible, within a timetabled period, for instruction of a single curriculum grade...(Little, 2001:482).

Little (2001) reviews the various reasons and conditions for multigrade teaching which are mostly concerned with the school being located in an area of low population density, insufficient to support a larger school and monograde teaching. This suggests a condition of *necessity* rather than *choice* on the part of the teacher. However, she also recognizes that there are schools where teachers have decided for pedagogic reasons to organize students in multigrade rather than monograde groups which are then a matter of *choice*. Where this choice is exercised, the classes are sometimes referred to as 'composite classes', 'multiage classes', 'vertical groups' or 'family groups' to distinguish them from monograde classes.

Those who are unfamiliar with multigrade teaching might wonder how teachers actually manage such situations. Three curriculum and timetabling practices have been described by Lungwangwa (1989) from experience in Zambia. The first is *common timetable* where all children learn the same subject in a given timetable period though each group does work according to their respective grade level. The second is *subject stagger* where groups learn different subjects in the same period. The teacher arranges for subjects requiring high teacher-pupil contact to be matched with those requiring little contact to accomplish this strategy. The third is called the *subject grouping* practice where all groups receive the same subject and instruction; this is particularly appropriate in subjects such as art or music. A common practice is for older children to guide and even teach the younger children in some subjects and this is known as 'peer tutoring'. For example, older children can read stories to younger children which is a learning experience for both if the stories are carefully selected by the teacher. In physical education classes, the older ones can help skill development of younger children in throwing and catching, for example. Provided that the teacher is overseeing the activities, it can be quite valuable for mixed-age groups of children to learn together.

A question that often arises in discussions of multigrade teaching concerns the relative achievement levels of students in multigrade versus monograde classes. So entrenched is the idea that monograde classes must be better for student learning that there is often skepticism about the value of multigrade teaching in that respect. Little (2001) has surveyed a range of research studies that reveal either no difference or a slight advantage for multigrade classes, particularly in the non-cognitive learning areas such as development of social skills. It is a myth, therefore, to conclude that monograde classes always produce better student learning.

**The Research Project**

Having clarified what we mean by multigrade teaching, we now turn to the research project. The project was carried out in schools in the Northern Areas (NA) of Pakistan over two years. The question being researched was: 'What is the reality of creating effective teaching and learning practices in multigrade schools in NA?'

The study was planned in two phases. In Phase 1, spread over six months, the situational analysis was done to gather data on the existing state of 15 sample schools out of 73 schools in the region. Based on the Phase 1 findings and recommendations, Phase 2 of the study was planned to make interventions in four selected schools and learn from the experience. The selection of four schools out of 15 was based on the following criteria:

- Schools from two regions should be a part of the sample
- A Field Education Office should be willing to participate in the intervention phase
- The number of teachers should be 2-3
- The two schools of a region should be in a radius of 5-10 kilometers for easy access for researchers as well as for teachers to meet each other.

Table 1 provides details of the schools in the project and highlights the ones selected for the Phase 2 intervention.

## Table 1
## Schools in the Project

| Regions | Schools | No. of teachers | No. of students |
|---|---|---|---|
| Gilgit | D. J. Primary school Aminabad Nomal | 2+3 | 66 |
| Hunza | D. J. Primary school Murtazabad | 3 | 40 |
| | D. J. Primary school Garelth* | 3 | 69 |
| | D. J. Primary school Rahimabad | 2+1 | 32 |
| | D. J. Primary school Faizabad* | 2+1 | 31 |
| Puniyal/ | D. J. Primary school Japuki | 4 | 102 |
| Ishkoman | D. J. Primary school Gulmoti | 2+1 | 74 |
| | D. J. Primary school Kuchdah | 3 | 80 |
| | D. J. Primary school Dain | 2+1 | 119 |
| | D. J. Primary school Shonus | 2+1 | 72 |
| | D. J. Primary school Bargjungle | 2+1 | 67 |
| Gupis/Yasin | D. J. Primary school Hakis | 4 | 197 |
| | D. J. Primary school Hamardass* | 3 | 91 |
| | D. J. Primary school Yasin* | 2+1 | 90 |
| | D. J. Primary school Bojayot | 2+1 | 64 |

*Indicates schools selected for the intervention.*

## Phase 1: Situation Analysis in Fifteen Schools

The following recommendations and questions arose from Phase 1 of the study:

- We propose an advocacy campaign for all stakeholders before making any intervention plans for improving multigrade practices.
- The teachers in multigrade settings should be the key role players in determining effective multigrade practices; these should stem from their own concerns and should include planned actions to confirm what works and why. All child-centered activities require a shift of thinking from the needs of the teacher to the needs of the learner; this shift also requires other conditions favouring the learner. What are those conditions and how can they be created?

- What are appropriate instructional strategies for effective multigrade teaching?

The study was carried out using action research methodology because it was intended that there would be interventions into the schools to support and encourage teachers to improve their teaching in the multigrade situations. We took guidance on action research methodology from Kemmis and Mctaggart (1988) who define it in these terms:

> Action research is a form of collective self-reflective enquiry undertaken by participants in social situations in order to improve the rationality and justice of their own social or educational practices, as well as their understanding of these practices and the situations in which these practices are carried out (p. 5).

In this study, the 'social situations' are schools and the 'practice' is multigrade teaching in those schools. According to this definition, action research seeks 'improvement' (this implies change) in the practice as well as increased 'understanding' of it through 'collective self-reflective enquiry'. There are two aspects of the methodology that we chose to guide the enquiry. Firstly, the concept of the action research cycle was helpful—the sequence of planning, enacting, observing (or data gathering) and reflecting was employed in the study. Furthermore, not only was it a cycle but also became a spiral when the research moved through a number of cycles with increased understanding arising from each one. Secondly, the features of cultural action identified by Kemmis and McTaggart (1988) provided a useful scaffold upon which to build the project. They suggest that 'improving education is not just a matter of individual action, it is also a matter of cultural action' (p. 34) and in relation to improving multigrade teaching it means changing:

- the *language* used to describe, explain and justify the practice of multigrade teaching;
- the *activities* which constitute multigrade teaching and learning;
- the *patterns of social relationships* which characterize multigrade schools.

The way we used those categories in the project was in terms of what teachers 'say' about multigrade teaching i.e. the language, what teachers 'do' in their classrooms i.e. the activities, and how they 'feel' about the experience of working with others i.e. the patterns of social relationships. In the project, those categories were used as the focus for interventions to improve the teaching and the basis of data gathering to ascertain if any change and increased understanding was actually occurring.

As well as literature on action research, the project also benefited from reports and research data on good practices of multigrade teaching (e.g. Miller, 1989). In the study, Rana Hussain adapted ideas and strategies from those sources as the basis for interventions, prepared teachers to practice some of the strategies promoted for effective multigrade teaching and encouraged teachers to reflect on their progress and claims of failure or success. The study not only provides examples of how teachers were learning and putting their learning into action but also helps in understanding larger questions such as:

- How do teachers learn?
- What learning spaces are required?
- What factors support learning?
- How do we know the impact of interventions?
- What is the chance of applying such learning in other situations?

One of the earliest understandings to arise from the project was that the development of expertise through action research requires major investments of time: 'time for talking'—to process information and develop a language for discussing practice; 'time for doing'—to provide experience of specific classroom activities relevant for learners; and, 'time for relating'—to get to know the researcher, other teachers and students in new ways consistent with a change in the practice of multigrade teaching.

A second understanding that arose early in the project was in relation to teachers' motivation to learn. It was clear that learning is more meaningful and lasting when there are intrinsic reasons for learning; such reasons are more motivating and learners will work hard for them. Learning takes place when the learner becomes an active searcher for knowledge and as learning occurs there is a feeling that the quest has been rewarded. Hurdles and obstacles can be seen as learning challenges that need to be negotiated with patience and understanding.

Amongst the teachers we found two types of learners. There were those who had a tendency to see challenges from the viewpoint that they should avoid errors and were fearful of making mistakes. The others were learners who took all challenges as learning experiences and failure was seen as a stage of learning. The latter focused on the usefulness of what they were learning and how the new learning could be put into use to do something that has an impact on others. This kind of learning leads to further motivation.

## Areas of Intervention during Phase 2

Four areas were selected to prepare a programme of intervention and subsequent study; curriculum, material resources, peer tutoring and community involvement. In order to create a workable curriculum for the learners, a reorganization of the existing curriculum was carried out. In multigrade contexts children require more resources than a basic textbook, so to improve instruction resources of 'low cost and high thought' were created. The experience of multigrade classes is that students can learn a great deal in social settings involving other students. Peers play an important role in supporting learning and therefore peer tutoring was an important area of intervention. Finally, since multigrade classes are the reality of remote areas and such schools have a very defined and close community, community involvement was another area of intervention. Teachers are the key role players in preparing multigrade teaching hence they were given instructional strategies like story telling, preparing work cards with instructions for children to do self-study and designing peer tutoring tasks.

In any social situation requiring change, it is helpful to share the change strategy with all stakeholders. In this study, teachers, parents, management and researchers were all regarded as stakeholders and sat together to study and understand the existing situation and plans for action. The researcher at first shared the action plans, which had been earlier negotiated with the manager of the Aga Khan Education Service, Pakistan (AEKS, P) who had responsibility for the schools, and later, the research findings.

## Working with Teachers for Implementation

During the teacher workshops, certain principles of learning were emphasized:

a. Whilst teachers may lack knowledge and experience of how to organize effective multigrade teaching, they do not lack reasoning ability and can reason with the knowledge that they have.
b. Learning new strategies is not easy; important is the sheer will on the part of teachers to be able to intentionally learn them.
c. Teachers need to value themselves as learners; they need to recognize and understand what it means to learn, who they are as learners, and how to go about planning, monitoring and revising. They also need to reflect upon their own learning and that of others. A question that they need to constantly ask themselves and others is: 'do I understand?'

Keeping in view the above principles, the findings of Phase 1 were shared so that teachers could see the existing practices and how some of them are supporting students' learning while others need to improve.

**Good Practices in the Existing Situation**

A number of good practices were identified in the existing situation:

- Teachers teach through split teaching and in such an approach individual grades get individual attention.
- Teachers keep other classes busy through assigned tasks like reading or writing.
- Occasionally teachers give students a chance to work in pairs and rarely is there any evidence of bringing resources into the classroom.
- The schools have a separate resource room that has many resources available for use in the classroom.
- The schools have a system of voluntary Village Education Committee (VEC) that look after students' welfare and administrative affairs; generally the members are happy with teachers and acknowledge their hard work.

## Some of the Key Issues

- Students have a lot of energy that could be tapped but the current curriculum organization and instructional strategies do not seem to encourage that
- Resources have to be brought into the classrooms and classroom organization has to be reconsidered
- Engagement of VEC will have to shift from an administrative role to a more academic support role
- Curriculum reorganization can best be done through thematic plans by engaging different classes at the start of the lesson and then moving to individual grade learning (currently each class is taught separately by subject and grade)
- Structured peer tutoring has to be introduced for effective teaching and learning, not incidentally as is currently done.

Through sharing these issues, the teachers realized that they were dealing with multigrade teaching out of necessity rather than as a model chosen for pedagogical reasons. With that in mind they wanted to understand how they could work with the researchers to improve their existing practices. Having made this shift, teachers showed an interest in working with researchers but were not very confident that they would be able to make improvements themselves. They constantly asked us to tell them 'how to do it' rather than believing that together we could find out best practices in multigrade teaching. It was encouraging to notice the support from Field Education Officers and AKES,P management in influencing the teachers to participate in this research project and assuring their full support during the study.

## Moving to Phase 2: General Discussion with Stakeholders

A significant shift in attitudes about multigrade teaching had to be created as the study moved to Phase 2. Unless all stakeholders at different levels had a strong belief in the philosophy of multigrade as an approach to teaching, no intervention would be sustainable. Some of the basic philosophies about learning in general and learning in a multigrade situation in particular, were discussed with the stakeholders. If the merits of multigrade are clearly understood by all engaged, then the myth that monograde is always the best approach to teaching and learning is challenged. In order to break this myth some principles were shared with the key stakeholders. For example, in a multigrade situation, a combination of two to three grades provides learners with a longer period to stay with their peers and teachers and to develop more mutual relationships. The teacher begins to understand the learners better and the grouping of two to three grades makes the teacher's role more stimulating and exciting. Multigrade is built on a model of cooperative learning; older students model vocabulary, behaviour, reading, writing, learning strategies and skills like interpersonal and leadership—while working in groups with younger students. Older children's greater general knowledge helps to extend the learning of the younger ones.

**Phase 2: Intervention in Four Schools**

The intervention period was spread over 15 weeks. This happened to be the final term of the school academic year, and therefore, a very thorough planning of teaching practices was required. Since the teachers were new in designing the planned activities they were supported by the researcher as well as the Professional Development Teachers (PDTs) in the four areas of intervention: curriculum reorganization, resource development, peer tutoring and community involvement.

The actions were layered at two levels. The first was at the level of the researcher who planned actions based on the findings of the situational analysis. This part of the research required planning a thematic curriculum, instructional strategies the teachers could use with ease and the organization of learning in the classroom with flexible scheduling and flexible grouping of grades. The second level was action in the schools where the stakeholders were lobbied through an advocacy campaign to support the intervention. Educational seminars and open discussions were planned to gain the commitment of all stakeholders.

During the intervention phase different role players' work was also discussed. For the PDTs, the focus was research methods for collecting data while for the teachers it was on implementing the plans as discussed with them. It was agreed that teachers would write a reflective diary. The role of PDTs to support the teachers in the field during the intervention phase and the communication strategies between PDTs and the researcher were also firmed up. PDT's designed a timetable of visitation to the sites that included activities like supporting the teachers by visiting their classroom, team teaching and conducting small scale workshops on identified needs.

The role of the principal researcher was to work with the PDTs through distance conferencing and meet them as and when possible to supply material and answer queries. The principal researcher was also responsible for analyzing the data as it was received from the PDTs and teachers and to suggest ideas to try when problems arose. In order to keep the academic managers and FEOs in the loop there were regular telephone conversations to ensure their participation and to receive their feedback on the research project.

**Action in Four Areas of Intervention**

**1. Reorganizing the curriculum**

The present curriculum was taught in different subjects through division of textbook pages. Teachers had received a syllabus from the head office that described the textbook break down. The first step was to help teachers understand the content required to be taught during the available period prior to the end of term and they were asked to look at different subjects and develop a plan of common concepts and skills to be learnt by the students. Since four schools were participating with a group of twelve teachers, the work of reorganization was divided among teams. This division helped in engaging all teachers and also in managing the task in the stipulated time. Once the teachers produced draft topics and skills to be learnt class-wise and subject-wise, they prepared themes that could be taught in a class of mixed grades.

The shift in curriculum planning was visible in each school's planner. New teachers were planning combined grade lessons and concentrating on activities whilst making use of teachers' guides in subjects like Science and English. Nevertheless, teachers struggled in planning daily lessons through a thematic approach. It is ironic that teachers were faced with a multigrade context but the academic centre provided them a single-grade syllabus that revolved around graded textbooks and teachers were required to teach a specific number of pages in a given timeframe. For example, in Science (taught in English) the syllabus to be covered for a period was presented as follows:

| Text book and classes | Pages | Topics: From | To |
|---|---|---|---|
| Oxford Primary Science 2 (For class III) | 1-35 | Your Body | Solids, Liquid Gases |
| Oxford Primary Science (For Class IV) | 1-41 | The Human Body | Vegetables |
| Oxford Primary Science V | 1-49 | Building units of the body | The Plant Kingdom |

The above table helps in understanding the curriculum organization in a particular subject for three classes. During the workshops, teachers were guided to make connections between the given topics of three grades and derive a common theme. It can be seen that the common theme in most of the topics is 'Living being'. Teachers were then asked to select those graded concepts that they would be required to teach grade-wise and list them. Finally, they were helped to plan activity-based instructional material from either the textbook or teacher guides and then teach through direct instruction or through suggested activities that learners could engage as a whole class. Similar planning exercises were done in all subject areas. The topics were divided amongst the teachers following the same principles of seeking a common theme, graded concepts, direct teaching and learning through resources.

At the level of planning, there seemed to be a good response but when they tried to implement it, they had difficulty in comprehending the instructional tasks and also in preparing new tasks. It should be noted that these teachers had been exposed to the teacher manuals for the very first time and the manuals were available in two subjects only. For subjects like Urdu, Islamiat, Mathematics and Social Studies, they only had textbooks. The data on the enacted curriculum reveals that teachers were facing difficulties in preparing grade-wise instructional activities. Reasons for such difficulties can be traced to the beliefs, practices and knowledge that teachers have of the 'unidimensional' learning environments that they have experienced throughout their careers.

Another dilemma in curriculum re-organization stems from the conventional curriculum approach, an approach that places high premium on verbal skills. This mindset is obvious in the way the syllabus is sent from the centre with an expectation of developing reading and writing skills and covering the number of pages. It is evident that the conventional curriculum concentrates on a very narrow range of skills, particularly reading and verbal skills, with little emphasis on alternative intellectual abilities such as art, athletics, creativity and thinking. Although the teachers report in their diaries that the story sessions, games and working with materials enhanced the thinking abilities and confidence, they were not able to design more instructional strategies of this kind.

The role of the PDTs as support teachers was also occasional, as they were not available on a daily basis. Hence, teachers felt that they were not very successful in planning new activities. A teacher wrote in her diary:

> Teaching one lesson to a class takes a lot of time, as both classes have to be taught together and sometimes senior classes find the lesson to be repetitive.

Another wrote:

> In the English subject, it is difficult to teach two grades together as the two lessons have totally different topics and to mix the two is not easy.

One of the teachers reported:

> When I teach the same topic to both the classes and ask oral questions, both the classes give the same response. Lower grades learning is extended as they are challenged but the upper grades need more challenging tasks and I have difficulty in making them.

Some of these comments and the actions taken during the research reveal that the teachers had understood curriculum re-organization as a concept and had begun to see how divergent materials could be helpful in learning, but were not ready to make such plans. This conclusion raises the issue regarding the need for preparing more detailed instructional plans with the teachers and provision of thematic material. There needs to be a well planned set of instructional strategies for combined grades and subjects to facilitate such flexible learning structures.

## 2. Resource Development

All schools were provided with teaching kits that included manipulative resources. Firstly, teachers audited the materials in the kit and prepared a list of activities that could be carried out with the resources. Then a workshop was held on how to use the materials from the kit and also on preparing new resource materials for children through low-cost and high thought. Teachers realized that resources are crucial in organizing children's learning and they are very necessary in multigrade teaching as the role of teacher in such teaching changes from knowledge transmitter to facilitator of learning. Some resources in the form of storybooks were also supplied to schools. Teachers found this exercise very informative and one commented:

> We have been given this resource and we were supported or guided as to how these are to be used.

## 3. Community involvement

Teachers were of the opinion that VECs are very supportive of their work. Not only are they involved in some administrative tasks, but are also a bridge between the schools and home. However, when they were asked to engage parents as para-professionals to work with them in the classrooms, one teacher's immediate response was:

> They cannot become teachers, how will they teach.

Another commented:

> Parents pay us fees to teach their children; we can't pass our responsibilities to them.

During a workshop, teachers came to realize that when children are given home tasks, they expect the parents to supervise the homework, which is difficult for parents who are unschooled and can't read or write. Generally, teachers felt that schooled parents give more support in academics than the unschooled ones.

Teachers collectively planned tasks for the parents who would come and work with teachers. These were:

- A talk on local history
- A talk about their own profession
- Doctors and nurses could come and talk about health and hygiene and give some medical assistance
- Some older students can support in listening to students' reading and help them in written work
- Parents can also help in creating low-cost, high thought resources.

With these possibilities, the teachers prepared a plan of engaging the parents through steps such as: sharing with parents the objectives of why they are invited; negotiating time and topics and also creating space in the classroom timetables for parental visits.

Community involvement was a promising area for change and there were many examples of community members being engaged in school teaching through lectures and providing support in teaching curriculum areas. These included health and hygiene, local administrative set up of the district, local history and some knowledge of social organization. Involvement of the community in this way surprised the teachers who commented in their diaries that when members of the community were approached to come to school and work with children, initially they were reluctant. They expressed their inability to speak in the official language (English/Urdu). Later, they were surprised to hear that language was not a major barrier and these people had a wealth of knowledge which could be drawn upon for making the school curriculum indigenous and rich.

The community involvement brought two positive changes; one was in the richness of school curriculum and the other was in building better working relationships. Some of them volunteered to support children during holidays; some went house to house to convince people that the two months holiday time could be used effectively and children could be put to work on home assignments. In one case, the community was mobilized to a level that they raised a sum of ten thousand rupees to support the school in purchasing a computer. Generally, in all the schools, the community began to own the school and accepted the change for the better.

## 4. Peer tutoring

Teachers were aware of this strategy, though the situation analysis revealed that there was some confusion in the minds of teachers about group work and peer learning. In the teacher workshops, literature on peer tutoring was shared and the approaches to plan such learning situations were discussed. It was interesting to hear teachers comment that the strategy is self-defeating for teachers: *'because if peers can be teachers why are we here?'*. One teacher commented: *'I think my parents will not like this approach as they believe schools are all about teachers teaching children'*. Any other organization of learning was seen by parents as a makeshift arrangement.

These apprehensions needed to be addressed, so a discussion was arranged on how children learn and examples of children learning outside the school such as in playgroups and family outings were discussed. Teachers then set about planning the peer tutoring timetable, selecting children who could perform the role of peer tutor and selecting children who actually required peer support.

Whilst teachers had heard about and discussed peer tutoring, they felt amazed to see it happen in their own classrooms. They initially struggled with its planning, choosing the students to be paired together for specific tasks but with the support of the PDT they were able to manage the peer tutoring schedule. They remarked how this approach had helped in completing the set syllabus and also realized the importance of such a strategy for developing non-cognitive skills of the students. This strategy had both positive and negative results and teachers have very succinctly expressed their opinions about this approach. Teachers felt that initially they were struggling as to how students should be paired, they stated that a child working with another child may lose out on his or her own learning time and such acts may not be acceptable to the parents. Later, reflections and the observation data on how this strategy worked in their classrooms proved that the teachers' assumptions were not totally correct. One teacher wrote:

> I am surprised on the power that this strategy has as I had never believed that students gain so much when they work with their peers and the gain is mutual.

About their relationship with supervisors, they feel more settled. The data were very promising as there were initial apprehensions with the teachers about the role of supervisors during the study period and a fear of getting bad appraisals. Engagement of supervisors at the early stage of intervention and their commitment to support the study can be seen as an important factor in the success of the study.

Initially, the process started late or randomly in two schools, but with the support from PDTs in planning the peer tutoring sessions, almost all schools made it a part of their teaching learning processes. There was no mention of older children bullying the young ones or children not learning. On the contrary, there were examples of how the older ones developed more confidence in the content while teaching the younger ones. There were examples of leadership amongst children and learning enhancement as a result of peer tutoring with no concerns or complaints from the parents as the teachers had initially feared.

**Teachers and Learning**

We know that there are both formal and informal ways of teacher development, some which liberate the teacher's mind, while others may shackle the teacher. In this project, we realize that genuine learning comes from within; the urge to feel, to know and to discern. This can happen only when the learner is willing to take some responsibility for his/her own learning and this learning is deeply dependent on the answers sought by the learner. The teachers in this project were made to realize from the beginning that they should seek answers themselves. The role of the action researcher was the true role of a facilitator that may be expressed in these words: 'I do not know how it's going to work in this particular situation but I do know that together we can find out'.

Despite this, there was pressure from the PDTs as well as from the teachers to 'tell us' or 'give us the right answers' and one of the earlier comments from a PDT illustrates this tendency:

> Things are changing but teachers are struggling, we are also not there most of the time, why can we not give them a local tutor who is knowledgeable about multigrade teaching. He can conduct workshops for them on multigrade teaching.

Such reflections created nervousness and insecurity in the mind of the Principal Researcher and she began to ask questions like: 'Why is it not working? How should I help the teachers to have faith in themselves? Should I allow interventions of a 'knowledgeable trainer?' How can I help the teachers to learn from their own practice?' These questions denoted the inner struggle of the researcher and were answered through talking about the process and realizing that more and better understanding of learning from practice had to be created. This was possible because we were working from a distance in this study and distance leads to delays and delays allowed time for trying things out. It was very interesting to read reflections from the PDTs who were initially very concerned about the slow change but who later wrote:

> I went to school and was very pleased to see that teachers have managed to plan peer tutoring timetable and there are good number of community people working with teachers in the classroom. Teachers are gradually grappling with the situation.

## Professional Aspirations and Teachers' Self-efficacy

Student attitudes, behaviours and accomplishments influence how teachers feel about their professional lives. Conversely, teacher perceptions and expectations shape students' attitudes and academic success. In this study teachers were required to reflect on their own beliefs about their children's abilities and potential to learn. Certain concepts about learning needed to be revisited; teachers' conceptions of children learning were based on 'telling' and no space was given for 'construction'. This was a challenge and addressing it was not easy. Teachers required time and models to see that children have innate learning abilities and need an environment to practice this. The role of a teacher is to provide a conducive environment for learning. This issue was slowly addressed as teachers started working with peer tutoring and the use of resources to engage the students. Both teacher diaries and those of the PDTs suggested the slow but steady change in students' achievement. A teacher said:

> I am happy to see how my children are progressing, they can work with the resources, other children are teaching them and I see the children enjoying this process, children are busy in their work and do not misbehave now.

Another teacher was surprised at the change she observed in the leadership roles exhibited by her students. She wrote enthusiastically:

> Now when I come in the morning, I observe children busy with preparing the classroom, laying out materials and I am surprised that instead of students running and playing, screaming aimlessly, they are engaged in reading or helping their peers with assignments.

Comments like these helped our understanding of how teachers were changing their attitudes about the abilities of children and also realizing the potential of learning from one another as a strong source in a multigrade setting. Later, there were examples of how they were able to plan a strong peer tutoring plan and allocate time for it.

Supervisors visited the schools and wanted to know how the students were engaged in learning. They seemed pleased with the progress and at times, tested student learning through formal questioning to which they received positive responses. This was a facilitating factor for teachers to continue with their initiatives. Teachers have written positively about the relationships of trust that were building among the supervisors, fellow teachers and community.

Teachers attribute this change in relationships to some of the approaches taken in developing good communication, engaging different stakeholders and importantly, they felt empowered. The process of changing the restrictive culture under which teachers generally operate, to one that is enabling and open, was most important. A teacher commented:

> I was working as a person who was always asked to do things and never consulted, now we are regarded as individuals that can make their decisions about classroom instructions, organization of learning and reaching to the community, this has helped me to do more then I was doing earlier. I have to be very vigilant in my actions as this is a big responsibility.

## Factors Facilitating Teacher Learning

Support, sharing, mentoring and working in their own classrooms were some of the facilitating factors. From the start, teacher isolation was broken as all planning of curriculum was done collaboratively. During the three weeks of initial intervention, the teachers of cluster schools attended workshops on curriculum planning. They worked on assigned subjects and grades and shared their plans with one another, receiving feedback from the PDTs and the Principal Researcher who played a mentoring role. Such collaborative exercises continued throughout the study period and combined sessions developed a better harmony among the teachers. They got inspiration from the good examples of their colleagues and made efforts to produce and develop new resources themselves. In one school, the teachers were ahead in planning homework tasks and when these were shared with the other schools they created their own plan and took initiatives in developing students' activities in the form of educational games. Teachers of one school brought their kit box and shared the missing tools with the other school that had misplaced them.

Teachers in general found collective work to be meaningful. They have written in their diaries that, although they were working in separate schools, they had similar topics and similar areas to work on and this similarity of cause brought them together and created a healthy cooperation.

The study was based on real classroom practices and was planned around teachers' own classrooms, curriculum instructional strategies and other support mechanisms like engaging the community. They had freedom to make choices about daily schedules and reorganizing topics. All these areas are very dear to any teacher who wants to work for their students' betterment. Other research also confirms that teachers learn best and accept new educational strategies when they see them working in their own context; otherwise, the new knowledge remains a theory and is not put into practice. Teachers not only participated most willingly in this process, but were also appreciative of how this part of the study was developing them into better teachers. They have commented favourably on the workshop models as they were realistic and addressed their own concerns.

Another facilitating factor stemmed from allowing teachers to continue with the practices that they felt were good and supported learning e.g. use of split teaching. In the current model they would begin the topics collectively for all children of different grades but would then continue either through self-directed tasks or teacher-directed tasks to enable children work at their own level. Initially, they were struggling with the organization of learning and some mentioned that when combined plans were used, the younger children's learning was broadened and the sessions were interesting for them but the older ones did not learn beyond the revision.

When confronted with this situation, the PDTs intervened and helped the teachers prepare lessons that would begin with common topics but would later split into topics to cater for specific class needs.

The important point here was the conversation between teachers and PDTs and the sharing of concerns and joint decision making that is at the hub of the action research project. The dialogues were helping teachers to look for solutions and suggest strategies for improvement. One teacher wrote is his diary:

> In Science, the topic for classes iv and v was the same (matter) but the concepts were graded, the students of grade v needed my attention and I decided to introduce the topic collectively and then with the higher class, I spent time explaining as these children will have to write an exam and will need correct statements to give their understanding. I will set some questions for them that they can work from home using their textbooks. I think from exams viewpoint children need to read and write at their own level and I plan to give them separate tasks.

There were a number of examples of teachers using a thematic approach but also helping children to learn at their own pace which was possible because teachers were trained to use split teaching. Teachers did not receive a manual or written document on thematic planning hence they were struggling:

> I began the lesson collectively in two grades but children in higher classes did not learn much as I could not plan the challenging tasks. I had to revert to teaching individual class as their learning had to be ensured.

**Hindering Factors**

Moving teachers from an approach to teaching bound up in authority, classroom control, teacher as expert, and students as 'empty heads', to an approach which engages with learners, is tumultuous. Traditional pedagogy rests on the assumption that children must learn knowledge selected by adults, but often children challenge this by teaching themselves whatever they desire to learn. This shift was not easily understood by all teachers. As the intervention began in the middle of the term and teachers had fear of external exams, at times they clung to old practices of split teaching.

Sometimes teachers were struggling with the language issue. Three subjects were mostly taught through Urdu (national language) and the other three in English. Imposing a second language on young learners has its own implications but this study was about more than a foreign language, it was also about learning Science and Mathematics through the English language.

**Table 1**
**Major Changes in Multigrade Practices as a Result of Intervention**

| Areas | Observable changes |
| --- | --- |
| Student ability | Fixed versus multi-dimensional. Every child could demonstrate an ability on some instructional task. Teachers created a variety of tasks to organize learning. |
| Teacher's role | Managing learning environment in the classroom, procuring resources be they human or material. Patient and reflective, good planner and honest. Seeking information. |
| Learner's role | Taking responsibility for their learning, learning from other sources besides teacher. Helping other learners in the classroom. |
| Basis of determining competence | Only reading and end tests are not the gauge of competence. Observing children in their engagement and involvement in different tasks and making judgements based on their performance in all areas. |
| Task structure | Moving away from teacher-centered to learner centered, variety and creativity, pairing children with specific tasks across grades, flexible scheduling—indoor and outdoor. |
| Learner assessment and evaluation | Final term exams and internal tests, recording learner's strengths/abilities across a wide variety of tasks. |
| Effects on learner | Balanced learners, happy learners, self-control and pride in what they have been asked to accomplish by taking control of their own learning. |

Lack of teacher training in multigrade teaching was a hinderance. Generally, it is assumed that teachers can teach in multigrade settings by adopting some organizational patterns, timetable and student grouping, and effective multigrade teaching will happen. The current study informs that such practices lead to 'quasi' multigrade schools with limited chances of success. In the situation analysis, examples of using textbooks grade-wise with some instructional strategies like use of blackboard, a few displays and questioning loaded with teacher talk were found. However, there was no pedagogical technique like 'peer-tutoring' or 'thematic approach', as suggested in the literature for effective multigrade teaching (Miller, 1989).

How the current study addressed the lack of teacher training in multigrade and the results of the intervention can be summed up using a model adapted from Miller (1989). He refers to multi-dimensional classroom characteristics and since our study is based in the classroom and the entire data is generated from classroom interaction, the same norms as suggested by Miller can be used to see what changes occurred in the multigrade teaching practices. Most important are the changes that we see in teachers' beliefs about students, their role and their learning.

**Conclusion**

We began this chapter by defining multigrade teaching, describing the context of such teaching in NA of Pakistan and the method of action research used to bring about more effective multigrade practices. While sharing the project findings, we have also addressed the facilitating and hindering factors that came in the way of learning. Since the project was implemented on a very small sample there are no claims of generalization yet it can be safely said that teachers' learning about effective multigrade teaching is evident in two particular areas: teachers' understanding and application of peer tutoring and community involvement in enhancing students' learning. The results in the other two important areas of curriculum re-organization and developing material resources were not as impressive. This could be attributed to a few factors like lack of teacher manuals for referencing, lack of time and money for developing resources during the intervention phase, and possibly, there were too many areas of intervention undertaken in the time available for the study. Conclusions on teacher learning were supported by their reflections; teachers openly admit that the empowerment, the support and above all, their experiences of seeing things happening in their own schools and classrooms were powerful learning experiences.

Finally, if this study reveals what teachers can achieve in designing multigrade practices it also highlights the complex nature of bringing such practices, to a bigger scale. Teachers would require constant support in developing resources and would need continuous teacher education in developing the right kind of repertoire to deal with effective multigrade teaching. Effective multigrade is possible when a well designed plan of action is created through engagement of stakeholders, when they work together to enhance and improve the teaching and learning processes in their schools and when they have a commitment to continue the same with support from the teacher educators as well.

### References

Kemmis, S. and McTaggart, R. (1988). *The Action Research Planner* (3rd ed.). Geelong: Deakin University Press.

Little, A. W. (2001). 'Multigrade Teaching: Towards an International Research and Policy Agenda'. *International Journal of Educational Development*, 21, 481–97.

Lungwangwa, G. (1989). 'Multigrade Schools in Zambian Primary Education. Cited in A. W. Little (2001). Multigrade teaching: Towards an international research and policy agenda. *International Journal of Educational Development*, 21, 481–97.

Miller, B. (1989). *The Multigrade Classroom: A Resource Handbook for Small, Rural Schools*. Portland: Northwest Regional Education Laboratory.

# 8

# PEDAGOGICAL LEADERSHIP IN PAKISTAN: TWO HEAD TEACHERS FROM THE NORTHERN AREAS

*Muhammad Memon and Zubeda Bana*

In the public sector in Pakistan, head teachers are recruited and promoted on the basis of their teaching rather than their leadership and management experience or qualifications. Hence, most schools are functioning without qualified and trained head teachers. A typical school head teacher is normally engaged in three kinds of tasks—academic, administrative and financial. In a study on understanding head teachers' roles in government and non-government schools in Pakistan, Simkins and his colleagues (1998) found that the majority of them tended to spend more time on administrative and financial tasks and performed their role as 'administrators' or 'chief executives' rather than as academic leaders. This suggests that leadership is missing from most of our public sector schools.

Despite their heavy administrative work, some head teachers work as educational leaders by providing academic leadership in their schools, especially in the private sector (see Memon, 2000). These head teachers have begun to transform their schools into learning organizations (Senge, 1990; 1992), which are continually engaged in expanding their capacity through generative learning; yet these schools still need to be transformed into learning communities (Mitchell and Sackney, 2000), to facilitate learning of all individuals in the school.

According to Mitchell and Sackney (2000), 'a learning community consists of a group of people who take an active, reflective, collaborative, learning-oriented, and growth-promoting approach toward the mysteries, problems, and perplexities of teaching and learning' (p. 9). Therefore, there is a need for head teachers to broaden their vision through re-conceptualization of their roles as educational leaders to transform schools into learning communities. Head teachers require a life-long learning approach for becoming 'perpetual learners' (Barth, 1997) and leaders need to develop a passion for learning. School leaders must learn about new leadership practices and discover their 'moral purpose' (Sergiovanni, 1998; Fullan, 2002b), in order to change schools into learning communities or 'professional learning communities' by creating and sharing knowledge (Fullan, 2002b).

In this chapter we first review the literature on leadership and management in order to show how they need to co-exist. Having done that, we point out a new role for school head teachers; the role of a pedagogical leader. In the final section of the chapter, we present two brief cases of pedagogical leaders in action in schools in the Northern Areas of Pakistan.

## Leadership and Management

The new millennium demands head teachers who can and will act as educational leaders for transforming schools into professional learning communities that result in teacher development and greater learning. Topping (2002) argues that many institutions or organizations have a good number of managers but do not have a good number of leaders; hence a leadership vacuum exists inside educational institutions and that has affected their institutional performance. Topping (2002) cites a viewpoint of one of the chief executive officers who differentiated between managers and leaders by saying that managers 'wait to be told what to do while leaders take initiative, figure out what has to be done, and then do it' (p. ix). This gives a loud and clear message to the policy makers to develop leaders in schools to enable them to inspire, motivate and lead others. This requires a process of unlearning old practices and developing new leadership practices through 'enlightenment, commitment, and a willingness...(to lead)' (Topping, 2002: xii).

Kouzes and Posner (1996) describe five competencies of an effective leader:

- challenging the process
- inspiring a shared vision
- enabling others to act
- modelling the way, and
- encouraging the heart.

These general competencies of leadership can generate and promote a culture of change (Fullan 2001a; 2001b) for the transformation of schools into professional learning communities. Goleman (1995) argues that leaders require intellect, technical ability and emotional maturity to lead any institution or organization. His notion of 'emotional intelligence' is based on five foundations—self-awareness, self-regulation, motivation, empathy and social skills which also seem to be the qualities of effective and enlightened leaders who are participative, encouraging and focused on the development of people. Covey (1990) highlights seven skills of effective leaders—be proactive, begin with the end in mind, put first things first, think win/win, seek first to understand then to be understood, synergize, and engage in continuous learning. Both Goleman (1995) and Covey (1990) emphasize the personal, social and moral acts of leaders who can create a culture of change and collective learning in organizations.

Goleman, cited in Fullan (2002b), mentions that emotionally intelligent leaders 'are aware of their own emotional make-up, are sensitive and inspiring to others and are able to deal with day-to-day problems as they work on more fundamental changes in the culture of the organization' (p. 414). We tend to agree with Fullan that the principal [head teacher] of the future has to be much more attuned to the big picture, much more sophisticated at conceptual thinking and focused on transforming the organization through people and teams. Leaders require new 'mental models' and shared vision to deal with the complexity of organizational change. Therefore, Fullan's (2002) work is of particular interest where he proposes a model of leadership that has 'moral purpose, understanding change, relationship building, knowledge creation and sharing, and coherence making' (p. 414).

The literature on leadership suggests that leadership styles and models vary from one context to another. Hence, leadership is a situational act; 'one size does not fit all'. This means that there is no *one* right leadership model to be followed and developed. Rather, what is required is the creation of situation-based leadership models that suit the specific environment and the institutional or organizational dynamics. Hughes et al. (2002) define leadership as 'the process of influencing an organized group toward accomplishing its goals' (p. 8). They further differentiate between management and leadership. Management deals with efficiency, planning, paperwork, procedures, regulations, control, and consistency, whereas leadership is concerned with risk-taking, creativity, change and vision. Bennis (1989) also draws some useful distinctions between managers and leaders:

- Managers administer; leaders innovate
- Managers maintain; leaders develop
- Mangers control; leaders inspire
- Managers have short-term view; leaders have along-term view
- Managers ask how and when; leaders ask what and why
- Managers imitate; leaders originate
- Managers accept the status quo; leaders challenge it.

Bennis and Nanus (1985) point out that managers 'do things right' whereas leaders 'do right things', while Kotter (1997) recommends a set of ideas for leaders: a) services to the public; b) fairness and honesty; c) teamwork for the common cause; d) untiring effort for improvement; e) courtesy and humility. This refers to the moral and educational purpose of school leadership. According to Bennis (1989), managers are concerned with the 'stability', whereas, leaders emphasize 'change'.

Looking at the above distinctions, it appears that the term management is used as a 'strategy' and leadership as a 'process' to achieve the institutional or organizational goals. It may be added that administration deals with operational matters whereas management deals with the matters at the tactical level though, generally speaking, the terms management and administration are now being used interchangeably. Hughes et al., (2002) argue that leaders must have managerial competencies to manage their institutions effectively: 'Leadership and management complement each other and both are vital to organizational success' (p. 10). Thus, both management and leadership are two sides of the same coin; they are not mutually exclusive. Whereas leaders are engaged in team-building for promoting accountability and creating a culture of shared decision-making so that everyone considers themselves part of a community of learners, managers are usually responsible for running their organizations where there is little or no sharing of power and decisions. Managers deal with the operational aspects of organizations, whereas, leaders deal with the visioning aspects. Topping (2002) suggests that in order to operate effective organizations, leaders should acquire 'managerial leadership' skills and knowledge and Memon (2002) argues for the acquisition of managerial skills for leaders. All of this suggests that effective leadership requires deep understanding of effective management and governance.

Like other practitioners in schools, head teachers initially learn to 'walk the tightrope'. Then, they gradually learn to make sense of their actions and practices and move towards maturity and stability in their thinking and actions. Later, they start demonstrating their clear vision, mission and values relating to school goals and policies. Our schools require leaders who can play a greater role in school improvement and use high leverage strategies based on high standards for themselves, as well as for others.

## Head Teachers as Pedagogical Leaders

In order to provide effective and practical leadership in schools, we need to develop head teachers as 'pedagogical leaders', with a concern for the professional and intellectual development of teachers and social and academic development of students. The success of any school is highly dependent on the quality of the leadership and school leadership has been identified as one of the major contributing factors to school improvement in both developed and less developed countries. In the context of Europe, Australia, North America and Asia, several professional development programmes are being offered to head teachers to improve their managerial and leadership skills, competence, attitudes and knowledge. Educational leaders play a most important role in managing change in schools. They are able to create schools as professional learning communities through organizational learning. Schools keep changing because of internal and external forces; therefore, head teachers must learn to work collaboratively with all stakeholders to develop and promote team-building as a first step towards organizational learning.

The head teacher's role is normally perceived as bureaucratic, visionary and entrepreneurial leadership but it is argued that this is not enough (Sergiovanni, 1998). In addition, they must make a substantial difference towards institutional capacity building if schools are to improve significantly. A prime responsibility of head teachers, then, should be to enhance teacher performance for improved student learning outcomes. They should not only expect effective performance from teachers and students, but should set high standards of performance for themselves. Leading and managing schools is not the job of just anyone; it requires a new perspective, vision and a deeper understanding of school culture along with adequate management experience. This requires a re-conceptualization of the head teachers' role as a pedagogical leader; a model which draws on the basic concept of transformational leadership (Leithwood, Tomlinson and Genge, 1996). Transformational leaders are charismatic; they possess good visioning skills, they develop emotional bonds with the staff and empower others to act on their vision and implement change. Transformational leadership is perceived as the best way to achieve school restructuring in the twenty-first century (Barnett et al., 2001).

Pedagogical leadership may be viewed in various ways. Some researchers prefer to use the term 'instructional leadership' e.g. Fink and Resnik (2001) and others use a structural model of leadership (Bolman and Deal, 1992) on the assumption that schools would improve provided head teachers bring about change in the internal structural conditions of schools. Hallinger (2004) differentiates between instructional leadership and transformational leadership. To him, the former deals with top-down approaches to school improvement, individual leadership, first order change and the latter deals with bottom-up approaches, group leadership and second order change. However, 'transformational leadership is not easier to demonstrate than instructional leadership' (Hallinger, 2004).

Despite its popularity in many parts of the world, it has been said that instructional leadership has a narrow view of teaching and learning (Fullan, 2002), whereas, pedagogical leadership has a more expansive view. MacNeill and Silcox (2003) define a pedagogical leader as one 'who has credibility with key stakeholders (teachers, students, parents, schools boards, the community, and the system administrators) because of informed school or classroom management practice and who has a high level of pedagogic knowledge and skills which, when applied in a learning environment, encourages others to pursue improved learning outcomes for students through appropriate pedagogies' (p. 18). They further mention that 'pedagogic leadership status cannot be decreed by well-intentioned educators; it is a badge of honour, earned and bestowed by colleagues...pedagogic leadership is about setting priorities and living with the dilemma of constantly needing to balance being involved in what happens in a classroom, against the demands of school management...pedagogic leadership has a 'hands on quality' (pp. 18–19). They argue that highly effective pedagogic leaders are passionate about learning and teaching.

Effective head teachers need to act as pedagogical leaders to create an enabling environment for teachers and students and be responsible for their learning and growth. Sergiovanni (1998) argues that bureaucratic, visionary and entrepreneurial leadership have failed to meet the demands of effective schools; therefore, he proposes pedagogical leadership as an effective alternative for improving schools through human capital development. According to him, 'pedagogical leadership develops human capital by helping schools become caring, focused, and inquiring communities within which teachers work together as members of a community of practice' (p. 37). He adds that 'pedagogical leadership invests in capacity building by developing social and academic capacity for students, and intellectual and professional capital for teachers' (p. 38). This kind of leadership will enhance student learning, teacher learning and classroom effectiveness. He emphasizes that leadership and learning should go together. Leaders and followers should reflect together, learn together, inquire together, and care together to form schools as professional learning communities. A modified form of Sergiovanni's (1998) concept of pedagogical leadership is presented in Figure 1.

## Two Cases of Pedagogical Leadership

Two schools in the Northern Areas of Pakistan were visited to gather data for this research. The schools are located in the extreme north of Pakistan and are characterized by isolation in a harsh, mountainous environment. A large part of the area in which the schools are located is affected by landslides which restrict mobility for much of the year. Despite rapid advancement in information technology, the area has poor communication links with other parts of Pakistan, though road and air access are both available.

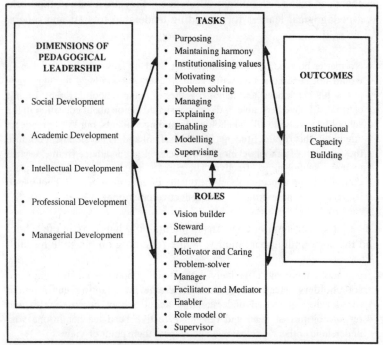

Figure1: Framework of Pedagogical Leadership (After Sergiovanni, 1998)

## Case 1: Head Teacher of a Community School

The first case is of a male head teacher of a community school. We will call him Tanveer Ahmed, though that is not his real name. At the time of the research, Tanveer had been head teacher for about two years and the school had 408 female students and 21 teachers. He described the school he inherited in these terms: 'I inherited the school where teachers used to work in isolation. Students were considered as empty vessels to be filled. Parents were considered as uneducated; therefore, less worthy. Support staff was treated as subordinates, therefore, considered as servants to obey orders…'. With these problems in mind, Tanveer set about improving the school

He has a clear vision of the purpose of education. His vision of the school is to 'work and learn together' and to share responsibilities for improving the quality of education. This notion seems quite similar to the idea of a school as a learning community. He believes that head teachers can make a significant difference if they are aware of their role as a pedagogical leaders for providing leadership to staff and others. As he said:

> No matter how powerful a head teacher is, if he lacks clarity of vision he would not become a successful head teacher. A good head teacher needs to use his head, heart and hands together to make school different. I don't claim that I have been able to develop a shared vision about education in the school by involving all stakeholders including students, but I have made an attempt in this regard. Students like this school and its development because they are part of school development process. I get an advice from everyone to make school more effective. The parents, teachers, and students share their voice and concerns about the quality of education in the school which has made me more proactive and reflective practitioner.

One of Tanveer's major concerns is maintaining harmony in the school and the surrounding community. While reflecting on his style he said:

> a school cannot run effectively without full support of all the concerned stakeholders. Head teacher has to create an enabling environment for developing shared understanding about school purpose, roles and responsibilities of head and others...Effective head teacher is one who understands others' perspective and respect their point of view.

He believes in team building for transforming his school into a learning community. To him, policies on school timings, school fees, curriculum, co-curricular activities, students' assessment, homework etc. are developed in consultation with parents and teachers. Teachers and parents are on the various committees to assist the head teacher in the overall development of the school.

He assigns top priority to building rapport among teachers, students and parents and he uses school assemblies as a means of building this rapport. He delegates tasks to teachers and students for leading school assembly proceedings. In the beginning, he was confronted with some challenges as he said:

> Out of 26 teachers, I succeeded to delegate tasks to 24 teachers. Two male teachers were found to be reluctant to accept any additional task. I tried to convince them through formal and informal conversation. As a result, I convinced one teacher who started participating in the school assembly and other ones remained reluctant but I did not surrender. School has a policy on fairness, transparency, merit, equity, access, quality, tolerance, respect

for each others' views, and respect for teachers and parents. Corporal punishment is strongly prohibited in schools which is supported by parents and teachers. Poor students are not denied of their right of education.

He claims that in his school there is a strong sense of support from parents and the wider community. For example, teachers organized a Mothers' Day in which almost 500 mothers participated. Morning school assembly proceedings gave him confidence. He learnt that students had a lot of potential to perform both socially and academically. Teachers are engaged in co-curricular activities and as an integral part of his professional development activities, he visits classrooms and provides support to teachers in the school. He seems to have created a climate of trust between himself and teachers that enables them to understand each other's perspectives. His approach is clearly 'learning together' for making a learning community in the school.

Tanveer is concerned about the low status of teachers in society and financial constraints that affect their performance. While reflecting on his role as a motivator, he remarked:

> The majority of the teachers are strongly motivated but sometime their level of motivation goes down due to their low social status in the society. Teacher salaries are low to such extent that in the second week of the month, they start borrowing money from their relatives to meet their family members needs. I am well conversant with the idea of school improvement and school effectiveness. I do not have any major problem in academic matters since my teachers are completely charged with their full enthusiasm and passion but I become helpless when my teachers face financial crises. I always think how to change climate of the school. I strongly believe in sustainable changes. To me, it is an attitude not the aptitude, which guides people towards success of any sustainable change.

For Tanveer, a head teacher can become successful if he works like a problem solver, firefighter and entrepreneur. He said: 'I see educational leadership as an investment in capacity building of teachers and students for developing school as a learning community... I started selling the idea of building community of learners in schools'.

He thinks that the head teacher should be flexible in his style so that he is able to create synergy for achieving the planned results. He found that teachers are willing and committed but need academic support so that they are able to solve their pedagogical matters more effectively. While reflecting on his leadership style, he said:

> I see myself as a critical friend of teachers and others. My doors are always open for parents, teachers and students. I do not provide solution to them but I work with them to get solutions to their problems. This approach has especially helped my staff to make the first attempt to solve their problems rather than coming to me every time. They don't hesitate sharing with me and others any academic problem, especially the subject matter.

According to Tanveer, pedagogical leadership does not happen by chance. He learnt how to 'walk the tightrope'. The qualities of pedagogical leadership are to be developed through working with people rather than applying any scientific formula. As he said, 'I always felt that a majority of head teachers are normally thrown into the field and as a result they are not able to perform their roles effectively'. He added,

> I decided to begin with 'stock-taking' of the present situation, it took me three to four weeks to assess 'where the school is now'. I found that the situation was not dismal and hopeless. Many young teachers wanted to change their existing practices and students' talents and potentials were tremendous. Most importantly, adequate support from the school system was available.

He decided to start with the willing workers and build rapport with them. He engaged senior teachers to discuss the school mission but he found that they sometimes started imposing their ideas. As he described the process: 'I waited for the right time for making intervention. My patience and firm determination helped me a lot to change the current scenario of apathy and ignorance. I started identifying and engaging like-minded teachers first'.

His 'stock-taking' exercise enabled him to diagnose several problems such as indiscipline, lack of punctuality among teachers and students, teacher-centered classes, students' passive participation, inter-teacher rivalries, absence of collegiality among teachers, lack of trust between teachers and administration, a gap in parents-teachers relationship, lack of professional expertise among teachers, lack of organizing co-curricular activities, unimpressive results of public examinations and lack of computer literacy in teachers and students.

To begin with, Tanveer delegated duties for conducting the school assembly to those teachers who volunteered and later asked others to participate as well. He cited an example of how he handled a particular problem with one of the teachers who initially resisted a request to conduct the school assembly. He negotiated with the teacher and eventually agreed to take a lead role in the school assembly. The teacher arranged the school assembly well and got appreciation from Tanveer. Later, the teacher bought a microphone system and donated it to the school for conducting more effective school assemblies. He publicly announced his donation to the school, which was considered as a major achievement and the teacher became a role model for others. Tanveer said:

> Teachers' attitude, regularity and punctuality make a real difference in the school. Teachers' isolation is broken down by discussing the material to be delivered next day in the assembly. Parents have noticed significant changes in the school. The most difficult teacher has now became the most vocal spokesperson for me. I also provide necessary explanation and guidance to teachers in their own professional development as well as their students' development.

Tanveer considers himself a pedagogical leader because he believes in capacity building through intellectual development of teachers. He is engaged in building capacity by developing social and academic capital of students and intellectual and professional capital for teachers. His role is to provide resources to enhance the teaching and learning process. He believes that the head teacher should spend more time on coordination, engage staff in building the vision and mission, provide an enabling atmosphere for translating the schools' vision into reality, motivating the team to put energy into planning, organizing, mobilizing resources and empowerment. He considers himself as a visionary leader. To him 'pedagogical leadership is concerned with building teams in schools. Teachers have started taking initiatives to strengthen and promote a culture of collective learning in the school'.

He was the first head teacher recruited on merit. He took it as a challenge and started working on bringing about changes. While introducing changes, he faced enormous difficulties. As he mentioned: 'I faced difficulties from my school colleagues. There are many senior male teachers in the school, who challenged my authority and power. Parents were also worried about me as a young and less experienced head teacher. Hence, I entered the school with resistance. I thought I would not be able to see my dream into reality by converting this school into an effective school, I succeeded'.

## Case 2: Head Teacher of a Government Girls' Secondary School

Hajira Bibi (not her real name) is the female head teacher of one of the largest government girls' secondary schools in Northern Areas. The school has a purpose-built building, with an enrolment of 850 girls and 25 female teachers. The majority of parents are illiterate. The school's mission is to serve humanity and promote values of tolerance and empathy.

Hajira was promoted to head teacher on the basis of her teaching experience and she joined the school without any orientation about school management or her role and responsibilities as an educational leader. She struggled to manage her school during the first year. Her focus had been on administrative rather than academic tasks which is common for head teachers in Pakistan (Simkins et al., 1998; 2003). In 2001, Hajira was nominated by the Department to attend a two-week professional development workshop at the Professional Development Centre (PDCN), in Gilgit. The workshop focused on themes such as re-conceptualisation of roles and responsibilities, reflective practice, action learning, understanding the purpose of education and curriculum, understanding teaching and management styles, understanding learners and learning styles and understanding issues related to students' assessment. She was encouraged to examine her current practices and discovered how both positive and negative experiences shaped her leadership style. She also conducted a small-scale action research project in the school. The workshop helped to develop and broaden her perspective as an educational leader.

Hajira is aware that school is not just the building but functions as a social unit of the community. Hence, her focus had been to impart quality education in the area. She created a sense of cooperation and collaboration among parents and teachers and sought their advice on academic and management issues. She believes that her democratic management style enabled the school to grow as a learning community.

Being a female head teacher, she struggled a lot for seeking recognition as an educational leader, in and out of school. Nevertheless, her dynamic personality and firm determination helped her to succeed in her mission. To her, the head teacher is the key to establish, maintain and transform schools into learning communities. As a pedagogical leader, she thought her prime responsibility is to provide maximum opportunities to all individuals in the school to learn and grow.

She believes that her participation in the two-week workshop was a turning point in transforming herself into a proactive and reflective professional. She is able to 'do first things first' in consultation with teachers and parents. She works closely with parents and teachers to develop a shared understanding about the overall purpose of education, the role of the school and its teachers. To her: 'A common goal for everyone in the school is how to improve students learning so that they should not be deprived of quality education. Parents and teachers work together to develop and review schools, long-term goals'. She feels that she has been instrumental in bringing parents and teachers together for the common goal.

Hajira believes that the most important person in school is the student, not the head teacher. Although the head teacher provides opportunities for teachers, parents and others to transform the school into a learning community, she provides opportunities for everyone to become a learner. She said: 'I strongly feel that head teachers need to be consensus builders and facilitators more than instructors and directors. The process of re-conceptualization of my role has compelled me to reach the level of maturity and realize the goals of pedagogical leadership. I have vision, mission, commitment and insight into my role. It is not the game of power and status, but it is the game of building relationships with all stakeholders, including schools, through mutual respect and trust'.

She seems to have succeeded in motivating and inspiring teachers and other community members. She claims that qualifications or experience are not essential for motivating teachers but the head teacher's commitment and understanding about school development will definitely help him or her to influence teachers. As she said: 'I don't direct teachers but seek their advice in day-to-day management affairs. I do delegate power to teachers and others to get things done. This has helped my teachers to become more willing and participative in educational and management matters'.

She has an ability to use metaphors to explain the purpose of education, childrens' learning and teachers' roles. She is able to relate new learning and ideas to her own school context. She feels a tremendous change in her attitude towards problem solving. She has developed a team of like-minded people and shares her thoughts for improving the teaching and learning situation in school. She said: 'My experience working with teachers suggests that if you provide any solution to teachers' problems it would not change their practice until they are engaged in seeking solutions to their own problems. I prefer to act as a 'problem shooter' rather than a 'problem solver'. In the beginning, teachers had some difficulties with my approach but now they have realized that somebody else's solution will not help them to change their practices'.

Hajira has been able to develop useful learning materials. She had learnt a few innovative ideas by attending workshops at the Professional Development Centre and provides on-going professional support to teachers on different matters. She explained that:

> Teachers decided to prepare learning material for classes 1-5 in all subjects but I advised them not to take all classes at the same time. I provided all necessary support in conducting brainstorming sessions with them to develop the overall proposal. We discussed this proposal with parents and the concerned government officials which was highly appreciated. Students brought some junk material from their homes. Parents were also requested to identify some relevant material available at their homes. It was encouraging to see that not only the material aids were prepared for teaching within a month but also tremendous learning occurred in classroom. The classes were full of materials; corridors were decorated with students' displays. Social study was taught outside the classroom in real community. Parents were invited to sit in their children's classes. The school became a place of learning for the whole community. Students' dropout ratio substantially decreased. The school is considered as one of the best schools. Students, teachers and head teacher received an 'award for excellence' from Education Department, the Government of Northern Areas. Thus, our school has become a pioneer institution for the development of material and quality education.

Hajira has developed a good rapport with the community at large. She invites parents, especially mothers, to visit the school and explains to them school plans for improving education and infrastructure of the school. By involving parents, she has managed to solicit their support as spokespersons for the school. She also shares information with students, teachers and concerned government officials. Some parents volunteered themselves to construct and renovate toilets and provide drinking water. Hajira mentioned that 'if there is a will, there is a way. Although parents have limited resources, they would like to contribute towards school development. Head teachers should not feel shy about sharing problems with the community otherwise the purpose of education would be defeated. There are great opportunities for head teachers and teachers to collaborate with the community to make school a real centre of community learning'.

Initially, she faced a lot of problems. Nevertheless, her firm determination and strong leadership enabled her to overcome the issue of teachers' passive resistance by working closely with them. She organizes professional development workshops for teachers on a weekly basis. Reflecting on the outcomes of the workshops she said: 'without trust you cannot build effective teams to make the most difficult things possible. Change in classroom teaching has brought about change in teachers' and students' beliefs. Parents also feel a change in their children's attitudes. Children are seen at home doing their homework. They also talk with their parents regarding their activities in school. Mothers seem happy to visit the school'.

She shares innovative ideas with teachers in staff meetings. Teachers seem ready to organize a Mothers' Day function. This has developed good rapport between teachers and parents. Hajira provides maximum opportunities for girls to participate in different programmes that have enabled them to develop their self-confidence.

Hajira believes that her students should get quality education and feel honoured to be the students of this school. She uses several strategies to develop a civic sense amongst students. She has formed a school council represented by students who are engaged in numerous managerial and leadership tasks. As she said: 'the government schools have lost their credibility not being quality education institution but we would like to ensure that all government schools are not equal. We would like to make this school different from others in a way that our students should promote a sense of collective learning among themselves. I think it all depends on the head of school. I don't claim that I am the role model for parents, teachers and students but we are in the process of influencing parents' thinking about their role in the school. I must say the parents are good role models for us. I have learnt a lot from them. My only advice to teachers and students is to respect others' views'.

She added that the style of senior government officers is still traditional and they see themselves as 'boss'. This needs to change since they have a critical role to play in the overall school development.

She concentrates on improving students' learning by enhancing teachers' classroom practices and has developed a systematic process of observation of classes by herself, parents and fellow teachers. Since the majority of parents are illiterate, they do not focus on academic aspects, however, they give critical inputs in moral and ethical issues related to girls' education in the community. She said:

> My style of supervision is clinical that enables teachers to improve their pedagogical content knowledge. Teachers now put less emphasis on chalk-talk method of teaching. Students have become inquisitive about observing, knowing and analyzing things. Teachers have introduced creative thinking in their classrooms which needs more efforts and time. I also work with teachers on the development of learning material and activities. Students' questions are very interesting which have compelled teachers to come with preparation in the classroom. Teachers and students' interaction is getting momentum to learn from each other. Now, teachers have also realized that they can learn a lot from their students who come up with different prior learning experiences.

## Discussion and Conclusion

Although the two head teachers are from different school systems; government and non-government, they both operate within the framework of pedagogical leadership. They seem to have been performing ten tasks identified by Sergiovanni (1998) — purposing, maintaining harmony, institutionalizing values, motivating, problem solving, managing, explaining, enabling, modeling, and supervising. They have performed a variety of roles to make their schools into professional learning communities. In addition, both head teachers deal with the tasks related to management which is the major demand of school systems. Both head teachers seem to have adopted innovative approaches to create a sense of community of professionals. They have both been able to create positive relationships amongst teachers, parents and students through non-traditional ways or what Sergiovanni (1998) terms, 'a narrative of social covenants'.

Their focus seems to be on teachers' professional growth for improving student learning. There are clearly common roles and tasks between these two head teachers; perhaps because of the influence of professional development programmes conducted at PDCN. These head teachers seem to be aware of their roles and responsibilities and related challenges and have learnt how to address these challenges and find their own ways and means. They seem to have a constellation of skills and knowledge of pedagogical leadership focusing on enhancing student learning outcomes. In these two cases, the head teachers seem to have assigned high priority to improving students' learning through enhancing teachers' classroom practices and their management tasks have not affected their ability to act as pedagogical leaders.

Both head teachers tend to focus on 'capital development' of teachers and students to improve students' learning. In the context of Europe, North America, Australia and some parts of Asia, head teachers' daily work is supported by deputy heads, but in Pakistan, especially in government schools, there is no budgeted position of a deputy who could assist head teachers in their various roles and responsibilities. Although this is the case in both schools, however, the head teachers have performed their role as pedagogical leaders through delegation of tasks and power to teachers and parents in their schools. This also reveals that both head teachers seem to have clarity of their roles and responsibilities. Both head teachers are working in the Northern Areas of Pakistan where there is not much professional support except their participation in some workshops or short courses in educational leadership and management at PDCN. It seems that both head teachers have benefited from PDCN courses, but need wider networking to share their experiential learning and challenges with head teachers in the other parts of country. This will also lead to creating professional learning communities in schools by sharing and creating knowledge.

Fullan (2002b) highlights the importance of knowledge and its links with the role of organizational leadership. Most organizations do not have the habit of sharing and creating knowledge. Some organizations have difficulty using new knowledge. Fullan (2002b) supports the idea of 'giving' and 'receiving' knowledge and considers this as critical to improvement. He further argues about sharing knowledge in organizations: '...change leaders work on changing the context, helping create new settings conducive to learning and sharing that learning' (p. 411). He suggests that professional learning communities can be developed through sharing and creating knowledge which lead to the development of teacher learning. Fullan (2002b) suggests that 'We now must raise our sights and focus on principals as leaders in a culture of change and the associated conditions that will make this possible on a large scale' (p. 419).

It is worth mentioning that due to clear vision, both head teachers have a 'big picture' of their schools though they have yet to develop a strategic plan for school improvement. It was found that both head teachers have taken several initiatives for transforming their schools into professional learning communities, but there does not seem to be any systematic school improvement plan and its monitoring and documentation. Beach and Lindahl (2004) mention that educational leaders must lead schools through school improvement plans. De Grauwe (2000) also argues that quality of teaching and learning is strongly influenced by the quality of leadership of head teachers. Both head teachers seemed to have all possible qualities of being effective head teachers (see MacNeill and Silcox, 2003; Fullan 2002b). They also engage teachers and parents, creating an enabling environment to support school improvement initiatives. Fullan (2002a) terms such leadership as high quality leadership. We tend to agree with Fullan (2002a) that massive attention should be given to the creation of leadership in schools. Fullan, (2002b) mentions that the moral purpose of leadership is to play a larger role in transforming and sustaining system change.

Fullan (2002b) argues that sustained improvement of schools is not possible unless the whole system is moving forward. He further argues that sustainability will not happen unless there are radically more enlightened policies and incentives: 'We should select leaders in terms of their capacity to create conditions under which other leaders will flourish, leaving a continuing effect beyond their term' (Fullan, 2002a:7). Finally, Sergiovanni (1998) reminds us that the head of a school should be committed to serving its purposes and acting as a guardian to protect the institutional integrity of the school. Policy makers and school trustees need to recognize the importance of pedagogical leadership for developing important strategies, practices and policies to improve schools in Pakistan.

## References

Barth, R. (1997). Foreword. In M. Fullan *What's Worth Fighting For in the Principalship: Strategies For taking Charge in the School Principalship*. Toronto: Ontario Public School Teachers' Federation.

Bennis, G. (1989). *On becoming a leader*. Reading, MA.: Addison-Wesley.

Bennis, G. & Nanus, B. (1985). *Leaders: The Strategies For Taking Charge*. NY: Harper and Row.

Barnett, K., McCormick, J. & Conners, R. (2001). 'Transformational Leadership in Schools: Panacea, Placebo or Problem. *Journal of Educational Administration*, 39(1), 24–46.

Bolman, L. & Deal, T. (1992). *Reframing Organizations*. San Francisco: Jossey-Bass.

Covey, S. (1990). *The Seven Habits of Highly Effective People*. NY: Fireside.

De Grauwe, A. (2000). 'Improving School Management: A Promise and a Challenge. International Institute for Educational Planning Newsletter, 18(4), 1–3.
Fink, E & Resnik, L. (2001). Developing Principals as Instructional Leaders. *Phi Delta Kappan*, 82, 598–606.
Fullan, M. (2001a). *Leading in a Culture of Change*. San Francisco: Jossey-Bass.
Fullan, M. (2001b). *The New Meaning of educational Change* (3rd ed.). NY: Teachers College Press.
Fullan, M. (2002a). 'Leadership and sustainability'. *Principal Leadership*, 3(4),1–8.
Fullan, M. (2002b). 'The Role of Leadership in the Promotion of Knowledge Management in Schools'. *Teachers and Teaching: Theory and Practice*, 8(3/4), 409–19.
Goleman, D. (1995). *Emotional intelligence*. NY: Bantam Books.
Hallinger, P. (2004, January). *Reflections on the Practices of Instructional and Transformational Leadership*. Paper Presented at the International Congress for School Effectiveness and School Improvement, Rotterdam, Netherlands.
Hughes, R., Ginnett, R. & Curphy, G. (2002). *Leadership: Enhancing the Lessons of Experience*. Boston: McGraw-Hill Irwin.
Kotter, J. (1997). *Matsushista leadership*. NY: Free Press.
Kouzes, J. & Possner, B. (1996). *The Leadership Challenge*. San Francisco: Jossey-Bass.
Leithwood, K., Tomlinson, D. & Genge, M. (1996). 'Transformational Leadership'. In K. Leithwood, J. Chapman, D. Corson, P. Hallinger, & A. Hart, (Eds.). *International Handbook of Educational Leadership and Administration,* – Vol. 2 (pp. 785–840). Rotterdam: Kulwer.
MacNeill, N. & Silcox, S. (2003). 'Pedagogic Leadership: Developing an Inclusive School Culture of learning'. *The Practising Administrator*, 2, 18–22.
Memon, M. (2000, January). *Preparing School Leadership for the Twenty-first Century*. Paper presented to the International Congress for School Effectiveness and Improvement, Hong Kong.
Mitchell, C. & Sackney, L. (2000). *Profound improvement: Building Capacity for the Learning Community*. Lisse: Swetz and Zeitlinger.
Senge. P. (1990). *The Fifth Discipline: The Art and Practice of the Learning Organization*. NY: Doubleday.
Senge, P. (1992). 'Can Schools Become Learning Organizations'? *Educational Leadership*, 50(3), 41–4.
Sergiovanni, T. (1998). 'Leadership as Pedagogy, Capital Development and School Effectiveness'. *International Journal Leadership in Education*, 1(1), 37–46.
Simkins, T, Garrett, V., Memon, M. & Nazir, R. (1998). 'The Role Perceptions of Government and Non-government Head Teachers in Pakistan'. *Educational Management and Administration*, 26(2), 131–46.
Simkins, T, Sisum, C. & Memon, M. (2003). 'School Leadership in Pakistan: Exploring the Head Teachers' Role. *School Effectiveness and School Improvement*, 14(3), 275–91.
Topping, P. (2002). *Managerial Leadership*. New York: McGraw-Hill.

# 9

# PARENTS AS PARTNERS IN THE LEARNING COMMUNITY

*Qamar Safdar*

A school door must open from both sides
(From a statement by Jana Matousova, school principal,
Czech Republic, interviewed by Walterova, 1996)

The connection between home and school is referred to in various ways such as parent involvement, home-school relations or community involvement in schools. In this chapter, I want to conceptualize that connection as a 'partnership' with parents being viewed as partners with teachers in the education of children. Parents send their children to school with the expectation that the children will learn. Schools teach the children and send them back to their families where it is assumed that they will be provided with the support that they need to grow and develop. This may be seen as a partnership, in which school and home share the responsibility for the child's education. The idea of such a partnership is one that has been the focus of attention and debate for quite some time, though it is not without tensions and problems in many countries. For example, whilst it is generally accepted in England that parental involvement in schools is in the children's best educational interests, Edwards and Alders (2000) explored the perspective of children and young people and found that they sometimes do not want their parents to be involved. In Pakistan, a large number of Parent-Teacher Associations and School Management Committees have been formed but a recent newspaper report (Amir, 2004) suggests that many are ineffective due to non-representative membership or are non-functional, existing only on paper. However, the report adds that those that are functional are delivering marked results in reducing teacher absenteeism and improving school facilities. Troublesome though it may be, few would argue that there should be no connection between home and school, so my purpose in this chapter is to explore some ways to strengthen the relationship between teachers and parents.

## The Nature of Partnership

Understanding the nature of 'partnership' is the key to developing the idea of parents as partners with teachers. A dictionary definition tells us that a partnership is 'a relationship between two people, organizations or countries that work together regularly' (Langman's Dictionary, p. 1032). Although 'partnership' often implies equality in a relationship, in the context of schools and parents it may not necessarily be so. Rather, different, but nonetheless valuable roles played by each partner might be a more useful idea than equality. It is usually the school that plays the more dominant role, though in certain situations, it is the parents who dominate.

Bray (2003), in a paper titled 'Community partnerships in Education: Dimensions variations and implications', speaks of two terms related to but not as strong as partnership: 'involvement' and 'participation'. Both involvement and participation are weaker forms of connection whereas partnership denotes a shared responsibility. According to Bray, 'Partners share responsibility for a joint activity, whereas participants may merely cooperate in someone else's activity'. Perhaps it is appropriate in many schools to begin with involvement, then move to participation and ultimately a partnership.

The significance of partnerships is well expressed in the synthesized report following the World Conference on Education for All:

> Whether through new organizational structures or through reopening existing structures to include a basic education component, local and national partnerships can help provide materials, facilities and personnel to meet the basic educational challenge. A special benefit of this broadening of participation is to focus greater public attention on educational issues and to establish a stronger societal commitment to the principles of the World Declaration (Windham, 1992:3).

## Historical Perspective

The concept of partnership is not new. From a historical perspective, Bray (2000) shows that prior to the twentieth century, education of children was mostly provided by families or religious bodies. It was in the nineteenth, and up to the mid-twentieth century in some countries, that the government started taking responsibility for education and schools were established for this purpose. This notion found impetus in the 1948 United Nations Universal Declaration of Human Rights including the clause (Article 20) that elementary education should be compulsory. This was followed by a similar clause in the 1959 Declaration of the Rights of the Child (Principle 7). It became the responsibility of the State to take the lead in education. But by the 1980s, due to the inefficiency of government schools in some countries, privatization was favoured because it is more client-centered. The government in low income countries welcomed the private sector in sharing some of the responsibility. This perspective was reflected in the 1990 Jomtein Declaration which called for strengthened partnerships. Three years later, it was reflected in the Delhi Declaration (clause 20):

> ...education is and must be, a social responsibility encompassing governments, families, communities and non-governmental organizations alike, it requires the commitment and participation of all in a grand alliance that transcends diverse opinions and political positions.

The role of the State underwent certain shifts both in developed and less developed countries. In England, the Plowden Report in 1967 stressed the importance of parental support for children in schools. A movement of Parent Teacher Association (PTAs) gathered strength and focused on cooperation between schools and homes. The 1980 Education Act took reform further still, requiring schools throughout the country to have governing bodies that included parents (Kogan et al., 1986).

In less developed countries, the context was quite different but at least some policy makers considered links between schools and community to be important for financial, pedagogic, political and other reasons. In the 1980s and 1990s the non-government organizations (NGOs) started gaining prominence, but not all of them had strong credibility. Thus, the historical perspective at the end of the 1990s gave partners working either independently or with governments, a much greater place than had been possible a decade earlier.

## The Problematic Nature of School-Parent Relationships

In Pakistan, the notion of school-parent relationships and its significance in the education of children is vaguely understood and there are many misconceptions and fears surrounding the relationships. In our educational context there is a constant tug-of-war between the school and the wider community. A great deal of mistrust is evident and it is a sorry state of affairs. Often the school only has contact with the parents through a parent-teacher meeting to inform them of their child's progress, to berate a parent whose child has broken school rules, to pay the school fees or any other dues, or invite them to a social gathering which is very formal and lacks personal communication. The parents often do not cooperate given the circumstances under which they are called. They do not feel satisfied or wanted and are quick to defend their point of view. The parent-teacher connection, instead of blossoming into a reciprocal relationship, has been stuck in a quagmire of mistrust, lack of clarity of understanding and holding on to boundaries of their own making. It is usually 'Your child' or 'My child' and not very often, 'Our child'.

The relationship between parent and teacher has never been smooth because there is a constant power struggle between parental influence and school influence in the lives of children. As Bastiani and Wolfendale (1996) state: 'Family-school relations by definition touch upon the boundaries where professional confidence and parent responsibilities meet, often exposing raw nerves on both sides' (p. 2). Whilst teachers have historically tried to keep parents out of the school, parents are now a force to be reckoned with and have become established on the educational scene (Wolfendale, 1993). Research and practice have demonstrated how effective parents are in supporting their children's learning and well-being. Many parents want to be recognized as responsible partners in education to ensure that the best interests of their children are realized.

However, this is not always the case. Parents have not always been receptive to invitations to come in to the school, or participate in school-home projects. Baker (1987) says:

We often talk about the partnership in education. Of course parents have a right to expect schools to provide good education, and that is why we understand radical reforms of the education system. But perhaps we lay insufficient stress on the responsibilities of parents in that partnership. Teaching is a difficult enough task, made even more difficult when parents don't take their responsibilities seriously enough (p. 111).

In most developing countries, the parent-teacher associations (PTAs) have been working with the aim of collecting resources to help the teachers and to disseminate information. The PTA is used as a platform to inform parents about their child's and the school's progress. It also involves them in social functions and gains their support to collect resources. Many schools are reluctant to involve parents beyond this realm. Some teachers are wary of parents' intrusion into their domain and suspicious of parents' intentions; the common refrain is 'We do not want to open a Pandora's Box'.

## Rationale for Parent Involvement

Perhaps the fundamental question that we need to probe is the rationale for parental involvement in schools. In a chapter titled, 'The advent of parents in education: a review of recent developments', Wolfendale (1993) says, 'All parents care about their children's welfare and well being' (p. 7). This is exhibited in a variety of ways. Generally, parents want to do what is best for their children. They want to cooperate and respond to invitations to participate in school if they can see a benefit for their child. Since parents are the first teachers of their children, they have vital information and insights about them which are most helpful for teachers. Involving parents provides schools with extra human resources to help the teachers in all sorts of ways, from raising funds to assisting in the classroom. It helps build bridges between home learning and school learning.

The influence of the family on the child's education has been mentioned by many writers. For example, Grotevant (1989) expresses four levels of analysis of the influences and effects of the family upon child development: the individual; dyadic relationships within the family; the whole family system; and the interface of the family and its contexts. Berk (1989) lists five functions of the family, which influences children's development: reproduction; economic devices; societal order; socialization and emotional support. Dunn (1989) asserts that, 'research indicates that the familiar world of the family, and especially conversation with an affectionate parent, provide contexts of special value for very young childrens' intellectual development' (p. 23). The research evidence that she cites is that of Tizard and Hughes (1984), which revealed much about the discourse between parent and child, as well as her own and a colleague's research into the development of children's understanding of feelings, motives and social rules. The point to note is that we must not overlook the unique characteristics of the different though complementary settings in which children learn.

Whilst parents have a lot to contribute to their children's education, they are not to be seen as merely duplicating the role of the teacher. Topping (1986) emphasizes, 'Instead of working to make parents pale mechanistic shadows of teachers, operating some transplanted fragment of 'professional' technique, modern projects focus much more on the unique contribution of parents to the development of their children — enhancing the naturalistic skills of parents and taking their views and priorities very much into account' (p. 38).

## The Idea of a School-Parent Partnership

Given the problematic nature of the relationship between parents and teachers, it is felt that a new concept is needed to put it on to a more positive and constructive footing. If schools are to be transformed into learning communities, parent-teacher relationships also need to be transformed. That is where the idea of the partnership comes in. Whilst this is not a new idea, it is evident that considerable work needs to be done to make it a widespread reality in schools. As Sanders and Epstein (1998) put it: 'In order for schools in any nation to effectively educate *all* youth, families and communities must become partners in the process' (p. 483).

Pugh (1989:104) defines partnership as 'a working relationship that is characterized by a shared sense of purpose, mutual respect and the willingness to negotiate. This implies a sharing of information, responsibility, skills, decision-making and accountability'. Such a definition is a useful starting point in our consideration of parents as partners with teachers in a learning community. Epstein (1995 cited in Sanders and Epstein, 1998) has identified six types of involvement between school and home that are important for underpinning the idea of a partnership. These are: 1) parenting—helping all families establish home environments that support children as students and helping schools understand families; 2) communicating—designing and conducting effective forms of two-way communication about school programmes and children's progress; 3) volunteering—recruiting and organizing help and support for classrooms, school functions and student activities; 4) learning at home—providing information, ideas and opportunities to families about how to help students at home with academic decisions, homework, and curriculum-related activities; 5) decision-making—including parents in school governance, and 6) collaborating with community—identifying and integrating resources and services from the community to strengthen and support schools, students and their families, and from schools, families and students to support the community (p. 483). Although most schools, especially in developing countries, are not implementing many of these six types of involvement, there are some schools where strong partnerships exist. They exist in the form of school management committees, parents' associations or village education committees in different regions and countries (e.g. Govinda and Diwan, 2003, detail the situation in five states in India and Bastiani and Wolfendale, 1996, provide coverage of the situation in Great Britain).

Bray (2003) emphasized the importance of partnerships between school and community and pointed out that each situation is different so a great deal of flexibility is required—what works in one setting may not work in another and what works at one point in time may not work later. He enunciated seven general principles that help to explain how partnerships may be developed:

1. Partnerships need trust (and this is built on positive relationships).
2. Partnerships need long-term commitment.
3. Partnerships need clear and mutually accepted goals.
4. Partners must focus on both big and small pictures.
5. Partnerships need nurturing.
6. Partnerships are relationships between individuals as well as institutions.
7. Genuine partnerships involve much more than mere contribution of finances.

Developing such partnerships is, however, no easy task and research from a number of countries points to some of the difficulties. Based on research in Australia, Crump and Eltis (1995 cited in Sanders and Epstein, 1998) remind us that 'there are deeply ingrained individual and institutional histories that need to be addressed for good partnerships to develop. These include some teachers' perceptions of a lack of support or interest from the home, and some parents' negative experiences with education, either their own or their children's' (p. 493).

With goodwill on both sides and the best interests of the children at heart, it is possible to overcome such difficulties and build constructive partnerships. Sanders and Epstein (1998) state that: 'In country after country, research, development and evaluation reports indicate that barriers are beginning to be dismantled and that schools are developing successful partnerships with families and communities' (p. 494).

## An Incident in Home-School Relations

Some years ago, I was the principal of a school in Karachi where I worked for around ten years. Every year, we would contact parents in specific circumstances such as admission, submission of fees or complaints about their children. Such times were often a source of depression, for unwittingly, the parents would blame the teacher straight away for any of their child's misdemeanors. On special occasions such as concerts, debates and observance of religious functions, we would invite parents to the school and these were much happier times.

I vividly recall an incident of a boy studying in Class 8 entering the school premises with the skin loosely hanging from the nape of his neck and bleeding profusely. On enquiry I came to know his father, who had come home on holiday, was angry with his child for allowing some creases to remain on the bed after spreading a bed sheet. When the child pointed out that there were just a few creases, the father took out his belt and beat the child. I decided to talk it over with his mother to influence the father to be gentle with the child. But I could hardly say a word, for the mother was already sporting a black eye. I ventured to approach the father but he protested that he was the innocent victim of a vile campaign and he could do as he pleased with his child. I reminded him gently that the school also has an interest in his child for the child's well being is also the well being of the school.

It was in connection with this incident, which I shared with my senior management of the school and with my teachers, that we realized the need to have a closer relationship between the school and home for the betterment of the child. As a small initiative, we decided to involve parents who were willing to spare some hours to take sessions in the subjects of their choice as a standby for a teacher who was absent. The form we designed carried both the options, voluntary and paid services for just two hours, twice a week, voluntary or paid according to their needs. At first, we did not get a strong response but at least it was a beginning. Twelve forms came back in which three were voluntary and the rest to be paid.

The teachers and the management decided that preferably these parents should handle classes in which their children were studying as a morale booster for their respective children. It worked like magic, for the other children not wanting to be left out, motivated their parents to also spare some time to handle their classes when their teachers were absent. But we realized that though it is quite easy to take an initiative, it needs a lot of hard work to keep it going. We had to hold some orientation sessions for these parents in handling classes. Some were adequately qualified, though some had barely finished high school. Still, the interest to learn was paramount in them. To an extent, this liaison catered to quite a few needs of the school and helped to solve the teacher absence problem, yet it had a long way to go before we could claim it was a complete success.

## Changing Times and Building Partnerships

With the changing times, the schools realize that they cannot work in isolation. They need to involve the parents for the common concern of both parents and school is the student. The crucial influence of parents upon their children's educational achievements has been widely recognized but at times they do not get the required support from the school. Now it is the school's task to involve the community in such a way that they are a part of the school. Jones (1993:49) suggests that a true partnership between home and school can bring about:

- Positive attitudes
- Positive self image
- Improved performance
- Improved effort
- Improved motivation
- Support for teaching

- Informed help from parents
- Better parental understanding
- A shared purpose and belonging.

To achieve this support, the school has to nurture and develop these relationships. It is vital that schools do all they can to ensure that parents work with them for the benefit of the children. Dean (2001) rightly advocates, 'Parents are their children's first teachers and should be regarded as partners in their children's education'. With this perspective the child, after being admitted in the school, becomes 'our' child and it would be a milestone in our relationship with parents and the community at large, if this was generally accepted.

However, it will not happen instantly and must be seen as a gradual process. The first step would be for school heads to change their perspective and try to come out of their fears and threats of thinking of parents as problems. The attitude of most school heads needs to change when dealing with parents. A good example of a positive attitude was at the 1999 International Conference for School Effectiveness and Improvement (ICSEI) Conference in San Antonio, USA, when the principal of a school from Melbourne, Australia shared an anecdote of his initiative to bridge the school-parent divide. Every day for half an hour before school time he would stand at the school gate and greet the parents with a smile and enquire about their welfare. He also made it a point to telephone parents to congratulate them on their child's success; be it just neat class work or getting good grades. Within a week, he had developed good relationships with the parent community, which positively affected the progress of the school.

Care and concern on the part of the school builds lasting relationships and its impact is visible on the students. In the Advanced Diploma in Education: Leadership and Management course at AKU-IED, I have had many discussions with teachers about this issue. One teacher expressed her feelings about how she perceived this school-parent relationship. Using the analogy of a light bulb she said 'when both the wires were properly connected the bulb would light up'. Similarly, when the school-home partnership was well set the students' faces would light up. But when there was a wedge dividing them, the student's face drooped in despair. Another teacher envisioned the future school as 'A Family Friendly School' (see Figure 1).

Teachers may also benefit from increased parental involvement as parents become more aware and supportive of classroom activities.

### Figure 1: Family Friendly School

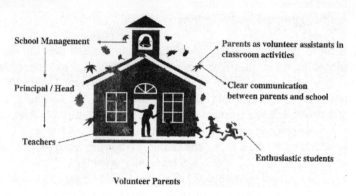

Staff development programmes could include how to involve parents in the classroom or conduct positive and meaningful parent-teacher conferences. Teachers can call on the voluntary support of parents in classroom activities. It could also help to solve the problem of large classes in developing countries.

Parents are a rich resource that can be tapped to assist with various school activities as shown in Figure 2. This was the result of an activity done by the course participants of the Advanced Diploma class when they were asked to identify possible areas where parents could help voluntarily. First, they listed them out in their respective groups, and finally, a consensus was built on the board.

Some of the activities mentioned above have actually been tried out in their respective schools. A head teacher of a private school mentioned that some parents who were good cooks volunteered to teach the students cooking as well as stitching in the Girl's Branch. In the Boy's Branch, woodwork, clay work and sports were regular features. It is also interesting that these were community schools where initial trust and knowing one another goes a long way in building bridges.

In another exercise, the course participants went a step further and identified areas in which they could develop closer links with the community and these are shown in figure 3. One of the areas was helping children who were struggling with their studies. An initial meeting with parents of these children set the ground for further action. It meant working closer with parents in the future. Volunteer parents who needed help in handling children and classes were provided

### Figure 2: School activities where parents could assist

professional support and guidance. It also worked in the school's interest for they were developing added human resources to assist in classes. Still, the number of schools taking these initiatives is very few and there is a need to involve many more schools.

### Figure 3: Areas for developing school-community partnerships

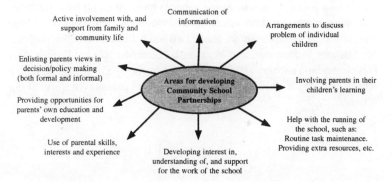

## Vignettes of Parental Involvement

Some vignettes (short case studies) have been selected to illustrate the effectiveness of involving parents in the school process. These vignettes are a result of the Whole School Improvement Programme (WSIP) of the AKU-IED Professional Development Centre, Northern Areas of Pakistan. The Centre is located in Gilgit in a beautiful purpose-built building and co-operates with all education systems (AKES,P, government and private) in their efforts to improve the quality of education. The mission is to develop and adopt activities and strategies that will lead to improvement in the quality of education in the Northern Areas.

The conceptual framework of the WSIP is derived from research on school effectiveness and school improvement. The main principles of WSIP are to treat the whole school as the unit of improvement rather than focusing just on individuals. Professional Development Teachers (PDTs) work alongside heads, teachers and students within their school context to improve opportunities for children's learning by focusing on the following areas:

- Quality of teaching and learning
- Leadership, management and administration
- Curriculum development and staff development
- Community participation, especially the involvement of mothers
- Building accommodation and resources
- Social, moral and spiritual development of students and health education.

It is 'community participation, especially the involvement of mothers' that is of a special interest. Some schools have taken up this challenge and have made genuine attempts to bridge the gap between home and school. I would like to share two such initiatives. The authors, Mr Shakoor Muhammad and Ms Khush Funer Murtaza are Professional Development Teachers (PDTs) involved in the WSIP in the Northern Areas and their initiative was to involve parents in improving schools.

## Vignette One
## Mothers and the Process of Teaching and Learning

To increase community involvement, the Whole School Improvement Project (WSIP) is trying to raise mothers' awareness and increase their participation in the learning process.

FGGM/S Hajigam is a WSIP project school at which there are 450 girl students, from nursery class to eight. With the collaboration of the Village Education Committee (VEC) and the school management, mothers were invited to attend a meeting, the first of its kind in the school's history. A total of 125 mothers attended and the following issues were discussed:

- Washroom problems
- Students leaving the premises during school hours
- Cleanliness
- Arrangements for the three classes that study in the open air
- Homework.

The following were the results of the meeting:

- The VEC solved the washroom problem within three days
- Girls no longer leave the premises during school hours and attendance has increased
- Cleanliness has improved
- Mothers provided handmade, low cost cushions to their daughters who were sitting on the ground. This keeps their uniforms clean and makes them more comfortable
- Homework, however, needs further attention.

At the second meeting, attendance of the mothers increased to 195. Furthermore, mothers started visiting the school where they discussed the teaching and learning process and promised to be more diligent in assisting their daughters at home.

We strongly believe that communication can be involved as vital partners in school improvement. Based on experience, we are convinced that parents'/mothers' involvement can make a real difference in improving the process of teaching and learning.

*By Shakoor Muhammad*

## Vignette Two
## The Community and the School

Communities can make a great contribution to improving schools. In WSIP, the faculty of PDCN encourages communities, especially mothers, to participate in school activities. Mother's days are celebrated at schools, where various issues are discussed—for example, cleanliness, homework, and the need for regular attendance. In our experience, these celebrations help to increase the participation of mothers in school activities. For example, we have seen mothers providing hand made cushions, which helps their children to keep their uniforms clean and makes them comfortable, especially in winter. Similarly, mothers have provided resources such as empty milk packs, tissue boxes, and bottles from which the teachers have prepared useful teaching materials.

Apart from this, some educated mothers come to school with their small children and teach in the classrooms. During the last academic year, we have seen various cases where this has been helpful. For instance, in one nursery class, a child was reluctant to come to school. His mother came to school every day, sat with him and taught in the classroom with the teacher. We found that the child gradually improved and finally moved up to first position in the class, all because of his mother's support. For us, this was further proof that where communities, especially mothers are involved, children will improve their performance at school. In other cases, we have seen students coming to school in clean uniforms with lunch boxes and have also seen them being provided with better opportunities to do their homework and study more. In conclusion, I can say that the involvement of community/mothers is a vital factor in improving students' learning.

*By Khush Funer Murtaza*

## Conclusion

The lessons from these vignettes are encouraging since they show a degree of success. The need now is to continue to build learning communities involving parents and teachers working in partnership with each other. It is recognized that building bridges between home and school needs marathon efforts from both the teachers and the parents, and what is absolutely vital is mutual understanding and cooperation on both sides. McLachlan (1996), in the conclusion to a research study, says: 'The main conclusions to emerge from the study highlight above all the need for both parties entrusted with the educational welfare of the child to listen actively to each other, and to hear what each is saying without allocating blame or pressure'. Parents and teachers can be partners and have an excellent opportunity to demonstrate what can be achieved when working together in the best interests of the student.

## Acknowledgement

I wish to acknowledge the guidance and input of my colleague Dr John Retallick in this chapter.

## References

Amir, I. (2004). *Parent-Teacher Bodies Rendered Ineffective*. Report in *Dawn* (newspaper), p. 4, 31 January.
Baker, K. (1987). 'The Churchill Lecture, Cambridge'. Quoted in P. Munn (1993). *Parents and schools: Customers, managers or partners?* London: Routledge.
Bastiani, J. & Wolfendale, S. (1996). *Home-school Work in Britain: Review, Reflection and Development*. London: David Fulton.
Berk, L. (1989). 'The parenting role and its influence'. In S. Wolfendale (1993). *Empowering Parents and Teachers: Working for Children*. London: Cassell.
Bray, M. (2000, April). *Community Partnerships in Education: Dimensions, Variations and Implications*. Paper prepared for World Education Forum, Dakar, Senegal.
Bray, M. (2003, August). *Community Partnerships in Education*. Paper presented at the International Conference on Impact: Making a Difference at AKU-IED, Karachi.
Crump, S. & Eltis, K. (1995). 'Schoolhome Connections: Political Relations in Policy implementation. Cited in M. Sanders & J. Epstein (1998). School-family-community partnerships and educational change: International perspectives. In A. Hargreaves et al. (Eds.). *International Handbook of Educational Change*. Dordrecht: Kluwer.
Dean, J. (2001). *The Effective School Governor*. London: Routledge.
Dunn, J. (1989). 'The Family as an Educational Environment in the Pre-school Years. In S. Wolfendale (1993). *Empowering Parents and Teachers: Working for Children*. London: Cassell.
Edwards, R. & Alders, P. (2000). 'A Typology of Parental Involvement in Education centering on Children and Young People: Negotiating Familiarization, Institutionalization and Individualization'. *British Journal of Sociology of Education*, 21(3), 435–55.

Govinda, R. and Diwan, R. (2003). *Community Participation and Empowerment in Primary Education*. New Delhi: Sage.

Grotevant, H.D. (1989). 'Child Development within the Family Context'. In S. Wolfendale (1993). *Empowering Parents and Teachers: Working for children*. London:Cassell.

Jones, J. (1993). 'What Governors Need to Know'. In J. Dean, *The Effective School Governor*. London: Routledge.

Kogan, M. J., Packwood, T. & Whitaker, T. (1986). *School Governing Bodies*. London: Heinemann.

McLachlan, K. (1996). 'Good Mothers are Women Too: The Gender Implications of Parental Involvement in Education'. In J. Bastiani and S. Wolfendale, *Home-School Work in Britain: Review, reflection and development* (pp. 28–38). London: David Fulton.

Plowden Report (1967, April). 'Children and their Primary Schools'. A Report of the Central Advisory Council for Education. In M. Bray (2000). *Community partnerships in education: Dimensions, variations and implications*. Paper prepared for World Education Forum, Daker, Senegal.

Pugh, G. (1989). 'Parents and Professionals in Pre-school Services: Is Partnership possible?' In P. Munn (1993). *Parents and Schools: Customers, Managers or Partners*. London: Routledge.

Sanders, M. & Epstein, J. (1998). 'School-Family-Community Partnerships and Educational Change: International Perspectives'. In A. Hargreaves et al. (Eds.). *International Handbook of Educational Change* (pp. 482–502). Dordrecht: Kluwer.

Tizard, B.& Hughes, M. (1984). 'Young Children Learning'. In S. Wolfendale (1993). *Empowering Parents and Teachers: Working for Children*. London: Cassell.

Topping, K. (1986). 'Parents as Partners'. In S. Wolfendale (1993). *Empowering Parents and Teachers: Working for Children*. London: Cassell.

Windham, D. (1992). 'Education for all: The requirements'. In M. Bray (2003, August). *Community Partnerships in Education*. Paper presented at the International Conference on Impact: Making a Difference held at AKU-IED, Karachi.

Wolfendale, S. (1993). *Empowering Parents and Teachers: Working for Children*. London: Cassell.

Wolfendale, S. (1996). *The Contribution of Parents to Children's Achievement in School Policy and Practice in the London Borough of Newham*. London: David Fulton.

# 10

# BUILDING COMMUNITIES OF PRACTICE IN PAKISTANI SCHOOLS

*Fauzia Shamim and Iffat Farah*

In-service teacher education in Pakistan has traditionally consisted of workshops and short training programmes conducted by experts, outside the classroom and school, to introduce particular teaching strategies or to train teachers to use new textbooks. Recent research, however, indicates that teachers learn best when their training is situated in the workplace and offers them opportunities to reflect on their practice in a supportive environment (Retallick, 1999). In addition, teacher learning becomes more sustained and has greater influence on practice, when they engage in conversations and share stories of their own practice with other colleagues (O'Brien, Newnham and Tinker, 2000; Kreshner, 1999; Lieberman and Miller, 1992). A number of institutions of higher learning now support teacher education which is school-based rather than university-based and emphasize partnerships with schools, so that most of the educational experience of teachers can be located in their own schools and classrooms (Kahne and Westheimer, 2000; Furlong, Barton, Miles, Whiting and Whitty, 2000; Jenlink, Kinnucan-Welsch and Odell, 1994). This new understanding of where and how teachers learn best is consistent with a view of knowledge as neither being fixed nor law-like or found only in institutions of higher learning i.e. external to the individual. It is also widely agreed that knowledge is socially constructed, that knowledge building is an ongoing process, and that teachers typically engage in knowledge building through dialogic inquiry into their own practice and conversations with colleagues and outsider critical friends in a mutually supportive environment (Wells, 1999).

International research on teacher learning and consequent developments in teacher education approaches suggest a need for exploring opportunities for on-going and school-based professional development of teachers in Pakistan, and developing partnerships between schools and teacher education institutions. AKU-IED implemented a model of 'partnershipping' with a number of schools, generally referred to as cooperating schools. These schools share AKU-IED's commitment to school improvement and send their teachers to various teacher development programmes offered by the Institute. The graduates of these programmes are expected to lead teacher development and other school improvement activities in the partner schools. As graduates from a number of programmes have returned to their schools, it has become evident that university-based programmes are not enough to sustain change in schools and that there is also a need for developing school-based structures and processes to support teacher development. The research and development study on which this chapter is based was an attempt to explore the possibility of establishing such a school-based process through the development of a community of practice of English language teachers.

## Communities of Practice: An Approach to Professional Development

A Community of Practice (COP), also commonly referred to in the literature as a professional learning community or a learning community, is typically defined as a group of people who have shared goals and are willing to engage, individually or collectively, in a systematic inquiry about their practice and to share it openly with other colleagues for collaborative reflection and improved classroom practice and student learning outcomes. Members of a COP are expected to be able to do things together and respond to each others' actions. They should understand the enterprise of a community of practice enough to engage in it and be able to use a common repertoire which is historically negotiated and developed over time (Wenger, 1998; DuFour and Baker, 1998).

Shaw (1999), Dufour and Baker (1998) and others find the concept very promising in its potential for teacher development and school improvement. According to Shaw, learning communities can provide the contexts for 'building the knowledge, skills, norms, habits and values necessary to adapt, renew, rethink and inform our classroom practice with respect to improving the learning of students'. Similarly, Hargreaves (2003) concludes that 'professional learning communities bring together the key knowledge-society attributes such as teamwork, inquiry and continuous learning'. However, he also points out that professional learning communities work best 'when they are combined with structures of caring and are grounded in long-term relationships of trust, foundations of security and commitments to active care among teachers and others'.

The role of a COP in transforming teachers, students and the schools of which they are part is now well established in the literature. However, as Wenger (1998) warns us, designing learning in a community of practice is a challenge. A number of studies have outlined design principles and processes used in learning communities in the whole school (Shaw, 1997), departments within a school (Wineberg and Grossman, 1998), networks of teachers across different institutions in higher education (Walker, 2001) and teachers from different schools forming a learning partnership with university colleagues (Palincsar et al., 1997). However, these studies do not give us enough understanding of the conditions, particularly contextual conditions that affect the design and development of such communities of practice. Recently, Hargreaves (2003) has drawn our attention to the fact that difference in context can be an important mediating variable in the success of different models of professional development. Comparing performance training sects[1] with professional learning communities, he argues that learning communities work best in contexts of 'high-capacity teachers in high-capacity systems', while the performance training models are suited to low-capacity systems 'where large numbers of teachers are uncertified and under-skilled, where schools have a record of poor performance and many teachers have lost belief in their capacity to make a difference, where too many leaders see themselves as managers more than instructional leaders, and where resources have been scarce and spread too thinly across too many initiatives...' (pp. 189–90).

In an attempt to explore whether communities of practice could offer a viable approach for teacher development and school improvement in varied school contexts in Pakistan, the authors of this paper launched a two-year long research and development project. The overall purpose of the project was to support the design and development of a community of practice of English teachers in a small number of selected schools and to study the process and outcomes of building these communities.

The key questions we asked in this study were: what is the process of building communities of practice in varied school contexts in Pakistan, and what factors contribute to, or hinder the process in our schools? In the remainder of this chapter, we respond to these two questions.

## Initiating the COP

The project team from AKU-IED approached several schools to participate in the project that had made an earlier study of the teaching of English in Pakistan. Each school was asked for a commitment to stay with the project for a period of two years and to make protected time of approximately 100 hours available for COP activities. Three schools; two private and one public, agreed to the conditions and were invited to participate. Although each school had a different organizational structure, all three had prior partnership arrangements with AKU-IED. This meant that a large number of their teachers had attended courses of various lengths at AKU-IED.

After entry negotiations with the head and school management were over, the project team held a meeting with all language teachers in each of the three schools to explain the purpose and nature of the project and request voluntary membership to a COP in the school. One member of COP in each school was appointed as the COP coordinator. In all three cases, the coordinator was a senior teacher with some management responsibility (such as head of department, deputy head, or professional development teacher), and was recommended by the head or principal of the school. The coordinators became the main channel of communication between the university faculty, teachers and school management.

## Developing the COP

COP membership in each school began with eight to ten teachers. However, in two schools, because of high teacher turnover by the end of the year, only a few of the original members were left and many new members had joined. In the public school, the membership remained constant and only one teacher left the school. Two persons from the AKU-IED project team joined each COP.

Although in our early negotiations with the principals and initial meeting with the teachers, we had emphasized that membership to the COP should be voluntary, teachers were directed by the management to attend COP meetings. In one school in particular, teachers had to be repeatedly called for a meeting. In each school COP, members quite obviously fell into two groups; active and enthusiastic members and, inactive and disinterested members.

## The COP Activities

COP activities started in all three schools at the beginning of the school academic year. A new school was included two months after activities began, when the original government school dropped out of the project. The main activities included fortnightly meetings of members of the COP in each school, inter-COP meetings and classroom observations.

## School COP meetings

Fortnightly COP meetings were planned at each school. Although this schedule could not be followed consistently because of other urgent priorities, on average, at least one meeting per month was held during the academic year; except in one school where no meeting could be held for several months. Frequency of meetings varied so that periods of fortnightly meetings were followed by periods of monthly meetings and 'lull periods' of two or three months, where no meetings could be held.

What happened in the meetings was determined by the University-based COP members' desire to 'create a COP' and the teachers' immediate needs, and the school management's priorities. Initially, a lot of time and energy was spent in identifying shared goals for the COP and in trying to develop a non-hierarchical, trusting environment and interaction patterns where teachers could share classroom stories, successes and challenges. Teachers told stories of what they had tried out in class. They identified specific problems, for example difficulties they faced in giving and assessing dictation, and they tried out solutions and reported them in COP meetings. A few of the classroom sessions were also videotaped and shared. In one COP, a lot of time was spent on planning the syllabus and the daily lessons in small groups and sharing with the whole group how the lesson went in the classroom. Other problems such as how to complete the syllabus in a short time were discussed and suggestions and experiences were shared. Sometimes, the University members' assessment of teachers' needs resulted in joint planning and joint teaching (with university members taking the lead role).

The school management's expectations and priorities also influenced what happened in the school COPs. Thus, in one school, the COP began with focusing on oral English which could not be continued because of the priority to complete the syllabus. In another school, the need to control and standardize teaching and to protect the school's image meant that few new ideas could be tried by individual teachers and only success stories could be shared in the meetings.

## Lesson observations

A number of lesson observations were carried out by University-based members in the classrooms of COP teachers. These came about in one school because of the principal's expectations and the teachers' requests for observation and feedback for building their own capacity. In one school, teachers began to observe each other's classes to learn and provide critical feedback. During the second year, one designated member of the team from AKU-IED made herself available in two schools to provide ongoing support to the teachers. However, the teachers were too busy to frequently take advantage of this opportunity. School schedules and priorities did not allow any time outside of the designated COP hours to engage in co-planning and co-teaching, even when the teachers desired it.

## Inter–COP meetings

Inter-COP meetings were planned to be held every quarter to bring school-based COPs together and have the opportunity for the heads of schools to learn about COP goals and activities, and challenges. However, because of difficulties in finding mutually convenient times for these meetings, only five meetings were held during the two years. None of the heads or principals attended any of the meetings. Instead of a session where some genuine sharing and reflection could happen, it was perceived as an opportunity for schools to 'show and tell'.

## Key Processes in COP Development

### Capacity of teachers

We had realized that COP was a new concept in schools. We, therefore, planned to conduct a workshop to help teachers become aware of some of the key aspects of a COP such as reflection and inquiry and to identify conditions which would facilitate or hinder the work of a community of practice in the three schools. Trust was identified as a characteristic of successful communities of practice and participants discussed and listed key issues and opportunities in building trust. Issues common to all schools included hierarchical organizational structures, status differences, lack of appreciation and respect for each other's work, fear of criticism and evaluation, and heavy workload. While there was some discussion at this stage on how to address these issues, it was clear that these were deep-rooted and would not have easy solutions.

During school COP meetings, the University-based COP members used various strategies to develop trust and confidence and open communication. These strategies included encouraging silence to give time for more reticent members to speak up, establishing a norm to allow each member to have a turn to speak even if they did not ask for a turn and did not use it, and giving verbal and non-verbal feedback to convey that what was shared was important and worthwhile.

As the COP meetings continued, we realized that each individual teacher's own proficiency in English and their knowledge, or lack of it, of language pedagogy were key factors affecting their participation in the COP. Based on needs identified by teachers, we conducted a few workshops on various topics such as teaching reading comprehension, or teaching writing to primary children. In two schools we supported selected teachers (at their request) by co-planning and co-teaching with them.[2] Nevertheless, individual teachers' capacity continued to be an issue and a certain level of content and pedagogical knowledge seemed necessary for active participation in the COP.

## Shared understanding of COP and its goals

Although considerable time was spent in each of the three schools to discuss the 'what', 'who' and 'how' of a COP, it was clear that different participants (heads, school coordinators, teachers and professional development teachers) were trying to make sense of COP in terms of their own experiences of professional development (such as learning from university experts), their personal agendas (improving language proficiency) and school's expectations from a university (make teachers learn to teach). Thus, teachers joined the COP to learn from the university experts and continued to expect them to demonstrate lessons, help develop curriculum etc. Others wanted to learn the English language by attending the COP.

Our attempts to develop shared goals for COPs met with different levels of success in different schools. In one school, a shared understanding was developed early on that the COP would focus on inquiring, reflecting and sharing ideas on improving students' English. However, the specific objectives and focus changed several times, particularly in the first year. The school first identified improving student oral English as a focus for the COP. However, teachers soon realized that they could not do this exclusively because they had to teach reading, writing and grammar as well. They then began to focus on integration and began co-planning lessons which they would implement and share in the COP meetings as they tried to refine their practice. Two things negatively affected this process; one, urgent school priorities such as completion of the syllabus, meetings and other school functions, and second, the high teacher turnover which made developing shared goals a regressive process.

In another school, the coordinator's own lack of understanding of COP goals remained dominant throughout the two years so that no shared goals could be developed. The COP meetings replaced the 'faculty meetings' which had been used for reporting to the head; now COP meetings were used to report to the 'experts' from AKU-IED. A majority of the teachers resented such reporting and avoided attending the meetings. The end of project interviews showed that teachers had thought of COP meetings as 'a burden' for them as they were unable to share classroom problems openly and were afraid of being reprimanded if they did so. Although the situation changed slightly in year two of the project, they began to understand that the COP could provide opportunities for inquiry, reflection and problem solving, they remained convinced that the goals and values necessary for forming a community of practice could not be nourished and sustained within the bureaucratic culture of the school.

In the third school, teachers' interest remained limited to using the COP to build their own proficiency in English. Although a few teachers moved on to making some effort to improve their practice for better student outcomes, this was neither consistent nor shared by other school-based members.

**Roles and relationships**

Developing COPs in schools required redefining existing roles and relationships between AKU-IED members and the schools, between teachers and their supervisors (heads, professional development teachers) and among teachers.

AKU-IED and its faculty were variously regarded as experts, resource persons and benefactors by schools. The COP project attempted to challenge some of these notions. For example, from the very beginning we tried to explain, both to the school managers and the teachers, that we would be equal members in the COP and would not be training the teachers. While schools said they understood and accepted this, it was clear that such a redefinition would not be easy. For example, in one school, at the end of the first year, a principal complained that the university members, particularly the senior members, were not active in educating teachers. The two schools continued to expect the university members to direct the meetings and to provide expert knowledge and classroom support. We could not ignore these expectations and so played a variety of roles based on need and level of readiness of school-based COP members to take on roles of facilitator during COP meetings, mentor and critical friend during co-planning and co-teaching, record keeper for the meetings, and occasionally, an 'expert' for conducting needs-based workshops. At the same time, we tried to slowly change our role and relationship by inviting other members of the COP to facilitate a meeting, listening carefully to others, asking questions, sharing our own problems and stories of our own classroom failure, and providing classroom support only when invited. Some of these strategies helped change our relationship as evident in the comments of a teacher which was echoed in many interviews in two schools:

I was scared at the prospect of having to talk in English in front of the experts, but now, you are just like friends. Now the teachers look forward to the COP meetings. When members from IED came and the teachers observed their behaviour and mannerism, their way of encouraging the teacher...so this attitude was gradually adopted; it penetrated into all the teachers so everyone has started changing their attitude.

The perception of a status difference between University and school-based members did not and could not completely disappear. For one thing, AKU-IED members were not affected by the school management; and did not have to become vulnerable by opening up their own teaching to others. They continued to be regarded as more knowledgeable and influential. It was obvious to us that a lot more time was required for new relationships to become established. Moreover, teachers' capacity, their perceptions of this capacity, AKU-IED members' own capabilities and difficulties in taking on a different kind of role also affected the development of new roles and relationships within the COP.

The COP meetings remained limited to the teachers from one department and despite some effort we were unable to engage fully in the process or to bring about any change in their role or relationship with teachers of other subject areas. In all schools, the principals and/or head teachers remained more or less informed about COP activities, primarily through the COP coordinator but showed little active interest. A lack of interest or time to develop an understanding of the goals and processes of the COP, how it might relate to school goals and processes, and what their own role in the process might be, meant that they took on the COP as another external demand. Although changes were made in the school timetable, substitution teachers arranged for classes of participating teachers and other school activities adjusted to facilitate teachers to attend the COP meetings, this was more to accommodate a project than for enhancing teaching and learning in the school. Thus, when other 'school priorities' such as administrative meetings arose, COP meetings were either cancelled or postponed. This kind of bureaucratic orientation is how schools commonly deal with externally driven innovations. In hindsight, COP development needed the leadership from within the school, preferably the head and the principal. Because leadership came from outside, the COP remained another project in the school which the head/principal agreed to accommodate.

As mentioned earlier, in each COP, one member, also nominated as COP coordinator, had a management role in the school. The management role affected the development of a relationship of co-learning and collegiality between the coordinator and the members. In two schools where these members were also the channel of communication between the teacher and the principals, the relationship remained much more of a supervisor and supervisees.

COP membership very positively affected teachers' relationships with each other. At the beginning of the meetings, teachers' relationships were personal and one to one. English teachers from different sections of the school hardly interacted. COP meeting brought them together. Mistrust and competition, which had characterized their professional relationships began to be replaced by trust and mutual learning as evident in the following reflection of a teacher.

> I think it is a good way of building trust amongst the teachers. I, as a teacher, feel free now and not previously, to share different stories of my class since I've been given opportunities to do so and I know that whatever is shared, I'm not going to be assessed on. ...We've been asked to attend so many meetings like this one but now I've found it somewhat different, because I know I will be given support instead of feeling guilty. By attending COP meetings I'm no more scared of saying, 'I don't know'. Rather, I can try. I am so excited that I've been given support by so many peoples as my colleagues...which I never expected. The most interesting thing I've found is that an era of change is taking place in me. People are listening carefully to what I'm saying and my ideas are taken seriously which I really like.... I've now been able to know the meaning of COP after attending so many meetings. (Teacher reflections, COP 3, written 19 November, 2001)

## Sharing and collaboration

The value of collaborative activities in teacher learning has received a lot of attention in recent literature on teacher learning (e.g. Hargreaves, 1997; McLaughlin, 1997, Kwakman 2003). According to Kwakman:

> The reasoning behind this call for collaboration is that feedback, new information or ideas do not only spring from individual learning, but to a large extent also from dialogue and interaction with other people. Moreover, collaboration is assumed to create a learning culture and helps to build a community in which further learning is supported and stimulated' (p. 152).

Kwakman cites four types of collegiality: story telling, help, sharing, and joint work. COP activities included opportunities for all these four kinds of collegial interaction. Collaborative learning through inquiry on one's own practice required almost a paradigm shift for teachers, particularly for those COP members who had previously held the responsibility for advising and supporting teachers such as heads of department and PDTs.

During the first year of the project, there was ongoing negotiation to clarify and establish the purpose and process of sharing classroom stories of both successes and challenges faced in the classroom with other colleagues in COP meetings. Teachers gradually began to understand that this story telling and discussion in the COP was purposeful. The following reflection by a teacher demonstrates this.

> When I joined the COP, I was simply unaware of its aims and objectives and the only idea, rather worry, I had was that it would simply increase the workload. But within the first few meetings I realized that these meetings would certainly enhance our teaching skills. But the question was 'how'—a really difficult question to answer. Since in the beginning we all lacked confidence to speak out, we talked about matters of little importance, we tried to mention only the positive points, i.e., the actual classroom scenario was not presented and all these things were not giving any meaningfulness to these meetings. But then we started to follow the right path gradually by focusing on one item only. We worked well on poetry teaching and really learnt how we can make it more interesting and much better in terms of students' interest as well. (Teacher COP 3)

Another teacher from a different COP reflected:

> When we discussed in COP meetings and shared our classroom activities and stories, it sometimes happened that when another teacher shared her story I thought that's how I can also do it...so their stories helped me a lot. Earlier, if we had a problem we would think how to solve it ourselves but now several points are highlighted through these discussions...earlier, whatever was done was on an individual basis. Now we discuss with each other our teaching plans and problems, someone asks me to look at her activity and suggest if it is applicable in our context or not—so we became 'strong' [improved] in this way. (Teacher Interview, COP 1)

The interaction pattern in all COPs changed over time from teachers being mainly quiet to sharing their success stories only, to raising issues and sharing problems faced at the classroom level when experimenting with new methodology and finding evidence of their teaching practices on student learning outcomes. By the end of year two of the project, teachers began to seek advice on how to make sharing in the COP more focused, and what to focus on in classroom observation in order to help a colleague.

## Sustaining the COP

In individual and focus group interviews conducted at the end of the project, we asked COP members and school management if they would like to continue the COP in their school and what it would take to do so. It was clear from the responses that while interaction in a COP was desirable for continuing professional development, it would be difficult to sustain because of lack of time, competing priorities, and high teacher turnover which made it difficult to establish trust and a common discourse over time. All schools expressed the hope to continue COP interactions within the existing structures in the school. However, our experience during the two years suggested that this would be difficult. The established roles, relationships, and goals of teaching were very strong and quite different from those we had been trying to establish in the COP. Continuing the COP in the schools would need strong advocacy and support from within, over a much longer period of time. Moreover, the COP will need to be opened to all teachers rather than a particular department. One group of teachers, trying to establish goals and norms quite different from the rest of the school, is bound to be challenged and hard to sustain.

## Lessons Learned

As we started the project, we were conscious that there was need to develop shared goals and a 'vision' for building a COP. Additionally, there was provision in the development design for ways of creating the context for teachers' professional development for improving student learning outcomes through a range of activities such as the school-based COP meetings. Efforts were, therefore, made to define shared goals with the schools in general and the COP participants in particular. However, teachers' goals for their individual growth and development were often incongruent with the institutional goals and priorities, such as conducting exams, the latter being driven more by administrative requirements than a long-term commitment to improving student learning outcomes. Furthermore, due to the participants' limited understanding of the purpose and process of COP or the characteristics of this reform effort, there was no compelling purpose to legitimize the time and resources required for teachers to engage in collaborative inquiry on their practice. Moreover, participation in the COP, unlike similar projects reported in the literature, was mandatory for the teachers who were nominated by the schools to participate in it. It also took a long time to build relationships of trust amongst the teachers themselves, but more importantly, between the school-based and University-based members of the COPs. The schools and COP participants had varying levels of commitment to the 'shared' goals, particularly when they were in variance with their own personal and professional and/or institutional goals and priorities at the time. Also, teachers were unable to focus on student learning outcomes through collecting evidence of their learning in a systematic manner. Thus, in contrast to the processes of other learning communities reported in the literature, where the communities are mainly driven and held together by a 'compelling purpose' (Shaw, 1997), where the membership of COP is voluntary and the driving force for collaboration is 'trust and reciprocity of exchanging ideas' (Walker, 2001), the COP project had limited success in creating a culture of collaborative inquiry on practice for improving student learning outcomes.

While there is significant evidence of teacher learning and empowerment through their participation in the COP, as indicated by their increased levels of confidence in engaging in professional dialogue, even with 'experts' and senior members of the school hierarchy, and their willingness and efforts to experiment with new teaching methodology with a focus on student learning outcomes, the project was not successful in infusing the characteristics of a COP into the school culture at large. Also, due to the limited life-span of the project, the practices developed in COP could not be institutionalised and despite various efforts to engage the participants and the school management in thinking about strategies for their continuation, the sustainability of the culture and practices of COP is highly unlikely after the exit of the project. Hargreaves (2003) cautions that 'Professional learning communities do not flourish in overly standardized systems which severely restrict teachers' discretion for decision making and self-initiated change' (p. 185). They would also not flourish in schools where teachers have very low professional capacity. This was found to be true in our study of building COPs in varied school contexts in Karachi, Pakistan.

## Acknowledgements

We are thankful to Roshni Kumari, faculty at AKU-IED and a member of our community of practice for her input and feedback during the writing of this paper. The research reported here was made possible by a research grant from the University Research Council, Aga Khan University.

An earlier version of this chapter was presented as a paper at the IATEFL conference, Brighton, UK, April 2003.

## NOTES

1. According to Hargreaves, the emphasis of reform initiatives, which he refers to as performance training sects, is on providing pressure and support to train teachers intensively in a limited number of given instructional priorities that will deliver rapid and significant increases in measured learning performances for all students.
2. Only some teachers showed interest in and requested for classroom level support mainly from the AKU-IED members of their COP. However, as indicated earlier when later one of the AKU-IED members made herself available for one day, a week for such consultation and support in three COPs, the teachers were not able to take advantage of this due to various reasons including competing priorities. It seemed that professional development of teachers and/or introducing innovative methodology and reflecting on its impact on student learning outcomes was a much lower priority than other school responsibilities such as preparing students for getting good grades in traditional exams focusing on rote learning, school administrative meetings etc.

## References

DuFour, R. & Baker, R. (1998). *Professional Learning Communities at Work: Best Practices for Enhancing Student Achievement.* Bloomington, Indiana: National Education Service.

Furlong, J., Barton, L., Miles, S., Whiting, C. & Whitty G. (2000). *Teacher Education in Transition: Reforming Professionalism?* Buckingham: Open University Press.

Grundy, S. (1999). 'Partners in Learning: School-based and University-based Communities of Learning'. In J. Retallick, B. Cocklin & K. Coombe (Eds.). *Learning Communities in Education.* London: Routledge.

Hargreaves, A. (1997). 'From Reform to Renewal: A New Deal for a New Age'. In A. Hargreaves & R. Evans (Eds.). *Beyond Educational Reform. Bringing teachers Back in* (pp. 105–25). Buckingham: Open University Press.

Hargreaves, A. (2003). 'Professional Learning Communities and Performance Training sects'. In D. Hopkins, M. Hadfield, A. Hargreaves & C. Chapman (Eds.). *Effective Leadership for School Improvement*. London: Routledge Falmer.

Jenlink, P.M., Kinnucan-Welsch, K. & Odell, S. J. (1994). 'Designing Professional Development Learning Communities'. In D. J. McIntyre & D. M. Byrd (Eds.). *Preparing Tomorrow's Teachers: The Field Experience*. California: Crown Press Inc.

Kahne, J. & Westheimer, J. (2000). 'A Pedagogy of Collective Action and Reflection: Preparing Teachers for Collective School Leadership'. *Journal of Teacher Education*, 51(5), 372–82.

Kreshner, R. (1999). 'The Role of School-based Research in Helping Teachers to Extend their Understanding of children's Learning and Motivation'. *Journal of In-service Education*, 25(3), 423–45.

Kwakman, K. (2003). 'Factors Affecting Teachers' Participation in Professional Learning Activities'. *Teaching and Teacher Education*, 19,149–70.

Lieberman, A. & Miller, L. (1992). 'Professional Development of Teachers'. In M. C. Alkin (Ed.). *Encyclopedia of Educational Research* (6th ed.) (pp. 1333–45). New York: Macmillan Publishing Company.

McLaughlin, M.W. (1997). 'Rebuilding Teacher Professionalism in the United States'. In A. Hargreaves, & R. Evans (Eds.). *Beyond educational reform: Bringing teachers back in* (pp. 77–93). Buckingham: Open University Press.

O'Brien, T. Newnham, G. & Tinker, L. (2000). 'Collaborative Practice-based Research in Supporting the Language Development of Primary Level Bilingual Children: A Case Study'. *Educational Action Research*, 8(1), 43–63.

Palincsar, A. S., Magnusson, S. J., Marano, N. L., Ford, D., & Brown, N. (1997, March). *Design Principles Informing and Emerging from a Community of Practice*. Paper presented at the Annual Meeting of the American Educational Research Association, Chicago IL.

Retallick, J. (1999). 'Teachers' Workplace Learning: Towards Legitimation and Accreditation'. *Teachers and Teaching*, 5(1), 33–50.

Shaw, P. (1999). 'Purpose and Process of Effective Learning Communities'. In J. Retallick, B. Cocklin & Coombe, K. (Eds.). *Learning communities in education*. London: Routledge.

Shaw, P. L. (1997). *Creating a community of practice: A case study*. Paper presented at the 6th International Conference in Education Research in Collaboration with the International Network, Faculty of Education, University of Oslo, Norway.

Walker, M. (2001). 'Collaboration With/In a Critical Community of Practice'. In M. Walker (Ed.). *Restructuring Professionalism in University Teaching: Teachers and Learners in Action*. Buckingham: Open University Press.

Wineberg, S. & Grossman, P. (1998). 'Creating a Community of Learners Amongst High School Teachers'. *Phi Delta Kappan*, 79 (5), 350–3.

Wells, G. (1999). *Dialogic Inquiry: Towards a Sociocultural Practice and Theory of Education*. Cambridge: Cambridge University Press.

Wenger, E. (1998). *Communities of Practice*. Cambridge: Cambridge University Press.

# 11

# NETWORKS OF LEARNING: PROFESSIONAL ASSOCIATIONS AND THE CONTINUING EDUCATION OF TEACHERS

*Sikunder Ali Baber, Zakia Sarwar, and Qamar Safdar*

> In Networked Learning Communities, teachers and other educational professionals are experimenting with new and innovative approaches in the classroom, working in creative partnerships within and across schools to develop and share good practice. Inspired and challenged by fellow professionals, they are learning together (National College for School Leadership: www.ncsl.org.uk/nlc).

This chapter draws on the notion of 'networking' and shows how a number of professional associations have been established as networks in Pakistan to encourage the continuing professional education of teachers. Case studies of three such networks are presented; the Mathematics Association of Pakistan (MAP), the Society of Pakistan English Language Teachers (SPELT) and the School Heads Association for Development of Education (SHADE). The formation and growth of these networks can be viewed as developing insights into the improvement of education in the developing world. The contributions of the associations may also add value to the learning of teacher colleagues in other parts of the world, while their experience may open possibilities for creating other networks of learning to assist reform efforts in education throughout the world.

The chapter consists of two parts. Part 1 will focus on a review of the literature regarding networks and their role in enacting and sustaining the culture of teacher learning among schools and different stakeholders in education. Part II will present case studies of three professional associations that are working for educational reform in Pakistan in the areas of mathematics, English and school leadership/management.

**What are Networks?**

It is difficult to find one all-encompassing definition of a 'network' given the range of purposes for which they are established. However, David Clark (1996) in his book *Schools as Learning Communities* quotes a useful definition:

> Networks constitute the basic social form that permits inter-organizational interactions of exchange, concerted action, and joint production. Networks are unbounded or bounded clusters of organizations that, by definition, are non-hierarchical collectives of legally separate units. Networking is the art of creating and/or maintaining a cluster of organizations for the purpose of exchanging, acting, or producing among the member organizations (quoted in Clark, 1996: 142).

He further says 'Networks and networking have a huge contribution to make to schools and other bodies wanting to become partners in learning. As structures geared to innovations, networks can stimulate schools and their partners to open up and explore their diverse ideologies and approaches to education. They can bring more isolated learning communities, such as the home, into a new educational relationship with the wider world' (Clark, 1996:143).

Networking provides strong support to schools in their reform efforts. For example, if a school has decided to embark on placing students at the centre and organizing the rest of resources (human, financial and material) to make this happen, then it has to create mechanisms to develop the capacity of all stakeholders to support the school's effort to bring about these changes over a period of time. Also, it has been recognized that no major reforms in schools take place without getting the required commitment of teachers and creating avenues to support their professional development on an ongoing basis. Given the enormity of the task of reforming schools, each school has to find partnerships and create networks to offset the high cost involved in development of teachers for reforms to happen. Networks are seen as being very important for these purposes.

Darling-Hammond and McLaughlin (1995) have stressed the importance of networks as a powerful tool in teacher learning as cited by the report named Networks@Work (Queensland Board of Teacher Registration, 2002). The report says: 'Networks provide the 'critical friends' or 'peers' that teachers need to be able to reflect on their own teaching experiences associated with developing new practices in their classrooms. Teacher networking often provides an opportunity for teachers to visit the various schools of participants and to gain 'practical pedagogical clues' (Moonen and Vooget, 1998:102), from other teachers' classrooms. Also, 'Professional relationships forged outside the immediate working environment enable teachers to gain valuable insights into new knowledge and practice beyond that gained from interactions with colleagues in their own schools' (Board of Teacher Registration, 1997:6-7).

Lieberman (1999), while quoting several educational change leaders (e.g. Darling-Hammond and McLaughlin, 1995; McLaughlin and Talbert, 1993; Cochran-Smith and Lytle, 1993), says that 'Networks are becoming popular, in part, because they encourage and seem to support many of the key ideas that reformers say are needed to produce change and improvement in schools, teaching, and learning'.

Networks seem to provide:

- Opportunities for teachers to both consume and generate knowledge
- A variety of collaborative structures
- Flexibility and informality
- Discussion of problems that often have no agreed-upon solutions
- Ideas that challenge teachers rather than merely prescribing generic solutions
- An organizational structure that can be independent of, yet attached to, schools or universities
- A chance to work across school and district lines
- A vision of reform that excites and encourages risk taking in a supportive environment
- A community that respects teachers' knowledge as well as knowledge from research and reform (Lieberman and Grolnick, 1997).

Various writers (e.g. Darling-Hammond and McLaughlin, 1995; Smith and Wohlstetter, 2001; Lieberman and Wood, 2003) have identified two distinctive features that teacher networks exhibit in their pursuit to better support teachers' learning on a regular basis:

- **Personal and Social Relationships:** improved relationships, flexibility, risk-taking, commitment, openness in interacting with each other and clarifying values and expectations.

- **Academic and Professional Aspects:** innovation, enriching practice, continual development of teachers focused on professional concerns such as student learning, sharing and getting relevant professional information (dissemination), developing healthy and shared norms, enriching curriculum and influencing policy makers.

Lieberman and Grolnick (1997) observe several themes that give networks their purpose such as 'creating purposes and directions; building collaboration, consensus, and commitment; creating activities and relationships as building blocks; providing leadership through cross-cultural brokering, facilitating, and keeping the values visible; and dealing with the funding problems' (p. 196).

**How are Networks Organized?**

Darling-Hammond and McLaughlin (1995) observe that successful networks operate with flexibility and this flexibility and dynamism enables them to maintain not only sustainability but also continually meet the changing professional needs of their participants: 'Networks are best managed through 'systematic ad-hocism'—a process of moving towards shared goals with enormous flexibility in strategy' (p. 5). They also recognize that the network has to be mindful of contextual needs in situations where they operate.

There are three important aspects of network organization:

- Networks have a loose structure. This loose structure is often associated with their flexibility to respond to the changing needs related to the purpose for which the networks are organized.

- Association with a network is on a volunteer basis. The focus of work in particular networks defines the nature and function of such membership.

- The boundaries of networks are permeable. This permeability supports the network to remain innovative in creating and sustaining new ideas and solutions to complex problems. Often the social problems that networks are trying to address require a multi-disciplinary approach.

However, whilst flexibility is a key idea in network organization, there is also a need for some structure, particularly in the case of professional associations. This is usually in the form of an elected executive committee that is empowered to make decisions about the effective operation of the group.

**What Challenges do Networks Face?**

A thorough review of networks in general and teachers' networks in particular, has revealed the following challenges that networks have to address on a regular basis:

**Sustainability:** This involves many aspects; two of the most important are financial sustainability and vitality of members in the network. For networks, financial sustainability has remained a perennial problem and there may not be any assurance that this would be addressed in a clean manner at the early stages of networking. However, it is suggested that if networks have developed credibility and a good reputation through providing quality services, they may attract good financial support through government or non-government sources. This directly leads to the second aspect of sustainability of networks, that is, the vitality of their members to continually get engaged in running various professional and administrative affairs of the network. Maintenance of optimal enthusiasm of members on an ongoing basis is a challenge for the distributed leadership of networks.

**Genuine collaboration:** No network can survive without creating a genuine collaboration both amongst their members and also with all the stakeholders who are direct beneficiaries of the network. In the case of teachers' networks, the ultimate beneficiaries are students. For students to get the real benefit of these networks, teachers have to consider themselves as learners so that students can take them as role models. Teachers may not be expected to behave as learners until schools and society, in which they work and live, also adopt a learner orientation. Ramsley (2002) suggested some of the features related to the importance of collaboration in networks as:

- A good collaboration will continue to evolve as a result of mutual learning. To be successful, collaboration should build on new patterns of information gathering, communication and reflection that allow all parties to participate in decision-making and learning. This requires time and face-to-face interactions.

- Like any other important effort, community partnerships must be accompanied by a strong commitment to a 'culture of evidence'. It is important to keep a running assessment of how well the partnership is working from the point of view of all participants.

**Leadership:** Teacher networks operate in a flexible and non-hierarchical manner. This brings an added complexity to manage the networks in a smooth fashion. It has been recognized that professional networks require a particular kind of leadership that should be distributed over the entire network. In this regard, Networks@Work (2002) has quoted the Queensland Board of Teacher Registration in Australia on the need to have a leader who is a respected person, as it says:

> Nominating a respected person to have responsibility for overseeing communication, coordination and administrative matters can facilitate this [complex working of a Network](Board of Teacher Registration, 1997: 15; McDermott, 1999:6).

> One of the greatest problems for successful collaboratives is for them to maintain their momentum. Ongoing, thorough planning and management are essential and this allows for the continued redefinition of roles, responsibilities, goals and timelines as the community progresses. This type of progressive planning ensures that the network remains successful and productive (Board of Teacher Registration, 1997:11)

> Communication is an essential element to any successful community of practice and allowances need to be made for the differing pressures on participants. For communication to be beneficial to the network it must be regular, honest and explicit and enable community members to be able to evaluate, consult, share, re-negotiate, and advocate (Board of Teacher Registration, 1997:13).

**Quality of networking:** The quality of networking depends on how well networks encourage a culture of trust to become established amongst the members. Without having openness and willingness on the part of members to contribute to the activities of the network, no network can claim to be genuinely contributing towards professional development of teachers. This requires transparent decision-making mechanisms and providing access to quality information to all their members so that an environment of trust and care can be established. McDermott (1999) has noted features of a successful network as:

> Mutual respect, trust and understanding are fundamental features of a successful community of practice. Without mutual respect teachers would not be able to freely engage in discussion or be willing to accept feedback (Hord, 1997). Sufficient time is required to enable network members to establish relationships with each other (McDermott, 1999).

Networks should also continually get engaged in the process of diversifying their activities and programmes so that evolving and changing needs can be accommodated. This requires training of network leaders in managing the complex relationships and meeting the evolving needs in an effective manner. Also, networks can be engaged with processes of follow-up of their professional development activities through engaging different individual and institutional members. These follow-up activities can also help participants to develop insights into the issues that the professional networks are supposed to tackle. This continual sharing of professional practice of teachers within the networks can help all the participants to develop the culture of evidence essential to develop teaching practice along professional lines.

## Why are Networks Important in the Context of Pakistan?

Within the context of supporting reforms in education to succeed, the importance of professional association networks, such as MAP, SPELT and SHADE, can be very well recognized. These professional associations have been very active in creating ongoing opportunities, not only for teachers, but also all the respective stakeholders to interact with each other. This will increase the likelihood of a conducive environment to be created to make reforms more possible in Pakistan.

For teachers to successfully engage in reform efforts, they need to be supported to change their beliefs about existing teaching practices and try to explore possibilities for adopting new teaching practices. In this regard, teacher networks can play a vital role to support teachers in their development as caring and competent professionals and can create many opportunities for teacher development through their different activities. For example, the Mathematics Association of Pakistan (MAP), through its regular monthly activities has been supporting mathematics teachers to not only get attuned with new teaching methodologies of mathematics, but also to help them experience these methodologies within workshop settings where they can see the potential benefits and challenges associated with teaching for understanding.

Recently, AKU-IED has supported six professional associations; namely, MAP, SHADE, Science Association of Pakistan (SAP), Pakistan Inclusive Education Association (PIEA), Association of Primary Teachers (APT) and Association of Social Studies Educators and Teachers (ASSET) to form a network called Professional Teachers Associations Network (PTAN). This network has some funding support from the Canadian International Development Agency (CIDA). The overarching aim of this Network is to promote an enabling environment for the professional growth and development of educators from diverse backgrounds, as a contribution to the improvement of education in Pakistan.

In the funding proposal of PTAN, an insightful assessment is made about the status of teachers in Pakistan. It states:

> Teaching in the context of Pakistan continues to remain as a neglected profession, thus leading to poor status for the teachers within society. This status quo also remains prevalent due to the absence of networking amongst Pakistani teachers and an authentic platform to raise genuine issues to broader audiences as well as to support their own professional development. Pakistani teachers today, find themselves as an ignored identity, in most educational reforms and quality improvement initiatives in the country. This despondency has further perpetuated nonchalance and lack of conviction within their profession leading to the educational system working in a dismal situation. The main victims, thus being the students, the so-called primary beneficiary of education (PTAN Proposal, unpublished, p. 1).

PTAN, through its constituent members, is helping teachers from different sectors (public, private not-for-profit and private for profit) to come together and discuss their professional matters in a more open manner and develop a collaborative strategy to approach their professional matters. For example, the composition of working committees of these professional associations is made up with fair representation of teachers from all the constituencies such as government and private and other non-governmental organizations that they are serving. This coming together of teachers from different sector schools helps members of these networks to understand their particular issues and develop a holistic approach towards creating greater cooperation to deal with these issues in a more sustained and focused manner.

**Summary**

At the end of Part 1 of this chapter, it can be seen that networks can play a crucial role in supporting teachers to develop themselves as lifelong learners but also help them to get ready to face the challenges of the fast changing professional landscape of teaching.

Networks can help teachers to change their conception of teaching and learning. They can conceive it as a cyclic process where one gets an opportunity to not only critically evaluate the information, but also develop a personal disposition towards becoming an independent professional ready to embark on the challenge of monitoring his or her own learning and supporting others to learn. In turn, this continuous interaction between self-learning and others' learning can lead to challenging our beliefs about the purpose of education and also contribute towards developing a healthy society which can be a better place for us to live a decent life.

In the next part, we provide case studies of three professional association networks—MAP, SPELT and SHADE. These cases provide an insight into the work of teachers as change agents in enacting reforms in education in Pakistan.

**Case Study 1:**

**Mathematics Association of Pakistan (MAP)**

*Sikunder Ali Barber*

MAP was established as a professional association of mathematics teachers to upgrade the quality of mathematics education, initially in Pakistan. Since its inception in 1997, it has been committed to providing a learning platform for all those related to the field of mathematics education whether directly or indirectly.

MAP has adopted a three-pronged approach to address the matter of the continuing development of mathematics teachers. Firstly, it has created and structured focused programmes for mathematics teachers to provide opportunities for them to interact freely with each other on professional matters. For example, MAP organizes a regular workshop every month on various topics such as teaching fractions meaningfully or geometry—making connections etc. Secondly, for children to develop a positive attitude towards mathematics, MAP has been very active in organizing separate programmes for them. In these programmes, children have opportunities to work in teams to experience mathematics as an interesting and challenging subject. The main focus of these programmes has been to help children to see that mathematics is a valuable subject for them to pursue. Also, through these programmes, MAP is helping mathematics teachers to see how they can teach children according to the new demands of teaching and learning for understanding. For example, MAP has so far organized three Olympiads for children of different grade levels to work on interesting and challenging mathematics in a collaborative fashion.

Thirdly, in order to create a strong support mechanism for teaching and learning worthwhile mathematics, MAP has been working on various projects where important stakeholders are being encouraged to re-learn mathematics so that they can see the broader role of mathematics in their daily life situations. In this regard, MAP has been actively engaged in the process of rewriting text books with Provincial bodies such as the Sindh Text Book Board. Also it is organizing workshops for parents so they can see what it means to learn mathematics and how they would be able to support children's mathematics understanding. This work with the wider society enables MAP to create greater synergy and networking amongst different stakeholders to achieve quality mathematics education within Pakistan and beyond.

If one looks critically at the work of MAP, it is clear that it has created several avenues where mathematics can be conceived of as a human activity and considered as a subject essential in daily life situations. Within this scenario the learning of mathematics can be seen as an important subject for making informed decisions in today's fast changing world.

## Activities and Organization of MAP

MAP offers a variety of approaches to upgrading the quality of mathematics education:

- It assumes the role of champion in furthering the goal of quality mathematics education in the contexts where it serves
- It encourages networking amongst its members and the wider society to deliberate on professional matters and issues in a sustained and effective manner
- It is proactive in influencing the policies of government concerning the goals of quality mathematics education within the country and beyond
- It has established an Institute of Math Olympiads intended to serve the development of mathematical thinking amongst students at all levels
- It develops partnerships for learning with similar professional associations in other countries.

The following are some of the specific activities that MAP has been arranging in its professional role of supporting the professional needs of its members:

- Maintaining it as a platform for the continuing professional development of teachers and providing follow-up support to the graduates and visiting teachers of AKU-IED in a variety of ways
- Providing opportunities for members to plan, conduct and evaluate the workshops of MAP
- Creating opportunities for members to meet renowned mathematics educators whenever they visit AKU-IED and Pakistan

- Assisting mathematics teachers to continuously update their pedagogical content knowledge of mathematics (Shulman, 1986)
- Assisting members to continuously update their career profiles; the success of this is evident in the preference given to MAP members for job opportunities at different schools in Karachi and other parts of Pakistan
- Creating opportunities for members to engage in the process of challenging each other's ideas of teaching and learning of mathematics in a non-threatening environment.

The working committee of MAP is responsible for all its affairs. It comprises of members representing various sectors such as private and government schools. Proportionate representation of different sectors enables MAP to cater to the diverse needs in an informed fashion whilst in committee meetings, the debates normally canvas professional issues as well as policy formulation concerning the activities of MAP. The Chair of MAP is responsible for the overall direction of the association and is accountable to its working committee for all the affairs ranging from policy implementation to setting the strategic directions to achieve the intended goals of MAP. Veuglers and Zijlstra (2002) have pointed out the importance of the role of the Chair of a learning network:

> Chairing such group means that all people should get involved, each voice should be heard. The chair must have the competence to analyze the experiences and ideas and place them in a theory that has clear links to the practice of the schools (Veuglers and Zijlstra 2002:172).

The General Secretary of MAP is responsible for all administrative affairs. MAP is also in the process of developing positions of coordinators with responsibility for different areas such as monthly Saturday workshops, summer workshops, organization of Math Olympiads, Interest Groups intended to serve teaching and learning of mathematics at different levels, financial affairs and membership, publications e.g. editor of MAP Newsletter, outreach activities of MAP and special projects of MAP.

## What is the Vision of MAP?

The members of MAP have been conscious of the need to define the vision in relation to the link of mathematics and the wider society. Through intense deliberations, the members have focused on issues related to the teaching and learning of mathematics in Pakistan. MAP considers that mathematics is an important human invention and can be conceived of as playing a vital role in all cultures in the world for a variety of reasons. Some of the reasons are:

- Mathematics is considered essential for all informed citizens, not only to make sense of available inflow of information, but also to make effective decisions on matters relevant to both personal and professional spheres where numbers are critically involved. For example, making day-to-day decisions about purchasing things from the market, choosing a school for children to attend, deciding about insurance or health policies and plans, and voting knowledgeably, all call for some quantitative sophistication
- Mathematics has been part of the cultural heritage humankind for several centuries. In this connection, it is essential for informed citizens to develop an appreciation and understanding of that achievement, including its aesthetic and even recreational aspects
- It has also been recognized that all careers require some foundation of mathematical knowledge, but there are some subjects where mathematics is pursued intensively, such as statistics, engineering or science.

It has been widely observed that teaching and learning of mathematics has received and continues to receive great significance in the development of human thought, especially critical thinking, logical thinking and creative thinking.

## What Qualities does MAP have as a Network?

MAP, as a community of professionals, would not have been playing such a constructive role towards the professional development of teachers without some of the important characteristics of networking. One of those characteristics is improving relationships and MAP has been pursuing that by developing and working in teams. Teams are necessary for the successful operation of most of its activities. As West-Burnham (2000) has said:

> Effective teams have come to be seen as one of the crucial characteristics of quality organizations and, equally significantly, one of the most powerful catalysts in an organization for implementing change (p. 15).

Another quality of networking is the culture of sharing. MAP has created such a culture where both the active members of MAP and other fellow colleagues share their professional knowledge and concerns in a very open and candid manner. They understand that their views would be well listened to and they would get useful suggestions from their fellow colleagues in a non-threatening environment, which MAP has created so far. This is in sharp contrast with a culture where alternative suggestions are not listened to and valued; this is often observed in the discourse of education in this country.

MAP has been contributing to the enhancement of the quality of mathematics education in Pakistan in a variety of ways. It has been created as a network to contribute to the development of different areas such as support to its members, involvement in curriculum development initiatives, actively disseminating the research results of various studies being conducted in mathematics education around the world and engaging in dialogue with professional organizations in the world.

**MAP's Role in Curriculum Development of Mathematics**

Efforts to bring change into mathematics teaching in Pakistan have to begin from the understanding that mathematics teachers are mostly text book driven. Generally, they teach from the text book, page by page, and their focus is on covering the syllabus rather than providing effective learning for students. A learning-for-understanding orientation should be considered important for the development of students to become informed citizens. To achieve that, considerable efforts have been made to devise a progressive curriculum with the involvement of the stakeholders of the schools. In Pakistan, there is little involvement of teachers in the development of the curriculum. Since they do not have an active involvement in curriculum development, normally mathematics teachers equate curriculum with the text book and this prevents them from experimenting and implementing new ideas in the classroom. As Barwell (2000) has rightly captured:

> In Pakistan, teachers' practice operates entirely at the implementation level of the curriculum. Teachers have little influence on the intended curriculum in the form of text books or government publications and there is no tradition of school-level curriculum planning in the form of schemes of work or similar documents (p. 37).

In that context, MAP has taken up the challenge to change the notion of curriculum as well as the teaching of mathematics. MAP normally plans its workshops in a manner whereby teachers become active learners while working on several diverse mathematical activities designed to enrich a meaningful understanding of mathematics. The question arises as to how teachers can be supported to become more resourceful in implementing these activity-based learning approaches in their respective school contexts. This requires rewriting the curriculum of mathematics for schools. In recognition of this need, MAP, with the support of AKU-IED, played an active role in the review of text books of primary grades of the Sindh Text Book Board, an official body of the Province of Sindh, established to create, publish and distribute text books in the Province. After successful review of these text books, MAP organized special workshops for mathematics teachers where reviewers shared their experience of reviewing the text books.

For MAP, it is an exciting challenge to play a proactive role in influencing the design and development of the curriculum of mathematics not only at the school level but also at the national level. Another aspect of curriculum development that MAP has been engaged in is the process of introducing Information and Communication Technology (ICT) in the teaching of mathematics. Through various workshops, MAP has encouraged mathematics teachers to learn possible ways to teach mathematics with the software packages such as *Cabri Geometre* and *Excel*. The advantage that these packages provide to students is to help them learn different concepts of mathematics in a more meaningful manner. For example, if they wish to explore different properties of angles and sides of a triangle, this can be done with simple dragging of the shape on the screen of the computer. Through dragging the shape they can see what effect it has to stretch the angle measurement of the shape if the vertex of one triangle is fixed etc. In this way students are getting engaged in the process of developing a conjecturing attitude towards mathematical propositions. This attitude may lead them to prove different mathematical propositions before accepting their truth.

## Challenges for MAP in Maintaining its Professional Norms and Values in the Context of Pakistan

Since its establishment, MAP has been successfully engaged in creating a collaborative culture of doing and investigating mathematics. Its presence is being felt at various levels from schools to governments. It has created several types of professional networking for the development of mathematics teachers and in terms of provision of meaningful experiences for children. Despite all its efforts, MAP faces a number of challenges:

- Sustaining a culture of 'volunteerism versus commercialism'
- On-going professional development of MAP leaders and active members
- How to meet the increasing professional needs of mathematics teachers in Pakistan with implications for resources and outreach
- Greater networking among sister organizations in the country and in the world
- Encouraging alternative assessment practices as opposed to heavily emphasized established summative assessment practices in Pakistan
- Planning and conducting research in mathematics education as all members are volunteers who take the responsibility for the completion and dissemination of research
- Establishment of the Math Olympiad Institute devoted towards creating a variety of innovative activities for the children on an on-going basis
- Having a sound infrastructure (office space, permanent office secretary, computer, record keeping mechanism)
- Sustained funding until its operations become sustainable through its sources of income
- Data-base management system for membership and other relevant categories of the work of MAP.

The MAP leaders feel that the acceptance of these challenges would not only develop a feeling of accomplishment but also help in creating and sustaining effective networking for mathematics teachers and teacher educators in Pakistan MAP, as a network of professionals, is definitely contributing towards improving the quality of mathematics education in Pakistan though much remains to be done.

Therefore, it is essential for a country like Pakistan to encourage networks like MAP to continually grow and sustain their operations. Their efforts would lead them to empower not only mathematics teachers to become caring and competent professionals, but also support society to adopt a learning mode to face the challenges of the Twenty-first Century in improving the quality of mathematics education in Pakistan.

**Case Study 2:**

**Society of Pakistan English Language Teachers (SPELT)**

*Zakia Sarwar*

**The Beginnings of SPELT**

In June 1984, four English language teachers sat together wondering how to initiate a forum that could get English language teachers (ELT) together. This was a long felt need since 1978, when one such attempt had been made. In that attempt, we tried to give equal representation to all provinces; the President was from Punjab, the Secretary from Karachi, Treasurer from NWFP and the Academic Secretary from Balochistan. Those were not the magic days of email. The plan never got off the ground and the committee never met again.

English teachers from all over Pakistan met at a conference in Islamabad in 1983, and again in 1984. The need for an ELT forum was voiced again. This time four teachers from Karachi decided to take the lead to meet and find a way to establish a language teachers' association. They started with questions like: how can we establish a difference between a professional forum and teachers' organizations which work like trade unions and have a bad reputation for squandering money? What makes associations begin with a bang and fade out in a whimper? What precautions should be taken to ensure that the established forum operates on 'professional' standards, which are internationally accepted? What kind of academic programmes should be considered to serve the ELT teaching community and community at large? After a lot of discussion, it became clear that it would be best if we followed these principles:

- A non-hierarchical system, based on merit and actual work of office bearers, would be required so that it would not hamper work that needed to be done, despite the continued dominance and deference demanded by senior teachers within the Pakistani culture
- Complete transparency would be needed in financial matters
- Meticulous programme planning and punctuality would be required for professional credibility
- The needs of the teaching community and the community in general would have to be kept in view while addressing academic issues.

The vision of how SPELT was to conduct itself was clear, but the initiators realized that the strong support of the teaching community and schools was necessary for its success. Self-help and teamwork became the motto. Those who worked selflessly in the first year of SPELT's inception were called the 'founder members' (eight in number). The policy was to network and acknowledge efforts of all those who helped in whatever little way they could. This built a trust in teachers who got to know about SPELT's activities. A teacher coming to one of the meetings reflected, *'On the way, I was thinking of our SPELT family...I feel lucky that as an English teacher, I have a niche—Poor other teachers!'*

## The Story of SPELT

The first SPELT activity was the 'Academic Session' and it has been held every last Saturday of the month. This has taken place since inception to this date without a break. In this two-hour free workshop, teachers share their classroom experiences with each other. It honours teachers' experience and exposes novice teachers to updated choices in pedagogy. It creates linkages through networking and grooms teachers as leaders and presenters. The SPELT Academic Sessions can be considered an excellent example of a forum for peer learning and support. Moreover, they are SPELT's window to the community. The sessions have helped to create an awareness in the teaching/learning community that ELT is a specialized field. It has impacted the way schools currently view English language teaching.

The Academic Sessions in their first year gained a prestigious reputation for quality presentations in the field of ELT and also for their punctuality and regularity, which gave a great deal of encouragement to the founder members. To celebrate the first anniversary, two initiatives; a SPELT Newsletter and an international ELT conference were launched. By this time, The Asia Foundation, British Council, OUP, PACC and USIS were all interested in SPELT activities as the need to upgrade expertise in ELT in Pakistan was also a part of their agenda. However, SPELT only asked for material support such as venue, speakers and conference materials rather than 'funding' for the international conference. The registration fee for the conference was only Rs.5 for two days of presentations, lunch and conference materials. It was held from Friday to Sunday and there was great uncertainty about whether teachers would sacrifice their weekend to come to the first ever privately organized conference. Over 200 teachers attended and it was a great success!

The SPELT conference has now become a major ELT event in the region drawing presenters from within Pakistan and neighbouring countries such as Malaysia, Indonesia, India, Bangladesh, Nepal, Singapore, Sri Lanka and also Australia, UK, USA and Japan. With the passage of time it has become a 'Traveling Chain Conference', attended by over 1600 school, college and university teachers from across the country. It is a great source of peer learning and networking for English teachers as they come in contact with teachers from different levels and different kinds of institutions. To maximize their exposure, presenters travel to different conference sites in Pakistan to give the same presentation, tailoring it to the needs of the audience. The conference is a strong indicator of networking, in which SPELTers use their personal resources for home hospitality of the outstation presenters. During the conference and stay in homely surroundings, the visitors and the host SPELTers both get a wonderful opportunity to network which enables the sharing of issues, current ELT methodology and research findings. Personal contacts with colleagues across the country are developed. Moreover, speakers' presentations at the conference are published in the SPELT Journal, and therefore, reach colleagues who are unable to attend the conference. The wider international community thus comes within the reach of SPELT members.

Another outcome of the first conference was that SPELT team members (mostly from the college level) for the first time met teachers from different schools from the public sector, and were able to understand the mismatch that exists between different levels. The theme of the first conference was 'Evaluation of compulsory English courses from Class 6th to the BA level.' It brought two concrete results. One was a systematic, analytical report of the conference proceedings with recommendations about the English courses, from a large body of teachers. Secondly, the teachers who were contacted to work on the school level asked the SPELT team to organize a training course to meet the challenges of teaching English. This is because many courses, such as the compulsory English courses, have not been revised for at least four decades. This brought to existence the SPELT Practical Teacher Training Course (PTTC) in 1985, and it has since been run every year. It has the singular distinction of being a course run by the teachers, for the teachers, in response to an identified need. It can be considered an extension of the original vision of the initiators, and also an indigenous model of teacher education suited to the Pakistani community's teaching/learning needs.

SPELT now runs long and short-term courses including Cambridge University's Certificate for Overseas Teachers of English (COTE). Besides transmitting updated ELT methodology, the courses provide an excellent opportunity to trainees to network and learn from each other. They visit each other's institutions and learn about different teaching and learning communities. They are able to see the difference in school cultures and are empowered to make considered decisions in their career choices. During the year-long courses, the isolation barriers are overcome. Sharing of problems, reflecting and finding solutions which would be acceptable to other colleagues as well, gives them confidence. They also develop a network of like-minded colleagues through continued association.

Another impact of the conference can be at the organizational level, since the training courses originated through it. Most of the SPELT office bearers/volunteers are 'harvested' from these courses. Once they have been in contact with SPELT long enough to see the work which is being done, some of the trainees volunteer to help out. A number of our trainees have leadership roles in the SPELT Working Committee as coordinators and sub-committee members, while others with their training have changed the learning culture of their institutions.

Simultaneously, on the occasion of the first conference in 1985, the first issue of the Newsletter was published in an effort to provide a wider dissemination of SPELT and its activities and gain a larger membership. The original four page cyclostyled Newsletter has now graduated to a quarterly refereed journal, adorning the library of many institutions around the world. Due to shortage of human resources, the issues sometimes get delayed, but come out nevertheless. The first editorial declared that the goal was to reach members who are unable to participate in SPELT's activities. It is a teacher friendly journal, which makes an effort to reach out to teachers who are mostly untrained and without any exposure to modern methodology. It reaches far-flung areas, where teachers have no other support. It also grooms Pakistani teachers to view themselves as 'writers', and in some instances contributes to their career development as publication in professional journals is a growing requirement for promotion in many institutions. Internationally, the journal is used for affiliate interaction with sister organizations, bringing Pakistani colleagues closer to the wider ELT world. Thus, the journal is a great source of networking, both nationally and internationally.

The most recent initiative of SPELT is promoting collaborative research among teachers. Professional development through classroom research has been recommended as a powerful tool for teacher growth. Recognizing its importance, SPELT has opened opportunities for teachers since 1996. Two research projects have been completed; one under the sponsorship of the British Council and the other through TESOL USA, undertaking to pilot the prestigious Tailor-Made Professional Development (TESOL-TMPD) in which 22 teachers from school, college and universities took part and researched a number of classroom issues. The aim of this initiative is to build a community of practitioners who would gain insight into classroom issues and take informed decisions on the basis of their research observations. Moreover, working together on projects would make teachers agents of change, not only in their immediate surroundings but also having an impact on larger teaching and learning communities.

SPELT has spread nationally and been institutionalized in different Chapters in cities of Pakistan. The founders of SPELT had seen the organization as a loose non-hierarchical structure, in which coordinators would work on different initiatives on their own, instead of getting bogged down under bureaucratic procedures. The same vision was used for establishing Chapters in different cities. As long as the SPELT Charter and the basic structure are followed, the Chapters function independently. However, there is a strong emphasis on transparency in annual elections, and yearly audit of accounts. One after the other, the Chapters started functioning in Abbottabad, Hyderabad, Lahore, Multan, Peshawar, Islamabad and Quetta, besides Karachi. They hold academic sessions every month, thus giving a chance to practitioners to gather and network with each other. The quarterly journal reaches the SPELT membership around the country, though it is published from Karachi. (A dialogue is on at this point to involve teachers from different Chapters to be included in the editorial process using e-mail). Annually, the Chapters are a part of the international traveling conference, in which they are fully responsible for all local arrangements, while Karachi networks with them regarding the presenters who will speak in their city. This has two far-reaching effects. Firstly, it grooms practitioners around Pakistan for leadership roles, and secondly, a wide ELT community has come into existence on a national scale.

## Conclusion

The journey of SPELT is a success story; creating networks, providing professional development opportunities to practitioners and creating a community of teachers as learners—a true learning community. Some of the successes can also be attributed to the positive support of schools that view the importance of teachers' personal development as complementary to their institutions' own growth. However, as a grass root organization, made by the teachers, for the teachers, SPELT also faces a number of issues and challenges.

First of all, SPELT is finding it difficult to maintain its non-hierarchical structure and its strong democratic traditions in a country where the culture of democracy is very raw. Secondly, it is also a struggle to involve the general membership in the administrative work and policy making, and to inculcate a spirit of 'ownership' in the upcoming leadership without losing the vision for which SPELT was created and to institutionalize structures and procedures so that its success does not depend on individuals. Thirdly, SPELT has to grapple with how to generate funds to continue its academic work while maintaining quality and still be within the financial reach of teachers. Last but not least, how to inculcate a spirit of 'volunteerism' so as to retain SPELT's academic experts and trained staff on lower rates than deserved is an issue that begs constant attention.

The challenges are daunting indeed. However, if we view a teachers' network as an agent of change in the learning communities of educational institutions, it becomes evident that the way ahead lies within the positive cycle of outcomes resulting from teachers' professional development. By networking and innovative use of resources, SPELT has maintained a brilliant track record of high academic achievement of teacher education through self-help for nearly two decades. However, it is easier to ascend than to maintain standards. SPELT can only sustain itself if the community of English teachers at large realizes the pivotal role being played by SPELT in the field of ELT in Pakistan, especially as there are so few avenues open for teachers to educate themselves in this field in this country.

Finally, what is to be learnt from the story of SPELT? We have learnt that maintaining and sustaining a professional network is no easy matter. It requires some dedicated individuals to begin with, but requires an organization of people with a strong sense of volunteerism to continue. We have also learnt that a network must meet the changing needs of its members, if it is to continue over an extended period of time. A complementary cycle of professional development and support from the schools in which the members teach, has enabled SPELT to succeed and forge the way ahead for academic excellence which is the ultimate goal of all teaching and learning interventions.

**Case Study 3:**

**School Head Teachers' Association for the Development of Education (SHADE)**

*Qamar Safdar*

**Introduction**

SHADE was formed as a voluntary network organization in 1998 by the graduates of the first Advanced Diploma in School Management (ADISM) course at AKU-IED. This was a pioneer course to assist head teachers to be better leaders with a vision for their school and to help them plan to work cooperatively to achieve the goal of a learning community. There is very little awareness in Pakistan and other developing countries of this need for vision and that head teachers need to be educated in the specific field of leadership and management in order to run an effective school.

Due to this lack of awareness, AKU-IED initiated a one-year professional development programme in school management and leadership for head teachers. The primary focus of the programme is to equip head teachers with new knowledge, skills and competencies that will help them to become instructional and pedagogical leaders. Head teachers as pedagogical leaders can then develop the capacity of schools as learning communities. Literature on school leadership indicates that the success of any school is largely dependent on the quality of school leaders. One well-known writer in this field, Sergiovanni (1998) says, 'Pedagogical leadership develops human capital by helping schools become caring, focused and inquiring communities within which teachers work together as members of a community of practice' (p. 37). He further says, 'pedagogical leadership invests in capacity building by developing social and academic skills for students and intellectual and professional capital for teachers' (p. 38).

At the end of the first ADISM course (now renamed Advanced Diploma in Education: Educational Leadership and Management) the class of 1998 decided to work together and form the SHADE association, exclusively for practicing and aspiring head teachers. SHADE was established to provide a network for ADISM graduates to share amongst themselves common concerns and challenges related to their role and seek help for the development of education in general, and for effective school management in particular. By including other head teachers in the network as well, SHADE seeks to share and interact on a larger scale to help all head teachers become caring leaders and managers.

**The Aims of SHADE**

The aims of SHADE are to:

- offer a forum for enhancing professional knowledge, experience, human and other resources required for the promotion of effective school management

- help the head teachers in mobilizing resources for their professional development
- provide professional support to head teachers for creating a knowledge based school management system
- establish appropriate communication channels for disseminating information on school improvement.

To achieve these aims, SHADE has a management structure and a range of membership categories. The structure comprises of a main Executive Committee and two sub-committees, namely, the Program Organizing Committee and the Editorial Committee. SHADE offers various kinds of membership; namely, founder members who are all the course participants of ADISM class of 1998, faculty members of AKU-IED affiliated to the course, general members who are current or aspiring head teachers, associate members who are persons actively contributing towards teaching, learning, research or resources in the area of school improvement and institutional members such as educational institutions or organizations involved in educational leadership and management. Additionally, there are life members and honorary members who are people with outstanding services rendered towards school improvement and effective school leadership and management practices.

We know that school improvement requires active commitment from head teachers who see their role as pedagogical and curriculum leaders, not just as administrators. Indeed, a recent report in the United States carries the title, 'the rise and stall of teacher education'. The main reason for the 'stall' was that those in positions of management were not sufficiently active or included in the reform agenda. To overcome this problem, SHADE provides a platform and focus for dialogue and professional development amongst heads, leading to a commitment to work with teachers in a collegial and collaborative manner. In this way, the influence of head teachers will be an integral part of the school improvement agenda, thus making a much needed contribution to the quality of education for children.

## The Activities of SHADE

SHADE promotes the professional development of head teachers through a range of activities and initiatives including bi-monthly full day workshops, publishing a newsletter, conducting conferences, seminars and symposia as well as extending professional support to other educational institutions.

The first activity of the Executive Committee was to brainstorm possible areas of interest to head teachers for SHADE workshops. The first two workshops were on 'School Discipline' and were of absorbing interest to all head teachers. These workshops focused on head teachers' perceptions of, issues and challenges related to, and possible strategies to maximize, school discipline. Following those successful workshops, SHADE members, realizing that schools have children with mixed abilities and learning difficulties, held three workshops on these topics. This has led to a better understanding of the needs of such children and now our head teachers are seriously reflecting on inclusive education which is indeed a milestone in change.

SHADE has helped head teachers to realize that improvement in education can only come when teachers are professionally developed, satisfied and treated with regard and respect. Normally, in developing countries, 'teacher appraisal' is a difficult area for heads because it is linked to annual increments and is confidential and judgmental. A SHADE workshop on teacher appraisal tried to explain that the process should be transparent and the main aim of appraisal should be to help the teacher minimize weaknesses and enhance strengths. This networking among school heads has led to the emergence of better developmental, rather than judgmental appraisal systems in schools that will enhance the teachers to work in a more professional environment.

A series of workshops on 'School Improvement Initiatives' allowed head teachers to share innovative practices of their respective schools that are enhancing the quality of education. One of the needs identified by head teachers was Early Childhood Education. Keeping in mind the importance of early childhood and its implications for the holistic development of the child, SHADE conducted two consecutive workshops where the focus was on Dr Marie Montessori's Seven Characteristics of a Normalized Child. Health Education also featured with a workshop on 'How Health Education can be used as a Vehicle for School Improvement'. The role that head teachers can play to develop health action schools and conduct a needs analysis of health practices in their own school, was emphasized. The combined efforts of educationists and health authorities have made a difference in the lives of many students.

SHADE joined hands with the AKU-IED library to hold a workshop on 'Encouraging Reading Habits in Children' and the importance of Information and Communication Technology (ICT) was stressed in a workshop on 'Tele-Education in the 21st Century'. Action research has been identified as a useful tool to empower teachers to systematically enquire into their practices and contribute to professional growth. A workshop on action research, simply defined as 'learning by doing', was held. In action research, a group of people identify a problematic aspect of their work, plan and then take action to resolve it, collect data on their action and reflect on their efforts. This forms a cycle of action research that is usually repeated after re-planning a new action to build a spiral of improvement and increased understanding of the particular aspect of their work.

## Workshops by Visiting Faculty from Canada and UK

AKU-IED sometimes has visiting faculty from international universities. Whenever they are available, SHADE convenes special workshops based on their expertise. For example, Dr Paul Shaw from the University of Toronto conducted a workshop on student assessment and the role of head teachers. To highlight the discrepancies in assessment criteria, he asked the participants to assess a piece of writing, on a scale of 1–10, by a twelve-year-old student and then compare with each other. The discussion generated from this activity and the marked difference in grading clearly brought out the message that we need to carefully design the criteria for assessment. He also shared the idea of portfolio assessment as an authentic way of assessing learning. Normally, in our existing practices of testing, the student's future is decided on a three-hour examination without considering the other factors that are involved in a portfolio such as evidence of learning skills developed over a period of time or the student's accomplishments in non-academic areas of school life. A portfolio can provide a more holistic picture of the student's learning. The role of the head is to mobilize teachers to question, reflect and act on current practices of assessment and evaluation to ensure that they provide useful and accurate information on the students' learning.

A second example was Professor Tim Simkins from Sheffield Hallam University, UK who led a workshop on 'Leadership and School Performance'. He started the workshop with the notion of an effective school and ended on ten important themes that constitute an effective school: a) School climate, b) Relationships, c) Classroom climate, d) Support for learning, e) Support for teaching, f) Time and resources, g) Organization and communications, h) Equity, i) Recognition of achievement and, j) Home-school link.

## SHADE Newsletter

One of the ways of disseminating information on innovative practices in school management and leadership has been through a half-yearly newsletter. SHADE has so far produced four newsletters and a recent edition created some positive ripples in countries abroad. We appreciate letters received from Professor Parshiadis, Texas University and Mr Padmaker Sapre, Professor Emeritus and President of the Council of Teacher Education, India.

## International Conferences

Members of SHADE have participated in four successive conferences of the International Congress for School Effectiveness and Improvement (ICSEI). Conferences held in San Antonio, USA (1999), Hong Kong (2000) Toronto (2001) and in Sydney (2003) were all attended by SHADE members. These experiences and papers have been incorporated in the SHADE workshops and university academic sessions to build the community of learners. For example, AKU-IED faculty as well as four CPs of the pioneer class of 1998 jointly presented a paper on the ADISM programme at the ICSEI Conference in San Antonio, USA, followed by a study tour of schools both in the USA and Britain. As a result, they presented a workshop in SHADE titled 'Best Practices in Educational Management', with the themes of leadership qualities of head teachers, school management, monitoring and evaluation, professional development, classroom management and assessment.

## Extending Support to other Educational Institutions

Apart from workshops, SHADE was instrumental in sending two of its members, namely Ms Bilquees Nasir, Principal Government Girls Secondary School, Sir Syed Town and Ms Rukhsana Haji, Principal, Qamar-e-Bani Hashim School, to represent Pakistan in the inter-visitation programme in Sheffield in 2002. The Department for International Development (DFID) managed by the British Council, Karachi under the higher education link between AKU-IED and School of Education, Sheffield Hallam University, England, funded the programme. These head teachers shared their experiences and learning along with some recommendations with the other head teachers, encouraging a healthy exchange of ideas that will further facilitate this community of learners to adopt and adapt according to their context.

It is heartening to note that some ADISM graduates have volunteered to take part in a mentoring programme and to be paired with members who are less experienced and would like to acquire leadership and management skills over a period of time. The mentor-mentee relationships are negotiated over a period of time from two months up to six months and the experience of these mentoring relationships will be shared in future workshops of SHADE.

Finally, SHADE is not limited to the precincts of Karachi, Pakistan but has opened chapters in the Northern Areas of Pakistan; Dhaka, Bangladesh; Mombasa, Kenya and Dar-us-Salaam in Tanzania. Here, I am reminded of a saying of Rabindranath Tagore: 'A teacher can never truly teach unless he/she is still learning him/herself. A lamp can never light another lamp unless it continues to burn its own flame'. It is true that SHADE and its members are striving to light as many lamps as possible in many parts of the world in the quest for quality education. Together we can enlighten the student world, which is very dear to all of us.

## Conclusion

It is clear that SHADE is an active and productive network that has provided a great deal of encouragement and support to heads in their development as pedagogical leaders. What we don't know much about, however, is the extent to which this personal development has been translated into capacity building in the schools. The real challenge is for the heads to use the knowledge and skills acquired through SHADE in building learning communities in their schools. Perhaps SHADE might consider investigating this matter in the next stage of their growth as a professional network of head teachers for the development of education in Pakistan and beyond.

## References

Barwell, R. (2000). *Mathematics Teaching in Pakistan and UK*. Derby: Association of Teachers of Mathematics.

Board of Teacher Registration (1997). *Partnership in Teacher Education*. Toowong, Qld: Board of Teacher Registration.

Clark, D. (1996). *Schools as Learning Communities*. London: Cassell.

Cochran-Smith, M. & Lytle, S. (1993). *Inside/Outside: Teacher Research and Knowledge*. NY: Teachers College Press.

Darling-Hammond, L. & McLaughlin, M.W. (1995). *Policies that Support Professional Development in an Era of Reform*. NY: National Center for Restructuring Education, Schools and Teaching.

Hord, S.M. (1997). 'Professional Learning Communities: What are they and why are they important?' In *Issues About Change*, 6(1), The Southwest Educational Development Laboratory, Austin, TX. http://www.sedl.org/change/issues/issues61.html retrieved on April 16, 2003.

Lieberman, A. (1999). 'Networks'. *Journal of Staff Development*, 20(3).

Lieberman, A. & Grolnick, M. (1997). Networks, Reform and the Professional Development of teachers'. In A. Hargreaves (Ed.). *Rethinking educational change with heart and mind* (pp. 192–215). Alexandria VA: ASCD.

Lieberman, A. & Wood, D. (2003). 'From Network Learning to Classroom Teaching' *The Journal of Teacher Education and Change*, 3(3–4), 315–37.

McDermott, R. (1999). *Knowing in community: 10 critical success factors in building communities of practice*. Retrieved from http://www.co-I-1.com/coil/knowledge-garden/cop/knowing.html

McLaughlin, M.W. & Talbert, J. (1993). *Contexts that matter for teaching and learning*. Stanford, CA: Center for Research on the Context of Secondary School Teaching.

Moonen, B., Vooget, J. (1998). 'Using Networks to Support the Professional Development of Teachers. *Journal of In-service Education*, 24(1), 99–110.

Queensland Board of Teacher Registration (2002). *Networks@Work: A Report of the Queensland Consortium for Professional Development in Education*. Toowong, Qld: Queensland Board of Teacher Registration.

Ramsley, J. (2002). Address at the Conference on Outreach Scholarship held at Penn State University. http://www.outreach.psu.edu/OutreachScholarship/keynote.htm retrieved on October 26.

Sergiovanni, T. (1998). 'Leadership as Pedagogy, Capital Development and School Effectiveness'. *International Journal of Leadership in Education*, 1(1), 37–46.

Shulman, L. (1986). 'Those who understand: Knowledge growth in teaching'. *Educational Researcher*, 17(1), 4–14.
Smith, A. & Wohlstetter, P. (2001). 'Reform through School networks: A New Kind of Authority and Accountability'. *Educational Policy*, 15(4), 499–519.
Veugelers, W., & Zijlistra, H. (2002). 'What goes on in a network? Some Dutch experience'. *International Journal of Leadership Education*, 5(2), 163–74
West-Burnham, J. (2000). 'Teams'. In E. Bird, J. Butcher & B. Moon (Eds.). *Leading professional development in education* (pp. 141–57). London: Routledge.

# INDEX

## A

action research, 9, 50-51, 59, 65, 67, 79, 81, 84-86, 143; getting started, 86; interest group, 67-68; levels, 81; methodology, 70
Aga Khan Education Service, 144, 146
AKU-IED, 23, 45, 47, 51-52, 63, 67-69, 75, 80, 87-89, 93-95, 101-105, 112, 114, 200, 202, 204, 206, 207, 208, 222, 237-239, 241, 243
Anderson, 20
Anderson, Bennett and Rolheiser, 128
Argyris, 13, 14, 16
ARIG, 69, 90, 91; aims, 68; purpose, 68

## B

Baker, 185
Beach and Lindahl, 180
becoming a teacher, 26
Bennis and Nanus, 165
Bennis, 165
Berk, 186
Bolman and Deal, 167
Bray, 183-184, 188
Bregman and Mohammad, 3
BRIDGES project, 46
Britzman, 59
bureaucracy, 5
Burke, 59

## C

Capacity, 9, 69, 119; building, 9, 14, 24, 69; mastery, 14; interpersonal capacity, 120; personal capacity, 119; institutional capacity building, 171; interpersonal capacity, 9, 69, 90, 119; organizational capacity, 121

Carre and Ovens, 49
Carr and Kemmis, 51, 100
case study, 26, 71
children with special needs, 79
Cochran-Smith and Lytle, 64-65
co-learning, agreement, 99; partnership, 93, 97, 99-100
collaboration, 22; collaborative partnership, 99-100
collegiality, 98
communication, 22
community, 6-7, 17-18, 171; involvement, 151-152; of learners, 26
competitive attitude, 116
constructivism, 48
content knowledge, 105
Cooney and Shealy, 111
cooperative learning, 7, 117, 119, 121, 123-127, 130, 131, 132
COP, 1, 11, 16-17, 19, 201-202; activities, 203; meetings, 209; developing the COP, 202; key processes, 205; shared understanding of COP, 208; initiating the COP, 203; sustaining the COP, 211
cover the syllabus, 17, 35
Covey, 164
Crump and Eltis, 189
culture, of collaboration, 99; of the school, 18
curriculum, 17, 149; development, 194

## D

Dalton and Anderson, 21, 23
Dalton, 20
Darling-Hammond and McLaughlin, 217
Davis and Sumara, 51, 52
Day, 113
De Grauwe, 181

Dean, 70, 191
deep understanding, 22
double-loop learning, 12-13
Dufour and Baker, 200
Dunn, 186

**E**

Edward and Stout, 121
Elbaz, 39
Ellis, 121
emancipatory learning, 15
enacted classroom practices, 55
Epstein, 189
family-friendly school, 192
Farah, 4
Fink and Resnik, 167
Friedman, 41
Fullan and Hargreaves, 113
Fullan, 98, 119, 127, 133, 163-164, 167, 180, 181
Furlong, Barton, Miles, Whiting and Whitty, 199

**G**

Goleman, 164
Grossman, 34, 36-37
Grotevant, 186
Guilbert, 45

**H**

Halai, 70
Hallinger, 167
Harber and Davies, 5
Hargreaves, 11, 45, 201, 209, 212
Hayes, 3
head teachers, 167, 169, 170, 172, 174-175
Hogan, 20
home-school relations, 182, 190
Hoodbhoy, 3
Hughes, 165, 187
human development, 22
Hussain, 138, 143

**I**

improving teaching and learning, 80
inclusive: classrooms, 79; education, 76
induction into teaching, 27, 33
inquiry, 22
in-service teacher development, 94
instructional leadership, 167
interpretive research, 101

**J**

Jackson, 113
Jaworski, 97
Jenlink, 199
Johnson and Johnson, 121
Jones, 190
Joyce and Showers, 119

**K**

Kagan, 48
Kahne and Wetheimer, 199
Kemmis and McTaggart, 67, 142
Kemmis and Wilkinson, 100
Kinnucan-Welsch and Odell, 199
Kizilbash, 46
Kotter, 165
Kouzes and Posner, 163
Kramer-Roy, 70
Kwakman, 209, 210

**L**

leadership, 163, 194, 220; and management, 163; styles and models, 164
learning architecture, 10
learning as a constructivist process, 7
learning community, 1, 4-8, 10, 19, 45, 52, 62, 75, 87, 118, 122, 163, 181, 183, 201, 216; as a metaphor, 5; theory, 6-7; journey towards becoming learning communities, 10, 23; student learning community, 122, 136; starting point of a learning community, 4
learning, 7-9, 12, 102, 116, 156, 199; organization, 1, 10-12, 16; professional development, 45; behaviour, 109

# INDEX 249

Lieberman and Miller, 199
life history, 26-27
lifelong learning, 6
Little, 139, 140
Lortie, 42
Lungwangwa, 139

## M

MacNeill and Silcox, 167, 181
Marsick, 15, 16
Mathematics Association of Pakistan (MAP), 215, 221-223, 225
McLaughlin, 209
McNiff, 100
Memon, 166
mental models, 15
meta-learning, 6
Miller, 143, 160
Mitchell and Sackney, 5-7, 9, 10, 69, 119-120, 162
Mithani, 70
moral responsibility, 38
multigrade, schools, 139, 141; teaching, 140, 144, 147, 160-161
multiple intelligences, 7
Mustafa, 3

## N

negotiation, 17
networking, 19, 215, 216, 221, 222
networks, 215-223, 222; organized, 218; challenges, 219

## O

O'Brien, Newnham and Tinker, 199
organization, 149; capacity, 9, 69, 119; planning, 149
Osterman, 18
outcome-based education, 7

## P

Palincsar, 201
Pardhan, 47

parent involvement, 182, 186, 191, 195; parent partnership, 187; parent relationships, 185
parent-teacher associations, 182, 184, 186
participation, 194-196
partnership, 183-184, 189, 190
patterns in teaching, 33
pedagogical content knowledge, 34, 49
pedagogical leaders, 6, 18, 163, 166-170, 173-175, 179, 180
peer, coaching, 122; tutoring, 154
personal, capacity building, 90; capacity, 9, 69, 119; mastery, 14
PLOT (Professional Learning Online Tool), 21
poverty, 2-3
Povey and Burton, 99
practical domain, 15
professional development teachers, 147-148
Pugh, 187

## Q

quality, education, 2-3, 47, 80; of life, 2; teaching and learning, 80

## R

recitation method, 33
reflection, 14, 56, 88, 90, 98, 99, 154
reflective, journals, 101; learning, 16; practice, 71-73, 75
Reindal, 41
relational autonomy, 41
resource development, 151
Retallick, 5, 20, 70, 79, 138, 197, 199, 214
Rogoff, 98
roles and relationships, 207
Rosenholtz, 120

## S

Sacca, 119
Sally and Monk, 113

Sanders and Epstein, 189
Schon, 12
schooling, 1
School Head Teachers' Association for the Development of Education (SHADE), 215, 238-244
school, 2; improvement, 68, 180; management committees, 182; community partnerships, 194
Scribner, 6
self: reflective learning, 16; responsibility, 22
Senge, 14-16, 162
Sergiovanni, 5, 163, 166, 168, 169, 178, 180, 238
Shaw, 200-201, 212
Showers, 119-120
Shulman, 45, 48-49, 64, 226
Skamp, 48
Slavin, 119
Smith and Andrews, 121
Smith and Neale, 49
Society for Pakistan English Language Teachers (SPELT), 215, 223, 231-237
special needs, 75
Starrat, 7, 79
Stenhouse, 50
subject matter, 36
systems thinking, 15

**T**

teacher, as action researcher, 61; development, 59, 62, 63; education, 83, 93; learning community, 119, 121

teaching, 32, 33; hindering factors, 158; and learning, 29, 154, 195; mathemathics, 86, 101; science, 45; order and class management, 36-37; role of the teacher, 131
teams, 121; learning, 15; work, 12
technical domain, 15
Thiessen and Anderson, 5
time management, 124
Tizard, 187
Topping, 163, 166, 187
transmission, mode, 63; view of, 103

**V**

village education committee (VEC), 145, 146, 195
vision, 15

**W**

Walker, 201
Wallace and Louden, 33
Warwick and Reimers, 46
Watkins and Marsick, 11-12
Watson and Kilcher, 120
Wells, 199
Wenger, 16, 18, 20, 200-201
whole school improvement project (WSIP), 194-196
whole school improvement, 47
Wineberg and Grossman, 201
Wolfendale, 185-186, 188
workplace learning, 12
Wyatt, 7